Dealing with Inflation and Unemployment in Canada

This is Volume 25 in the series of studies commissioned as part of the research program of the Royal Commission on the Economic Union and Development Prospects for Canada.

This volume reflects the views of its author and does not imply endorsement by the Chairman or Commissioners.

Dealing with Inflation and Unemployment in Canada

W. CRAIG RIDDELL

Published by the University of Toronto Press in cooperation with the Royal Commission on the Economic Union and Development Prospects for Canada and the Canadian Government Publishing Centre, Supply and Services Canada

University of Toronto Press
Toronto Buffalo London

Grateful acknowledgment is made to the following for permission to reprint previously published and unpublished material: Agathon Press; *American Economic Review*; Bank of Canada; *Challenge*; MIT Press.

Printed in Canada
ISBN 0-8020-7268 /2
ISSN 0829-2396
Cat. No. Z1-1983/1-41-25E

CANADIAN CATALOGUING IN PUBLICATION DATA

Riddell, Craig.
Dealing with inflation and unemployment in Canada

(*The Collected research studies / Royal Commission on the Economic Union and Development Prospects for Canada*,
ISSN 0829-2396 ; 25)
Includes bibliographical references.
ISBN 0-8020-7268-2

1. Inflation (Finance) — Canada. 2. Unemployment — Canada — Effect of inflation on. 3. Wage-price policy — Canada. 4. Canada — Economic policy — 1945– I. Royal Commission on the Economic Union and Development Prospects for Canada. II. Title. III. Series: The Collected research studies (Royal Commission on the Economic Union and Development Prospects for Canada) ; 25.

HG655.R53 1985   332.4'1'0971   C85-099611-2

PUBLISHING COORDINATION: Ampersand Communications Services Inc.
COVER DESIGN: Will Rueter
INTERIOR DESIGN: Brant Cowie/Artplus Limited

Contents

FOREWORD

When the members of the Rowell-Sirois Commission began their collective task in 1937, very little was known about the evolution of the Canadian economy. What was known, moreover, had not been extensively analyzed by the slender cadre of social scientists of the day.

When we set out upon our task nearly 50 years later, we enjoyed a substantial advantage over our predecessors; we had a wealth of information. We inherited the work of scholars at universities across Canada and we had the benefit of the work of experts from private research institutes and publicly sponsored organizations such as the Ontario Economic Council and the Economic Council of Canada. Although there were still important gaps, our problem was not a shortage of information; it was to interrelate and integrate — to synthesize — the results of much of the information we already had.

The mandate of this Commission is unusually broad. It encompasses many of the fundamental policy issues expected to confront the people of Canada and their governments for the next several decades. The nature of the mandate also identified, in advance, the subject matter for much of the research and suggested the scope of enquiry and the need for vigorous efforts to interrelate and integrate the research disciplines. The resulting research program, therefore, is particularly noteworthy in three respects: along with original research studies, it includes survey papers which synthesize work already done in specialized fields; it avoids duplication of work which, in the judgment of the Canadian research community, has already been well done; and, considered as a whole, it is the most thorough examination of the Canadian economic, political and legal systems ever undertaken by an independent agency.

The Commission's research program was carried out under the joint direction of three prominent and highly respected Canadian scholars: Dr. Ivan Bernier (*Law and Constitutional Issues*), Dr. Alan Cairns (*Politics and Institutions of Government*) and Dr. David C. Smith (*Economics*).

Dr. Ivan Bernier is Dean of the Faculty of Law at Laval University. Dr. Alan Cairns is former Head of the Department of Political Science at the University of British Columbia and, prior to joining the Commission, was William Lyon Mackenzie King Visiting Professor of Canadian Studies at Harvard University. Dr. David C. Smith, former Head of the Department of Economics at Queen's University in Kingston, is now Principal of that University. When Dr. Smith assumed his new responsibilities at Queen's in September 1984, he was succeeded by Dr. Kenneth Norrie of the University of Alberta and John Sargent of the federal Department of Finance, who together acted as Co-directors of Research for the concluding phase of the Economics research program.

I am confident that the efforts of the Research Directors, research coordinators and authors whose work appears in this and other volumes, have provided the community of Canadian scholars and policy makers with a series of publications that will continue to be of value for many years to come. And I hope that the value of the research program to Canadian scholarship will be enhanced by the fact that Commission research is being made available to interested readers in both English and French.

I extend my personal thanks, and that of my fellow Commissioners, to the Research Directors and those immediately associated with them in the Commission's research program. I also want to thank the members of the many research advisory groups whose counsel contributed so substantially to this undertaking.

DONALD S. MACDONALD

INTRODUCTION

At its most general level, the Royal Commission's research program has examined how the Canadian political economy can better adapt to change. As a basis of enquiry, this question reflects our belief that the future will always take us partly by surprise. Our political, legal and economic institutions should therefore be flexible enough to accommodate surprises and yet solid enough to ensure that they help us meet our future goals. This theme of an adaptive political economy led us to explore the interdependencies between political, legal and economic systems and drew our research efforts in an interdisciplinary direction.

The sheer magnitude of the research output (more than 280 separate studies in 70+ volumes) as well as its disciplinary and ideological diversity have, however, made complete integration impossible and, we have concluded, undesirable. The research output as a whole brings varying perspectives and methodologies to the study of common problems and we therefore urge readers to look beyond their particular field of interest and to explore topics across disciplines.

The three research areas, — *Law and Constitutional Issues*, under Ivan Bernier; *Politics and Institutions of Government*, under Alan Cairns; and *Economics*, under David C. Smith (co-directed with Kenneth Norrie and John Sargent for the concluding phase of the research program) — were further divided into 19 sections headed by research coordinators.

The area *Law and Constitutional Issues* has been organized into five major sections headed by the research coordinators identified below.

- Law, Society and the Economy — *Ivan Bernier and Andrée Lajoie*
- The International Legal Environment — *John J. Quinn*
- The Canadian Economic Union — *Mark Krasnick*

- Harmonization of Laws in Canada — *Ronald C.C. Cuming*
- Institutional and Constitutional Arrangements — *Clare F. Beckton and A. Wayne MacKay*

Since law in its numerous manifestations is the most fundamental means of implementing state policy, it was necessary to investigate how and when law could be mobilized most effectively to address the problems raised by the Commission's mandate. Adopting a broad perspective, researchers examined Canada's legal system from the standpoint of how law evolves as a result of social, economic and political changes and how, in turn, law brings about changes in our social, economic and political conduct.

Within *Politics and Institutions of Government*, research has been organized into seven major sections.

- Canada and the International Political Economy — *Denis Stairs and Gilbert Winham*
- State and Society in the Modern Era — *Keith Banting*
- Constitutionalism, Citizenship and Society — *Alan Cairns and Cynthia Williams*
- The Politics of Canadian Federalism — *Richard Simeon*
- Representative Institutions — *Peter Aucoin*
- The Politics of Economic Policy — *G. Bruce Doern*
- Industrial Policy — *André Blais*

This area examines a number of developments which have led Canadians to question their ability to govern themselves wisely and effectively. Many of these developments are not unique to Canada and a number of comparative studies canvass and assess how others have coped with similar problems. Within the context of the Canadian heritage of parliamentary government, federalism, a mixed economy, and a bilingual and multicultural society, the research also explores ways of rearranging the relationships of power and influence among institutions to restore and enhance the fundamental democratic principles of representativeness, responsiveness and accountability.

Economics research was organized into seven major sections.

- Macroeconomics — *John Sargent*
- Federalism and the Economic Union — *Kenneth Norrie*
- Industrial Structure — *Donald G. McFetridge*
- International Trade — *John Whalley*
- Income Distribution and Economic Security — *François Vaillancourt*
- Labour Markets and Labour Relations — *Craig Riddell*
- Economic Ideas and Social Issues — *David Laidler*

Economics research examines the allocation of Canada's human and other resources, the ways in which institutions and policies affect this allocation, and the distribution of the gains from their use. It also considers the nature of economic development, the forces that shape our regional and industrial structure, and our economic interdependence with other countries. The thrust of the research in economics is to increase our comprehension of what determines our economic potential and how instruments of economic policy may move us closer to our future goals.

One section from each of the three research areas — The Canadian Economic Union, The Politics of Canadian Federalism, and Federalism and the Economic Union — have been blended into one unified research effort. Consequently, the volumes on Federalism and the Economic Union as well as the volume on The North are the results of an interdisciplinary research effort.

We owe a special debt to the research coordinators. Not only did they organize, assemble and analyze the many research studies and combine their major findings in overviews, but they also made substantial contributions to the Final Report. We wish to thank them for their performance, often under heavy pressure.

Unfortunately, space does not permit us to thank all members of the Commission staff individually. However, we are particularly grateful to the Chairman, The Hon. Donald S. Macdonald; the Commission's Executive Director, J. Gerald Godsoe; and the Director of Policy, Alan Nymark, all of whom were closely involved with the Research Program and played key roles in the contribution of Research to the Final Report. We wish to express our appreciation to the Commission's Administrative Advisor, Harry Stewart, for his guidance and advice, and to the Director of Publishing, Ed Matheson, who managed the research publication process. A special thanks to Jamie Benidickson, Policy Coordinator and Special Assistant to the Chairman, who played a valuable liaison role between Research and the Chairman and Commissioners. We are also grateful to our office administrator, Donna Stebbing, and to our secretarial staff, Monique Carpentier, Barbara Cowtan, Tina DeLuca, Françoise Guilbault and Marilyn Sheldon.

Finally, a well deserved thank you to our closest assistants: Jacques J.M. Shore, *Law and Constitutional Issues*; Cynthia Williams and her successor Karen Jackson, *Politics and Institutions of Government*; and I. Lilla Connidis, *Economics*. We appreciate not only their individual contribution to each research area, but also their cooperative contribution to the research program and the Commission.

IVAN BERNIER
ALAN CAIRNS
DAVID C. SMITH

PREFACE

The Royal Commission's Macroeconomics Research Studies Program was designed to shed light on the macroeconomic evolution of the Canadian economy over the postwar period and particularly over the last two decades, on current macro policy issues, and on overall prospects for the Canadian economy. The results of the research program provided background for the Commission's Final Report. The individual studies which constituted the research program are contained in volumes 19 to 25 in the Economics Section of the research publication series.

Volume 25 is the only monograph included in the Macroeconomics volumes; it was prepared by W. Craig Riddell, who also served as the Research Coordinator of the Labour Markets and Relations Section of the Commission's Economics Research Program. As its title suggests, the volume covers much of the subject matter of macroeconomics. It includes brief surveys of the interacting evolution of experience and academic analysis of the relationship between inflation and unemployment (chapter 1), and of the use of demand-management policy to respond to the inflation-unemployment issue (chapter 3). Further discussion of the latter area may be found in volume 21, *Fiscal and Monetary Policy*. It also reviews the record, and surveys empirical analyses, of wage inflation in Canada (chapter 2). This complements the survey of the record of price inflation in Canada by O'Reilly, White and Ford in volume 20. Finally, Professor Riddell's monograph provides extended surveys of price and wage controls as a macroeconomic policy tool (chapter 4), of incentive-based incomes policies (chapter 5), and of structural changes to wage-setting mechanisms which might ease problems of inflation control or of cyclical instability in the economy. These extended surveys cover the general analytical literature, and the international and, where relevant, Canadian experience.

JOHN SARGENT

ACKNOWLEDGMENTS

This monograph grew out of three papers written for the Commission's macroeconomics research program: "Dealing With Inflation and Unemployment in the Future"; "Wage Inflation in Canada" (essentially chapter 2 of this study); and "Incentive-Based Incomes Policies: Survey and Assessment" (essentially chapter 5 of this study). I am grateful to John Sargent, the research coordinator, and to Clarence Barber, John Crowe, Caroline Digby, Wendy Dodson, John McCallum, Keizo Nagatani, Douglas Purvis, David Slater, Gordon Sparks, and Bill White for helpful comments on those papers. I have also benefitted from the valuable suggestions of several anonymous referees and from several people who read the entire manuscript: John Helliwell, Stephen Jones, George Kahn, Richard Lipsey and Frank Reid.

Chapter 5 of this book draws on an earlier study carried out for the Department of Finance, Ottawa. I thank John Lester, Philip Smith and Hugh Young for their comments and advice on that study.

Special thanks go to Rosemary Shipton who skilfully and cheerfully edited the book and to my wife Rosemarie and son Chris for their support and patience.

W. CRAIG RIDDELL

Chapter 1

Inflation and Unemployment: *Events, Ideas and Issues*

Inflation and unemployment have been dominant policy concerns for the past two decades. They remain major challenges facing policy makers today. Over the past several years a substantial reduction in inflation has been achieved through a determined policy of demand restraint. In Canada, wage and price inflation has declined from the 10–12 percent range in 1980–81 to approximately 4 percent in 1984–85. Similar reductions have occurred in other countries. The costs of this policy have been enormous. Unemployment rates rose to levels unseen since the Great Depression of the 1930s. High interest rates and weak product market conditions forced many firms and farmers into bankruptcy. Some soul searching about the choice of policy instrument (demand restraint), if not policy objective (ending inflation), is clearly in order. But the more important issue is how best to face the challenge of dealing with inflation and unemployment in the future. The purpose of this study is to examine the main policy alternatives and to summarize the state of knowledge about their probable effectiveness.

An enormous amount has been written about inflation and unemployment, their causes, consequences and cures. The issues are complex and controversial. As stated by Nobel Laureate James Tobin (1972, p. 1) over a decade ago: "Unemployment and inflation still preoccupy and perplex economists, statesmen, journalists, housewives and everyone else. The connection between them is the principal domestic economic burden of presidents and prime ministers, and the major area of controversy and ignorance in macroeconomics." This study does not attempt to cover all aspects of this complex subject. Its focus is on the policy options — the costs and benefits to society of alternative ways of dealing with inflation and unemployment. Nonetheless, no informed discussion of public policy can take place without some understanding of the causes of the phenomena in question and the consequences for society of alternative outcomes. This introductory chapter and the next provide the necessary background material, leaving for remaining chapters the detailed assessment of policy options.

The organization of chapter 1 is as follows. A brief summary of the Canadian experience is provided first. The next section sketches the evolution of events and ideas with respect to inflation and unemployment. Our current understanding of these phenomena, the way that understanding has evolved in response to macroeconomic experience — the effect of events on ideas — and, reversing the causality, the influence of ideas on events are described. The following section provides a summary of the nature of the inflationary process and the relationship between inflation and unemployment. These two sections emphasize the important advances in knowledge made in this area, the existence of a core body of consensus among macroeconomists, and the remaining areas of disagreement and controversy. The chapter ends with an outline of the options for dealing with inflation and unemployment in both the short run and the long run.

Wage inflation plays an extremely important role in the inflationary process. Empiral evidence on the determinants of wage inflation in Canada is discussed in chapter 2. This chapter thus complements the analysis of price behaviour carried out by Howitt (1985), O'Reilly (1985) and O'Reilly, White and Ford (1985). It also is key to much of the policy analysis which follows, for most policies for controlling inflation assign a high priority to wage settlements.

The remaining chapters discuss policy options. A number of events — the build-up of inflation since the mid-1960s, the apparent momentum that inflation had attained, and the experience of stagflation (the co-existence of high inflation and high unemployment) during the 1970s — combined to create considerable alarm about economic developments and resulted in a variety of proposals for reducing inflationary pressures. Some of these proposals involve quite radical reforms of existing institutional arrangements. While this study does not promise to examine every such scheme, it does attempt to canvass those that, on the basis of existing knowledge, appear to be the main contenders. The following are discussed in turn: demand restraint (chapter 3), programs of wage and price control or restraint (chapter 4), incentive-based incomes policies (chapter 5), and structural reforms to wage-setting mechanisms (chapter 6). The final chapter summarizes the main conclusions of the study.

An Overview of the Canadian Experience

The Canadian experience with inflation, unemployment and some other key dimensions of macroeconomic performance is summarized in Fig-

FIGURE 1-1 Inflation in Canada, 1914-84

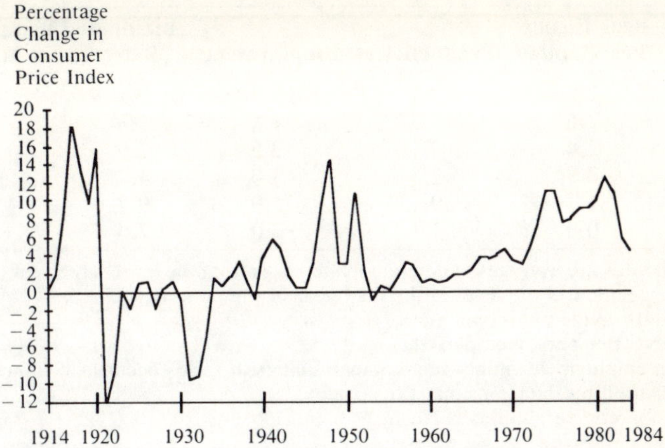

Sources: Statistics Canada, *Historical Statistical Compendium,* prepared for the Royal Commission on the Economic Union and Development Prospects for Canada (Ottawa: Statistics Canada, 1985); and Canada, Department of Finance, *Economic Review* (Ottawa: Minister of Supply and Services Canada, various years).

FIGURE 1-2 Unemployment in Canada, 1921-84

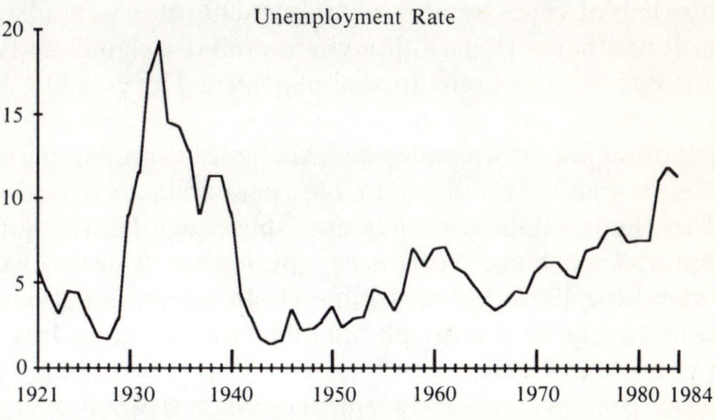

Sources: M.C. Urquhart, ed., *Historical Statistics of Canada* (Toronto: Macmillan, 1965); and Canada, Department of Finance, *Economic Review* (Ottawa: Minister of Supply and Services Canada, various years).

ures 1-1 and 1-2 and in Table 1-1. To abstract from cyclical effects, Table 1-1 shows average performance between the postwar cyclical peak years of 1956, 1966, 1973 and 1981.[1] (More detailed data are provided in Table 1-2 in the next section.) Average data for the period prior to 1946 are also included for historical perspective. However, as Figures 1-1 and 1-2 make clear, there is considerable variability underlying these averages.

TABLE 1–1 Key Economic Trends, 1927–84

Period	Growth Rate[a] of: Real Income Per Capita[b]	Productivity[c]	Employment[d]	Annual Average: Inflation Rate[e]	Unemployment Rate[f]
1927–46	2.2	2.1	1.4	0.1	8.1
1947–56	2.6	3.5	1.8	4.3	3.2
1957–66	2.4	2.1	2.5	2.0	5.5
1967–73	3.9	2.5	3.0	4.4	5.2
1974–81	1.7	0.1	2.9	9.7	7.3
1982–84	0.0	1.1	0.0	7.0	11.4

a. Growth rates are averages of compound increases from the level in the year before the period specified to the level in the final year of the period specified.
b. Real GNE divided by population.
c. Real GNE per person employed.
d. Civilian employment; minor non-comparabilities in series occur in 1946 and 1966.
e. As measured by the Consumer Price Index.
f. Minor non-comparabilities occur in 1946 and 1966.

Prior to World War II both the price level and unemployment rate fluctuated considerably. With the onset of the Great Depression dramatic declines in prices and employment occurred. During the war unemployment fell to very low levels and prices rose. Two bursts of inflation occurred in the early postwar period, one immediately after the war and the second during the Korean War. Otherwise, inflation rates were low by the standards of both previous and subsequent experience and displayed no obvious trend. Unemployment rates were also low by the standards of other periods, although they did rise significantly during the 1957–58 recession and remained above normal levels until the early 1960s.

Overall economic performance was excellent during the period from 1947 to 1973. Productivity and real income per capita grew at rapid rates compared to those attained earlier and subsequently. The growth in employment was also high. With the exceptions noted — the two bursts of inflation and the 1957–58 recession — both inflation and unemployment were relatively low, although inflation had begun to drift upward beginning in the mid-1960s.

The deterioration in economic performance since 1973 is evident from Table 1-1. The coexistence of high inflation and high unemployment during the 1974–81 period was the most dramatic departure from the past. A sharp decline in productivity growth also occurred. Real income growth slowed considerably. Only employment growth remained healthy.

The final period is dominated by the severe recession of 1982–83. Unemployment rose dramatically and has declined only modestly in the recovery to date (Figure 1-2). The recession also coincided with a steep decline in inflation, a fall which has continued at a more modest pace during the recovery.

This brief sketch of Canadian experience necessarily omits many important developments. The Canadian economy, like that of many other Western countries, underwent considerable structural change as well as growth during the postwar period. Two salient developments were the demographic changes associated with the "baby-boom" generation and the dramatic increase in female labour force participation, especially that of married women.[2] As a result, the composition of the labour force changed significantly: women and youth accounted for a larger proportion and adult men a much smaller proportion. Simultaneous with and connected to those trends, the industrial composition of employment changed, with rapid growth in the service sector and slower or negative growth in agriculture, primary industries and manufacturing. In addition, there were other important developments during the postwar period which affected economic performance and the well-being of Canadians — for example, the development of a legal framework which facilitated unionization and the adoption of collective bargaining as a mechanism for determining wages and working conditions; the increase in unionization, particularly in the public sector; the widespread adoption of long-term fixed wage contracts in the unionized sector; and the expansion of the welfare state in such areas as health care, public pensions and unemployment insurance. These developments are described in detail elsewhere;[3] their implications for inflation and unemployment will be noted as appropriate.

The Evolution of Events, Economic Thought and Policies

This section outlines the main events associated with the experience summarized above and describes the evolution of economic thought regarding the relationship between inflation and unemployment. Many aspects of the postwar experience and the evolution of knowledge, which are necessarily described only briefly here, are discussed in more detail in subsequent chapters.

The general public may view the evolution of policies respecting inflation and unemployment with considerable bewilderment; however, to a considerable extent the policies adopted have reflected the evolution of economic thought regarding the relationship of these key variables. Keynes's (1936, p. 383) view of the influence of economic thinking is worth recalling:

> [T]he ideas of economists and political philosophers, both when they are right and when they are wrong, are more powerful than is commonly understood. Indeed the world is ruled by little else. Practical men, who believe themselves to be quite exempt from any intellectual influences, are usually the slaves of some defunct economist. Madmen in authority, who hear voices in the air, are distilling their frenzy from some academic scribbler of a few years back. I am sure that the power of vested interests is vastly exaggerated compared with the gradual encroachment of ideas.

Three main phases of economic thought can be distinguished, discussed here under the headings of the Keynesian dichotomy, the Phillips Curve, and the natural-rate hypothesis.[4] This evolution is perhaps as good an example as any of the application of the scientific method — the confrontation of theory with evidence — in economics, and the resulting accumulation of knowledge and understanding. Although the process is of considerable interest in its own right, the main reasons for sketching the evolution of ideas is their role in the unfolding of events — Keynes's hypothesis at work.

The Keynesian Dichotomy

The first phase in economic thought covered the period from the end of World War II to the early 1960s. This period was characterized not only by extraordinarily good economic performance, as noted previously, but also by the increasing acceptance of Keynesian macroeconomics. By the late 1950s the basic model which guided thinking included the notion of a full employment level of output (potential output) with the associated unemployment consisting of frictional, structural and seasonal components. Inflationary pressures were dichotomized into "demand-pull" and "cost-push" forces. Demand-pull inflation would only occur when aggregate demand exceeded potential output; that is, when the economy was at full employment. Cost-push inflation could occur below full employment, but there was considerable debate about both the theoretical foundations and the empirical relevance of cost-push inflation. Graphically, the relationship between inflation and unemployment was viewed as "L-shaped" (see Figure 1-3a); zero rates of inflation were predicted up to potential output (or full employment, U_f in Figure 1-3a). Any rate of inflation could occur at potential output, depending on the amount of excess aggregate demand. In this model, the role of macroeconomic policy was straightforward — to achieve full employment without an "inflationary gap" (i.e., manipulate aggregate demand such that total output is equal to, but not greater than, potential output). Cost-push forces, if they existed, required policies other than aggregate demand management; for example, direct controls or other restrictions on firms or unions with market power. There was, according to this perspective, no conflict between the goals of full employment and price stability and thus no cost to society of pursuing the goal of full employment. Thus, the existence of unemployment (above some minimal level) was viewed as implying the existence of excess capacity in the economy, and therefore the need for stimulative aggregate demand policy.

The commitment to full employment was expressed formally in the 1945 White Paper on Employment and Income (Canada, Department of Reconstruction and Supply, 1945) and in similar statements in other countries. This paper crystallized society's desire never again to experi-

FIGURE 1–3 Evolving Views of the Relationship Between Inflation and Unemployment

(a) The Keynesian "L-shaped" Relationship

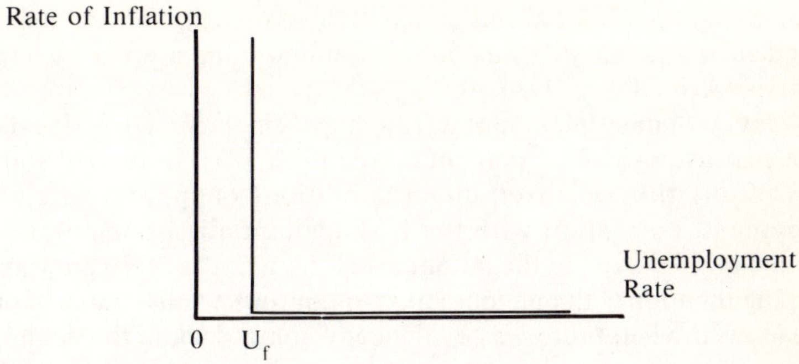

(b) The Phillips Curve

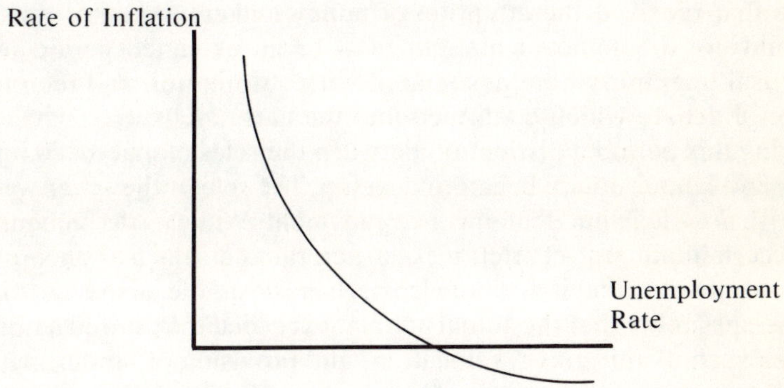

(c) Short-Run and Long-Run Phillips Curves

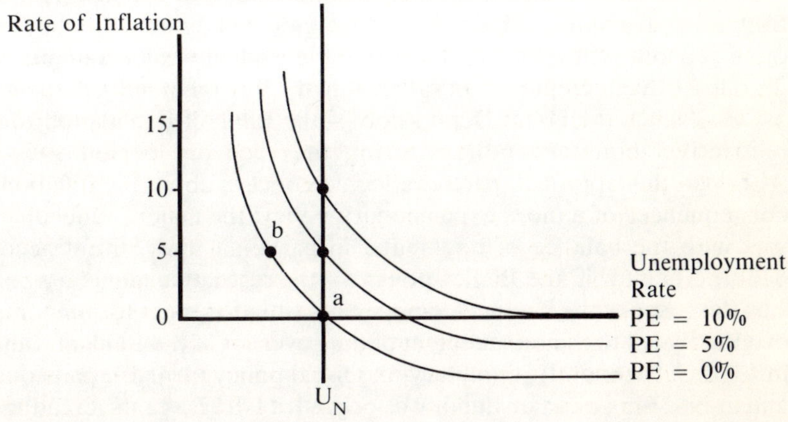

ence the horrors of the Great Depression. However, it was also based on existing views about what was attainable as well as desirable. In particular, it reflected the view that there was no conflict between the goals of full employment and price stability, and that unemployment beyond a certain minimum frictional and structural level (usually called "deficient demand unemployment") was both involuntary and a waste of human resources (Ashenfelter, 1983).

Low levels of unemployment were achieved in the first decade following the war (average of 3.2 percent — see Table 1-1). The two substantial bursts of inflation occurred under conditions of approximately full employment, consistent with the L-shaped inflation-unemployment relationship. However, in the latter part of the 1950s concern grew about "creeping inflation," the phenomenom of low but positive rates of price increase even when there was evidence of some slack in the economy. The experience of the 1957–58 recession — during which inflation fell but remained positive — added to these concerns. The high levels of unemployment experienced during the late 1950s and early 1960s and the creeping inflation of the 1950s were two aspects of economic performance that received the attention of policy makers. Another was the possibility of a significant amount of — or an extended period of — structural unemployment associated with automation and technical change, a debate which continued into the early 1960s.

During this period a distinction between the roles of macroeconomic policy and labour policy began to develop. The role of the latter was to deal with non-deficient demand unemployment. While it was recognized that a certain amount of frictional, structural and seasonal unemployment was not only inevitable but also perhaps desirable, also recognized was the possibility that the actual amount exceeded the desired amount. Policies such as retraining, relocation, and provision of labour market information were discussed as means for reducing the full-employment unemployment rate.

The severity of the recession in the late 1950s and the slow recovery from it led to a major debate about the conduct of monetary policy in an open economy (Sparks, 1985). Despite the evident weak economic conditions — the unemployment rate reached 7.9 percent in 1958, the highest level since the Great Depression — the Bank of Canada followed a restrictive monetary policy during the recovery period 1959–61. Although this approach partly reflected concern about the inflationary consequences of a more expansionary policy, the major preoccupation was with the balance of payments, in particular the current account deficit. The flaw in the Bank's policy — the restrictive monetary policy was the cause of the balance-of-payments situation, not the cure for it — eventually led to the replacement of the governor of the Bank of Canada in 1961. Subsequently, monetary and fiscal policy turned expansionary, and in 1962 the Canadian dollar was pegged at US 92.5 cents, creating the conditions for a boom in exports and investment expenditure.

The experience of the 1950s had pointed to one clear defect of the basic Keynesian macro model outlined above. Inflationary pressures began to emerge well before the economy was operating at high levels of output. As Burns (1951, p. xxi) succinctly put it, "Inflation does not wait for full employment." The dichotomy implied by the L-shaped inflation-unemployment relationship was too sharp. The stage was set for a more continuous relationship between inflation and employment (or output) — the Phillips Curve.

The Phillips Curve Tradeoff

The second phase in economic thought was the decade of the 1960s during which the Phillips Curve, or tradeoff between inflation and unemployment, became incorporated into macroeconomic thinking and models (see Figure 1-3b). This phase began with the seminal papers by Phillips (1958) and Lipsey (1960); there followed a period of intense empirical investigation during which Phillips Curves were estimated for any countries that collected the relevant data. In Canada, the notion of a permanent tradeoff between inflation and unemployment had become widely accepted by policy makers by the mid-1960s. The study by Bodkin et al. (1966) provides a good illustration of this view, as well as of the type of evidence this view was based on.

The incorporation of the Phillips Curve into macroeconomic thinking had significant implications for policy. No longer was there a well-defined notion of full employment. Rather, policy makers could choose between various unemployment rates and the associated rates of inflation. The role of macroeconomic policy was to choose (by weighing the costs of inflation against the costs of unemployment) and maintain (by demand management policies) the socially preferred combination of inflation and unemployment. As an empirical matter, "full employment" was generally regarded in the 1960s as involving unemployment in the 3 to 4 percent range. According to estimated Phillips Curves, achieving this outcome implied accepting a low but positive rate of inflation.[5] Governments, reflecting the advice received at the time, accepted this inflation as the "price" of attaining lower unemployment.[6] Stating this point in a different way, policy analysts viewed the cost of reducing inflation as being too high; for example, the tradeoffs estimated by Bodkin et al. (1966) implied that an increase in unemployment from 4 to 5 percent would reduce inflation by about 0.6 to 0.7 percent.

The extent to which policy makers could, through monetary and fiscal policy, maintain the economy at the preferred point on the Phillips Curve remained a matter of debate. The gradual acceptance of Keynesian economics and the development of econometric models of the economy generally led to optimism that such "fine-tuning" might increasingly become feasible. However, there was also recognition of the difficulties created for stabilization policy by the variability and unpredictability of the lagged responses to monetary, fiscal and other policies, as well as by the lags in recognizing and responding to deviations from full employment.

The potential role of labour market policy (such as improved information, training and relocation incentives) was to shift down the Phillips Curve; that is, to permit the economy to achieve less inflation at each unemployment rate. Holt et al. (1971) is a good example of this view. In addition, there was growing interest, largely based on the experience of several European countries, in the potential role of incomes policies to restrain inflationary pressures while maintaining high levels of employment.[7]

The Natural-Rate Hypothesis

By the late 1960s the notion of a permanent tradeoff between inflation and unemployment was being seriously attacked on theoretical grounds (the seminal papers were those of Phelps, 1968, and Friedman, 1968). In addition, the empirical support for such a relationship was rapidly diminishing; the upward drift of inflation beginning in the mid-1960s resulted in rates of wage and price increase well above those predicted by estimated Phillips Curves, given the unemployment rate (see Table 1-2). The third phase in economic thought, the widespread acceptance of the natural-rate hypothesis, had begun.

One source of inflationary pressure in the late 1960s was the rise in inflation in the United States. This in turn was largely due to the strong demand conditions associated with the Vietnam War and its financing primarily by printing new money rather than by taxation. The fixed exchange-rate regime in operation at the time meant that the U.S. inflation was transmitted to Canada.[8] However, even in the absence of the Vietnam War, it is highly likely that inflation would have accelerated. The policies based on the notion of a stable Phillips Curve tradeoff — accepting a positive (albeit low) rate of inflation in order to maintain the economy at high levels of employment — led to expectations that positive rates of inflation would continue in the future. As these expectations fed into wage and price setting behaviour, as well as interest rates, the Phillips Curve began to shift up, as Phelps (1968) and Friedman (1968) had predicted.

The central point made by Phelps and Friedman was that the short-run relationship between inflation and unemployment differs from the long-run relationship between these variables. In the short run, with given inflationary expectations, it is possible through (unanticipated) expansionary aggregate demand policy to reduce unemployment, thereby increasing inflation; to move from a point like "a" to "b" in Figure 1-3c. But doing so results in a higher rate of inflation than expected; thus, the position reached (point "b") is not an equilibrium position. The long-run relationship shows equilibrium combinations of inflation and unemployment, those for which actual and expected inflation are equal. Phelps and Friedman further predicted that wage and price setters would tend to take inflationary expectations into account on a "one-for-one" basis; that is, increase wage and price changes by the full amount of expected inflation in order to preserve the planned real wage or price increase. In these circumstances, the long-run relationship between inflation and unemployment is vertical at the natural unemployment rate U^n (see Figure 1-3c).

Two other developments may have played a role in the acceleration in inflation in the late 1960s. The sharp rise in prices meant a decline in real wages, relative to those previously experienced or expected, leading to pressure in wage negotiations for "catch-up" increases to restore real wages. At the same time there was an increase in worker militancy as measured by strike activity, which increased substantially in the late 1960s relative to earlier periods.[9] A wave of strikes and high wage settlements which occurred in a number of European countries is also generally attributed to declines in real wages (Flanagan, Soskice and Ulman, 1983). This increase in "grass-roots" worker militancy resulted in the breakdown of the tripartite incomes policies that had been used in several of these countries in an attempt to maintain high levels of employment without rising inflation. (The European experience with tripartism is discussed further in chapter 4 of this study.)

In addition, the rate of growth of unions in Canada began to rise in the mid-1960s.[10] In 1965 union density (union membership as a percent of all non-agricultural paid workers) was approximately the same as in 1946, about 30 percent. By 1983 union density had climbed to 40 percent. Much of the growth occurred in the public sector (public administration, health, education, and related services). Newly organized workers often receive above-normal wage increases in the first few contracts as a union/non-union wage differential is established.[11] For this reason, an increase in unionization may result in (temporary) additional inflationary pressures.

The acceleration in inflation was an embarrassing development for econometric predictions based on the stable Phillips Curve methodology and a source of considerable consternation for policy makers. The possible use of some form of incomes policy was actively discussed. The Economic Council of Canada commissioned a study of the foreign experience by Smith (1966) and devoted much of its third annual review to the issues of inflation, unemployment and incomes policy. The Task Force on Labour Relations also addressed these issues in its final report (Canada, Task Force on Labour Relations, 1968). Although both these advisory bodies cautioned against the use of an incomes policy, the federal government in its white paper *Policies for Price Stability* (Canada, Department of Consumer and Corporate Affairs, 1968) expressed concern that conventional monetary and fiscal policies were insufficient for

TABLE 1-2 Inflation, Unemployment and Related Economic Aggregates, 1960–84

	Rate of Change[a] of									
Year	Currency and Demand Deposits (M1)	Currency and All Chequeable and Notice Term Deposits (M2)	GNE Deflator	Consumer Price Index (CPI)	CPI Less Food	CPI Less Food and Energy	Negotiated Wage Rates[b]	Real Wage Rates[b]	Employment[c]	Unemployment Rate[c]
1960	1.3	—	1.3	1.4	—	—	—	—	1.6	7.0
1961	5.2	—	0.4	0.9	—	—	3.3	2.4	1.5	7.1
1962	3.3	—	1.4	1.1	0.9	—	3.5	2.4	2.8	5.9
1963	5.9	—	1.9	1.8	1.2	—	3.7	1.9	2.4	5.5
1964	5.1	—	2.4	1.8	1.8	—	4.7	2.9	3.7	4.7
1965	6.4	—	3.3	2.4	2.4	—	5.4	3.0	3.8	3.9
1966	6.8	—	4.4	3.7	2.8	—	7.9	4.2	4.2	3.4
1967	9.8	—	4.0	3.6	4.4	—	8.4	4.8	2.9	3.8
1968	4.4	—	3.3	4.0	4.5	—	7.5	3.5	1.9	4.5
1969	7.1	10.6	4.4	4.6	4.5	—	7.6	3.0	3.1	4.4
1970	2.4	7.2	4.6	3.3	3.9	—	8.7	5.4	1.1	5.7
1971	13.0	12.6	3.2	2.9	3.4	—	7.9	5.0	2.3	6.2

1972	14.4	10.8	5.0	4.8	3.7	3.9	8.8	4.0	3.0	6.2
1973	14.5	14.7	9.1	7.5	5.1	4.6	11.0	3.5	5.0	5.5
1974	9.3	20.5	15.3	10.9	8.8	8.3	14.7	3.8	4.2	5.3
1975	14.0	15.2	10.7	10.8	10.0	9.6	19.2	8.4	1.7	6.9
1976	8.0	13.0	9.6	7.5	9.4	8.8	10.9	3.4	2.1	7.1
1977	8.5	14.3	7.4	8.0	7.8	7.3	7.9	−0.1	1.8	8.1
1978	10.1	11.1	6.7	9.0	6.4	6.1	7.1	−1.9	3.5	8.3
1979	6.9	15.7	10.3	9.1	7.9	7.6	8.8	−0.3	4.1	7.4
1980	6.4	18.9	11.4	10.1	10.0	9.4	11.1	1.0	3.0	7.5
1981	3.8	15.2	10.6	12.5	12.8	10.9	13.3	0.8	2.8	7.5
1982	0.6	9.3	10.3	10.8	11.8	10.7	10.0	−0.8	−3.3	11.0
1983	10.3	5.7	5.5	5.8	6.4	6.3	5.6	−0.2	0.9	11.9
1984	2.4	4.2	3.0	4.3	4.0	4.0	3.5	−0.8	2.5	11.3

Sources: Statistics Canada, *Historical Data Compendium* prepared for the Royal Commission; Department of Finance, *Economic Review*, 1984; and calculations by the author.

a. Year-to-year percentage change.

b. Compound annual average percentage increase in base wage rates in new settlements. Data for 1961–66 are from the Bank of Canada Review, December 1971, and may not be strictly comparable to those for 1967–84.

c. Data for 1960–66 are based on the former Labour Force Survey. Data for 1967–84 are based on the revised Labour Force Survey.

restoring price stability without incurring unacceptably high costs in the form of reduced employment and output. Subsequently the federal government created the Prices and Incomes Commission "to inquire into and report upon the causes, processes and consequences of inflation and to inform those making current price and income decisions, the general public and the Government on how price stability may best be achieved" (Canada, Prices and Incomes Commission, 1972). The commission attempted to achieve agreement among business, labour and government on a program of wage and price restraint. However, as discussed in chapter 4 of this study, this attempt failed to win the support of organized labour.

The fixed exchange-rate regime in effect since 1962 severely constrained any attempt to employ monetary policy to reduce inflationary pressures. Maintaining the fixed exchange rate in the face of a rising rate of inflation in the United States resulted in rapid expansion of the Canadian money supply in the late 1960s (see Table 1-2). In 1970 the government allowed the Canadian dollar to float, and a rapid appreciation followed. The rate of growth of the money supply was then sharply reduced, unemployment rose to almost 6 percent, and the rate of price increase fell. Wage settlements, however, showed no tendency to decline (Table 1-2).

The government's attack on inflation was short-lived. Freeing the Canadian dollar allowed the authorities to pursue a lower rate of inflation than in the United States. However, concern about the rise in unemployment to over 6 percent in 1971 and about the effect of the appreciation of the Canadian dollar on the competitive position of exporting industries prevented this opportunity from being exploited. The latter, at least, was misguided (Sparks, 1985). Both fiscal and monetary policy turned expansionary and a period of rapid growth followed (Purvis and Smith, 1985; Sparks, 1985).

In its final report issued in 1972, the Prices and Incomes Commission attributed the rise in inflation in the 1960s to the building of strong demand pressure associated with pegging the Canadian dollar at the level of 92.5 cents in 1962, the expansionary monetary and fiscal policies pursued in Canada in the early 1960s, and the inflationary pressures emanating from the U.S. economy in the latter part of the decade. The persistence of inflation in 1970–71 despite slack demand, the report suggested, was due to lags in the response of wages and prices to variations in demand and to the inflationary expectations formed during the rise in inflation during the 1960s. The commission rejected "living with inflation" as an option and was skeptical of the potential for using manpower, regional development, and related policies for reducing the level of unemployment consistent with stable inflation, which they estimated to be 4.5 to 5 percent. Demand management and incomes policies were the commission's preferred policy instruments for dealing with inflation. Although demand management was to play the primary role, the commission did see potential for a temporary incomes policy:

> In conjunction with policies aimed at creating and maintaining a more stable demand environment, temporary resort to controls offers a means of bringing cost and price increases more promptly and reliably into line with the changes in demand conditions. This can speed up the process of adjustment and reduce the transitional loss of jobs and output in bringing inflation under control. (Canada, Prices and Incomes Commission, 1972, p. 7)

The commission added prophetically: "It may be that before long the march of events will bring Canadians to the view that serious consideration should be given to a temporary program of controls" (p. 7).

The Prices and Incomes Commission was clearly influenced by the Phelps-Friedman natural-rate hypothesis; their final report thus represented a significant departure from policy advice of the previous decade. Several aspects of this departure stand out. The commission rejected the notion that accepting some amount of inflation would enable the country to achieve lower levels of unemployment on a sustainable basis. It also cautioned against an overoptimistic view of the extent to which the "critical range of unemployment at which cost and price inflation [tends] to accelerate" had been or could be reduced. Their estimate of this critical unemployment rate — 4.5 to 5 percent — was significantly higher than the full employment targets recommended in the 1960s by the Economic Council of Canada, the Carter Royal Commission, and other advisory bodies. Further, the Prices and Incomes Commission noted that the costs of overly expansionary policies consist not only of the redistributive effects of the resulting unanticipated inflation but also of the reduced output and employment that would eventually be needed to reverse the inflation in costs and prices. To emphasize this point, the commission cited the following statement from the Economic Report of the President of the United States for 1971:

> We have now come to see more vividly than ever before how long and painful is the effort to halt the inflationary process once it has been let loose. The avoidance of inflation is always, of course, an objective of national policy, and was an objective in 1965–66 when the present episode began. But this objective may not get its proper weight because of failure to foresee the losses of output and employment that will later be entailed in ending the inflation. Remembering the experience of 1969–71 should help to correct this error.

The commission was clearly warning that the short-run costs of expanding the economy above potential output — the immediate increase in the rate of inflation — are less than the long-run costs. The corollary is that the short-run benefits of restrictive aggregate demand policies — the immediate reduction in inflation — are less than the long-run benefits, which accrue when inflationary expectations decline and the Phillips

Curve shifts down. This distinction between the immediate and longer-term benefits of a policy had not yet, however, become part of the accepted wisdom. After the brief flirtation with an anti-inflationary stance in 1970–71, both monetary and fiscal policy became expansionary.

In retrospect, monetary and fiscal policies were overly expansionary during the period 1971–73. However, this development was less evident at the time. The error in aggregate demand management appears to have had two main sources. The first was noted earlier — the Bank of Canada was apparently reluctant to allow the exchange rate to appreciate in order partially to insulate Canada from inflationary developments abroad. Expansionary monetary and fiscal policies were being pursued in most industrial countries; intervention in the foreign exchange market to prevent further appreciation of the Canadian dollar resulted in large increases in the money supply in 1972 and 1973 (see Table 1-2).

The second source of error resulted from the heavy reliance on the aggregate unemployment rate as a measure of slack in the economy, an inheritance from the Keynesian dichotomy.[12] Several important developments in the Canadian labour market caused the aggregate unemployment rate to become less meaningful as a measure of excess economic capacity. Most significant were the demographic changes in the labour force, in particular the increasing importance of women and youth, and changes in social legislation, such as the dramatic changes to the Unemployment Insurance (UI) Act in 1971–72. In addition, there were significant increases in minimum wages relative to the average wage throughout this period, a trend which began in the late 1960s. The effect of these various developments was to raise the natural unemployment rate by a significant amount.[13] Figure 1-4 provides one perspective on the magnitude of the changes between 1971 and 1974. Between 1971 and 1973/74 the unemployment-job vacancy relationship (the U-V curve) shifted dramatically to the right. The magnitude of the shift suggests an increase in non-cyclical unemployment of approximately two percentage points;[14] that is, if the Prices and Incomes Commission's estimate of the natural unemployment rate (4.5 to 5 percent) were correct, this rate would have increased to 6 to 7 percent in 1972/73. Subsequent empirical studies have tended to confirm the rough estimates suggested by Figure 1-4.[15] Thus, although the levels of unemployment in the early 1970s — 6.2 percent of the labour force in 1971 and 1972 and 5.5 percent in 1973 — were high by historical standards and were generally viewed as indicating an economy operating below its potential and requiring further stimulus, by 1973 the economy was evidently well past the point at which additional stimulation was appropriate. The extraordinarily rapid employment growth in 1972 and 1973 (see Table 1-2) was another indicator of developing demand pressures.

The early 1970s were also characterized by some dramatic price increases in food, raw materials and, in 1973, energy. These increases

FIGURE 1-4 The Unemployment — Job Vacancy Relationship, 1953–78

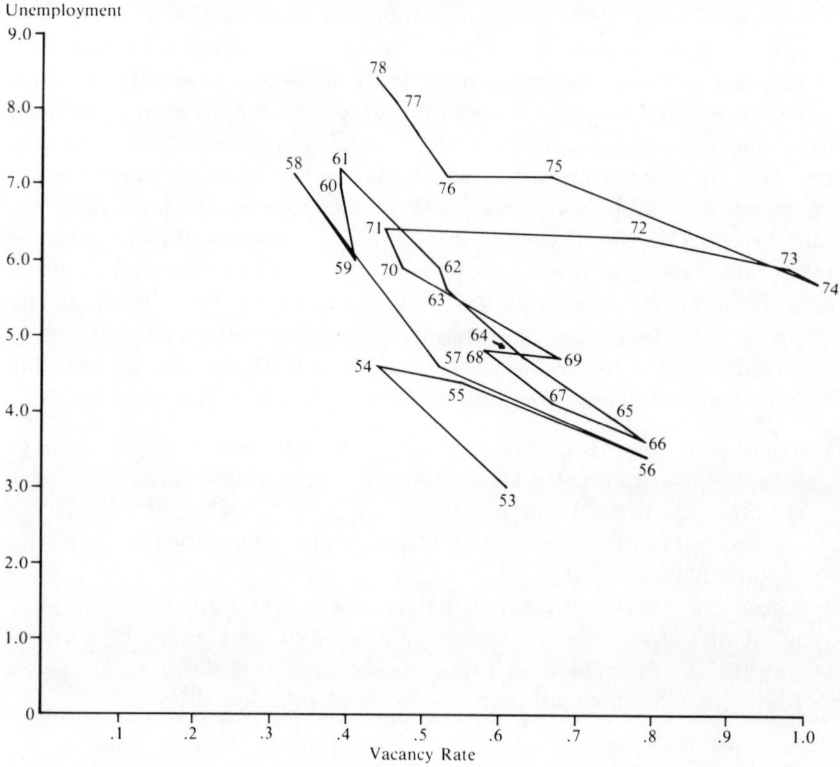

Sources: Unemployment rate: Statistics Canada, *The Labour Force;* job vacancy rate: Statistics Canada, *Job Vacancy Survey*. 1971–78, and F. Denton et al., "Patterns of Unemployment Behaviour in Canada," Discussion Paper No. 36 (Ottawa: Economic Council of Canada, 1975).

resulted both from random events — such as major crop failures and the disappearance of the anchovy harvest (a major source of animal feed) off the coast of Peru — and the rapid growth in world demand due to the coincident expansion in most industrialized countries. These developments in turn affected wage settlements. The sharp rises in consumer prices led to pressures for "catch-up" increases to restore real wages to their previous or anticipated levels. The dramatic increases in product prices which increased profitability in many exporting industries may have had an additional impact on wage increases.

The developments in the private sector coincided with an independent source of "wage push" — the rapid growth of unions in the public and quasi-public sectors (health, education and related services). As a result of this combination of events — buoyant demand conditions, sharp unanticipated increases in consumer and product prices, and unusually high wage increases for newly organized employees — wage increases accelerated rapidly from 1972 to 1975 (see Table 1-2).

Although some of the increase in inflation could be attributed to these various special factors, it was also becoming evident that inflation had developed considerable momentum in the form of a wage-price spiral in which individual wages and prices increase because prices in general are expected to increase, an expectation which becomes self-fulfilling. For this reason, the natural-rate hypothesis, highly controversial only five years earlier, had become fairly widely accepted by economists by the mid-1970s. The theory was compelling in the sense that the role of inflationary expectations was evident to even the most casual observer of wage and price determination. With the addition of data from the late 1960s and early 1970s, econometric tests had become increasingly favourable to the hypothesis. The mainstream view of the relationship between inflation and unemployment now had the following features:

- There is no long-run tradeoff between inflation and unemployment or total output. As illustrated in Figure 1-3c, the long-run Phillips Curve is vertical at the natural unemployment rate U^n. This unemployment rate is also referred to as the non-accelerating inflation rate of unemployment or NAIRU.
- There is a short-run tradeoff between wage inflation and unemployment or output, and between price inflation and unemployment or output. As illustrated in Figure 1-3c, there is a different short-run Phillips Curve for each expected rate of inflation, PE.

Accepting these features as a description of the operation of the economy had significant policy implications. There is no longer an argument for accepting somewhat more inflation in exchange for less unemployment. Using demand management to maintain the economy at an unemployment rate below the natural rate or NAIRU will lead to a continually increasing inflation rate.[16] Since operating the economy at potential output is consistent with any steady rate of inflation, that rate may as well be zero (or whatever target rate is deemed optimal). Moving to this optimal rate involves temporary costs (for example, it may involve maintaining the economy above the natural unemployment rate for some time until inflationary expectations decline) in return for permanent benefits (a permanently lower average rate of inflation). Compared to the implications of the Phillips Curve tradeoff view, the natural-rate hypothesis implied that macroeconomic policy should give a higher priority to reducing inflation and, once achieved, to the maintenance of price stability. Economic policy since the mid-1970s has reflected this view. At first, the gradualist approach to reducing inflation was tried. This was followed later in the decade by a much more determined anti-inflation policy. Before discussing these attempts to reduce inflation, a digression — forced by the unfolding of events — on stagflation is in order.

Stagflation and Productivity Decline

In the aftermath of the 1973 OPEC oil price shock there was a deep recession in the Western economies, accompanied by high rates of inflation. In Canada this downturn was less severe than in many countries, in part because the policy stance remained fairly accommodative and in part because Canada was a producer as well as an importer of oil.

The experience of stagflation — rising prices (or inflation rates) in a period of falling output and employment — caused considerable alarm. Although first-year economics students now learn routinely that increases in the price level can be caused by either a demand or supply shock, and accompanied by either rising or falling output and employment, this was not the conventional mode of thinking prior to 1973. As a result there was considerable speculation that the economic models inherited from the past were obsolete — that "the old rules no longer apply" — and confusion about appropriate policy. As stated by Solow (1978, p. 203):

> Practical people have been led to believe, first, that economists knew all the answers, and now they seem to believe that economists know absolutely nothing or perhaps even know negative amounts about the determinants of inflation. I guess many practical people would like to know what the truth of the matter is, and whether economics offers any guidance out of what they perceive to be a mess.

In retrospect, too much attention had been devoted to the demand side of macroeconomic models and too little to the supply side. Subsequently, considerable research effort has been devoted to correcting this imbalance.[17] With allowance for supply shocks, the basic expectations-augmented Phillips Curve or natural-rate model remained intact. The impact of supply shocks on potential output and the equilibrium real wage have also received increased attention.

Around 1973 in Canada and many other countries the growth in productivity slowed considerably (see Table 1-1), although it was not until later in the decade that it became apparent that a lower trend rate of growth had been established. The cause of this important development remains a matter of debate and controversy (Denny, 1985). Two factors which are generally agreed to have played a role are the rise in the relative price of energy and the generally greater amount of slack in the economy after 1973 (see, e.g., Helliwell, MacGregor and Padmore, 1985). However, most analyses suggest that these two factors cannot account for all of the decline, and a variety of additional explanations have been offered. Nonetheless, both stagflation and the decline in productivity growth appear to have resulted to a considerable extent from the 1973 oil price shock.

Disinflation I: Wage and Price Controls and Monetary Gradualism

Although the increase in inflation during the early 1970s was initially due to an important extent to external forces, by 1974/75 an ongoing domestic wage-price spiral had developed. Compared to other countries, Canada's 1974 recession was relatively mild; however, the rate of inflation was also relatively high. Price inflation exceeded 10 percent in both 1974 and 1975 and wage settlements rose to 15 percent in 1974 and over 18 percent in 1975. The government had increasingly indicated its concern about inflation but had rejected severe monetary and fiscal restraint as an appropriate response to the problem. Beginning in late 1974 attempts were made by the minister of finance, John Turner, to reach agreement with business and labour on wage and price restraint. These attempts, discussed in chapter 4, did not succeed. Faced with the continuing escalation in wage settlements and deteriorating demand conditions associated with the world recession, the government introduced the Anti-Inflation Program (AIP) in October 1975. The key ingredients in the program were mandatory wage and price (or profit) controls and gradual reduction in the growth in nominal aggregate demand through monetary and fiscal restraint.

The rationale behind this combination of policies was clearly stated at the time by both the government and the governor of the Bank of Canada.[18] Because of lags in the response of wages and prices to changes in demand and because of the strength of inflationary expectations, the immediate impact of restraint in aggregate demand alone would be primarily on output and employment. Only after a prolonged period of high unemployment and weak economic conditions would the desired reduction in wage and price increases occur. Combining demand restraint with temporary controls, it was hoped, would impact directly on wage and price increases as well as on expectations, thus reducing the transitional costs of attaining a lower rate of inflation. This rationale for a temporary incomes policy was clearly based on the natural-rate hypothesis, illustrating again the influence of ideas.

Monetarism and the Bank of Canada

The rise in inflation in the 1960s and 1970s increasingly focussed the attention of economists and policy analysts on the rate of growth of the money supply. A proposition common to all macroeconomic models was that inflation would not continue unless the price increases were validated by increases in the money supply. In this sense there was widespread agreement with Milton Friedman's dictum that "inflation is always and everywhere a monetary phenomenon." However, this proposition alone tells us little about the forces which cause monetary growth to be excessive — or at least rapid enough to validate a sustained inflation.

The experience of the 1960s and early 1970s caused the Bank of Canada to reassess the conduct of monetary policy. As early as 1973 the governor of the Bank expressed some sympathy for a policy approach focussed more on the control of monetary aggregates and less on credit conditions and the exchange rate (Sparks, 1985). By 1975 the Bank of Canada had become convinced that this approach was appropriate. Shortly after the introduction of the Anti-Inflation Program, the central bank adopted monetary targetting. The complementary nature of the two policies was stressed.[19]

Impact of the Anti-Inflation Program

During the three-year Anti-Inflation Program, wage settlements declined dramatically from about 18 percent in 1975 to about 6 percent in 1978. Price inflation also declined, although less dramatically. A gradual decline in the rate of increase of the GNE deflator and the CPI less food is evident in Table 1-2; the behaviour of the CPI including food is more erratic. The period was also characterized by much slower growth in output and employment, reflecting both external and internal forces. The unemployment rate rose to over 7 percent in 1976 and over 8 percent in 1977 and 1978.

Chapter 4 provides a more detailed description of the AIP and an assessment of its contribution to the observed decline in inflation. Most studies conclude that the program of temporary controls played a part in the moderation of inflation, particularly wage settlements.

The Resurgence in Inflation

Although world inflation moderated after the 1974/75 recession, it nonetheless remained high by the standards of earlier decades. In the United States the rate of CPI increase fell to almost 5 percent in 1976, but in the subsequent recovery moved sharply upward. In Canada, despite gradually declining targets (which were generally achieved) for the rate of growth of the narrowly defined money supply (M1) and any residual effects of direct controls, both wage and price inflation crept upward following the end of the AIP. In 1979 the second oil price shock occurred. By the end of the decade rates of inflation exceeded 10 percent in both the United States and Canada. A variety of aspects of economic behaviour suggested that expectations of continuing inflation were deeply entrenched.

Disinflation II: Severe Monetary Restraint

The consequence of these developments was the adoption of a much more determined anti-inflationary stance by the monetary authorities in the United States and subsequently in Canada. The general results of this policy change are evident from Table 1-2. (The response of wage changes on a quarterly basis are shown in Table 2-1 in the next chapter.) Initially, the impact of the reduced growth in nominal aggregate demand fell primarily on output and employment. As the unemployment rate climbed in late 1981 and early 1982, wage and price inflation moderated only slightly. However, as the impact of the severe recession became more widely felt, inflation began to decline dramatically. The adoption of the federal "6-and-5" wage restraint program and related provincial programs which limited the wage increases of public sector employees may also have played a role in the decline in wage increases. By 1984 the rates of wage and price inflation were the lowest since the 1960s. The restrictive monetary policy, possibly with some additional contribution from the public sector wage control programs, had clearly achieved its objective of ending a deeply entrenched inflation. Equally clear was the enormous cost — high unemployment, business failures, mortgage foreclosures, and reduced output.

The severity of the recession may well have been greater — perhaps significantly greater — than anticipated. Nonetheless, both the monetary and fiscal authorities had on numerous occasions emphasized the very high costs of reducing inflation by demand restraint alone. Why then was a policy chosen which had previously been rejected? One possible explanation involved recent developments in the theory of expectations.

Rational Expectations and Monetary Policy

The contributions of Phelps (1968) and Friedman (1968) had focussed considerable attention on the role of expectations in the inflationary process. Even those who were skeptical of the natural-rate hypothesis agreed that expectations of future inflation played an important role in wage and price determination. The long-run Phillips Curve, if not vertical, was thus considerably steeper than its short-run counterpart.

Given the importance of expectations in an ongoing inflation, a natural policy question follows: How can expectations be altered? The answer depends on how expectations are determined, an issue which has increasingly occupied economists. Although at first expectations had often been assumed to depend in a fairly mechanistic way on past behaviour, economists increasingly found attractive the notion that individuals would form their expectations rationally in the sense of Muth (1961); that is, expectations would represent an optimal forecast based on the individual's understanding of the process generating the variable being anticipated. A key feature of such rational expectations is that they are endogenous; that is, they depend on the behaviour of the system which generates the variable being anticipated. In the case of inflation, this implies basing expectations on one's understanding of the inflationary process, which would include the policy stance adopted by the monetary and fiscal authorities. Thus, one way that expectations could be altered was by changing the policy stance. However, simply announcing a change in the policy stance — for example, announcing that restrictive monetary and fiscal policies were to be adopted in order to reduce inflation — would not necessarily work. To affect behaviour the announced change in the policy stance would have to be credible.

This reasoning, which is discussed further in chapter 3, leads to the conclusion that estimates of the cost of reducing inflation based on past experience may not be reliable predictors of the potential cost.[20] According to the rational expectations hypothesis, such estimates are conditional on the policy stance in operation at the time — which over the previous two decades was a fairly accommodative one. If a credible commitment to a disinflationary policy were to be made, the costs of reducing inflation may be substantially less. As stated by Fellner (1980, pp. 763–64), models which ignore this credibility effect "involve a strong bias . . . toward overstating the difficulties of getting the price trend under control by consistent demand disinflation."

The fact that some economists predicted that the costs of disinflation might turn out to be significantly less than had previously been believed may have played a role in the adoption of severe monetary restraint in the United States, the United Kingdom and Canada.[21] For example, in his annual report for 1980, the governor of the Bank of Canada observed (Bank of Canada, 1980, pp. 7–8):

> It is sometimes said that the reduction of inflation in Canada through market processes is not practical in that markets are too unresponsive because of the degree to which power to control supply and prices lies in the hands of particular businesses or of trade unions or of marketing boards or of regulatory agencies. One cannot deny that there is some such unresponsiveness and that it intensifies the problem. But the Canadian economy has operated without significant inflation in the past, and the current problem may be more manageable than it looks. For one thing, we might be agreeably surprised at how well our markets would react if they were exposed to restrained demand over a considerable period of time and were convinced that the public authorities were serious and determined in their anti-inflation policy.

Wage and Price Inertia

A salient feature of the inflation of the past two decades has been its persistence. This characteristic was evident by the early 1970s, and appeared to contrast with the earlier postwar experience. In its 1972 final report, the Prices and Incomes Commission identified two major sources of the persistence of inflation in the face of variations in aggregate demand: lags in the adjustment of wages and prices and inflationary expectations. The determinants of both have since been high on economists' research agenda. The hypothesis of rational expectations was the major development in the theory of expectations; some implications of this hypothesis were briefly noted above, and these and others are discussed further in subsequent chapters. Two general sources of wage and price inertia have received substantial attention: implicit and explicit contracts and imperfect information.

These sources of persistence in wages and prices are at the heart of modern theories of the business cycle. Because of these rigidities, variations in aggregate demand have real effects — that is, effects on output and employment — in the short and medium term even though their ultimate impact according to the natural-rate hypothesis is solely on wages and prices. The extent to which changes in aggregate demand affect employment and outcome versus wages and prices — and how this division changes over time — depends on the strength of these sources of wage and price inertia.

Contract-based explanations of the business cycle stress the significance of understandings and agreements which (temporarily) set wages and/or prices in nominal terms. These may be explicit, for example, collective agreements in the unionized sector, or implicit, such as understandings regarding how frequently wages will normally be adjusted in the unorganized sector. The long-term nature of attachments between employers and employees make such understandings an efficient way to deal with changing economic circumstances. (Labour market contracts are discussed further in chapters 2 and 6.)

Information-based explanations of the business cycle emphasize the inability of individual firms and workers to distinguish temporary from permanent and aggregate from individual or localized changes in demand. Because of this uncertainty about the nature of the disturbance, the immediate reaction differs from the eventual response to the shock.

Sources of wage and price inertia are obviously central to the costs of disinflation via demand restraint. The view that these costs are extremely high is the main reason for considering additional policies such as wage and price controls. The experience of the recent severe recession has confirmed the large magnitude of these costs and their very uneven distribution across society. For this reason, economists have recently begun to examine possible institutional reforms which might increase the responsiveness of wages and prices to variations in aggregate demand. This increased interest in institutional reforms reflects more than the poor economic performance of the past decade.

TABLE 1–3 Alternative Schools of Macroeconomic Thought

		Nature of Expectations Formation	
		Adaptive (Backward-looking, Exogenous) Expectations	Rational (Forward-looking, Endogenous) Expectations
Wage and Price Adjustment	Continuous Market Clearing	Monetarist	New Classical
	Non-Market Clearing	Neo-Keynesian	Modern Keynesian

Recent research (discussed in chapter 6 of this study) indicates that the responsiveness of wages and prices varies across countries in ways that appear to be related to institutional mechanisms for wage determination.

Areas of Disagreement and Controversy

Clearly there have been significant advances in our understanding of the behaviour of inflation, unemployment and related economic aggregates. Nonetheless, important areas of ignorance remain. Two key sources of disagreement and controversy are the nature of expectations formation and the extent to which wages and prices adjust to equate demand and supply in labour and product markets. A classification of alternative "schools of thought" based on these two dimensions is presented in Table 1-3.[22] Like any such categorization, this necessarily glosses over subtleties and complexities in order to focus on the salient differences among these scholarly perspectives.

The observed inertia in wages and prices can be theoretically justified in terms of imperfect information, wage and price rigidities that prevent continuous market clearing, and slow adjustment of expectations. There is thus considerable scope for different views about the relative importance of each factor. The new classical school emphasizes imperfect information, and models macroeconomic behaviour as if labour and product markets are perfectly competitive and continuously in equilibrium (given current information and expectations). Modern Keynesians emphasize nominal wage and price rigidities due to implicit and explicit contracts and other institutional factors in labour and product markets, while neo-Keynesians see considerable potential for slow adjustment because of both backward-looking expectations and non-market clearing.

Empirical testing of these alternative perspectives continues. The available evidence favours the non-market clearing hypothesis over the assumption of continuous market clearing (O'Reilly, White and Ford, 1985). The evidence on the nature of expectations formation is more equivocal. This book will reflect this assessment of the current state of knowledge; that is, relatively little attention will be paid to the continuous market-clearing approaches to macroeconomics and both backward- and forward-looking expectations will be considered.

Summary and Conclusions

This section has sketched the main features of the postwar experience with inflation and unemployment, described the impact of these events on economists' understanding of these phenomena, and discussed the effect of the evolving accepted wisdom on the choices of policy makers.

One central theme is the influence of ideas on events. Three aspects of this theme stand out:

- the adoption of overly expansionary policies in the 1960s and early 1970s, in part based on a stable Phillips Curve perspective;
- the movement toward a policy of disinflation in the mid-1970s, partly associated with the increasing acceptance of the natural-rate hypothesis; and
- the adoption in the late 1970s and early 1980s of a strong anti-inflationary stance, perhaps reflecting in part the predictions of some economists that disinflation could take place at relatively little cost if a clear and widely understood commitment to such a policy were made.

A second theme is the influence of events on ideas — the accumulation of knowledge by discarding theories that appear inconsistent with observed behaviour and the devising of new or amended theories that appear capable of explaining the "facts." Although much remains to be learned about the relationship among inflation, unemployment, and related phenomena, and important controversies currently exist, there has nonetheless been significant progress in this area. Three aspects of this progress stand out:

- general acceptance of the natural-rate hypothesis as a reasonably good first approximation to the behaviour of the economy and rejection of the Keynesian dichotomy and the stable Phillips Curve tradeoff as inconsistent with observed behaviour;
- incorporation — or at least more widespread recognition — of the implications of supply shocks for macroeconomic behaviour and policy; and
- increased recognition of the importance of expectations for economic behaviour and of the implications of endogenous expectations formation.

One additional observation should be made. It is tempting to compare the economic performance during the first two decades of the postwar period with that subsequently, or perhaps the period prior to 1973 with that subsequent to 1973. Such a comparison might suggest that a variety of exogenous events — such as the Vietnam War, the food price shocks of the early 1970s, and the OPEC oil price increases in 1973 and 1979 — are largely responsible for the sharp deterioration in economic performance. Although these events clearly played an important role, this conclusion mistakenly treats the periods as independent of each other and ignores the role of macroeconomic policy. In fact, it appears that a significant component of the poor economic performance over the past 10–12 years may represent the "price" of the overly expansionary policies followed during the 1960s and early 1970s.

Dealing with Inflation and Unemployment: Options and Issues

The postwar experience illustrates many of the difficulties which policy makers face in dealing with inflation and unemployment. There are two central challenges:

- how to maintain desirable levels of employment without steadily increasing inflation; and
- how to stop or reduce in severity an on-going inflationary spiral should one develop.

The remaining chapters deal with key aspects of these challenges. As an introduction to the rest of the book, this section outlines the economic framework which underlies the analysis and lists the options available to policy makers.

A Framework for Policy Analysis

The previous section described the postwar experience and sketched the evolution of recent economic thought with respect to inflation and unemployment. Although a formal model is not developed here, a summary of the current understanding of these phenomena will provide a useful background for the policy analysis of subsequent chapters.[23] The framework which appears most consistent with the available evidence — and which will therefore be used here — has the following general features. Aggregate demand and aggregate supply jointly determine the price level (or rate of inflation) and output and employment, both in the short run and the long run. The long run allows for all necessary wage and price adjustments to take place in response to unanticipated shocks; in the short run there are wage and/or price rigidities due to implicit or explicit contracts, imperfect information, or other causes. The long-run Phillips Curve or aggregate supply curve is vertical; potential output and employment depend only on real variables. The short-run aggregate supply curve is upward-sloping and is "expectations-augmented." The following are the main propositions implied by this framework:

- Beginning in long-run equilibrium, an increase (decrease) in aggregate demand will raise (lower) output and employment in the short run, but will alter only the wage and price levels in the long run.
- The extent to which nominal demand shocks alter output and employment versus wages and prices in the short run and the speed of adjustment to the long-run equilibrium depend on the nature of expectations formation, the extent to which the shock was anticipated, and the nature of wage and price rigidities.

- Adverse supply shocks such as those that occurred in the 1970s result in stagflation — a rise in the price level and a decline in output and employment — in the short run. They may also alter potential output and the equilibrium real wage. The recession brought on by an adverse supply shock can be offset by an accommodating increase in the money supply, in which case the primary long-run impact of the disturbance is a rise in the price level (although, as noted, potential output and employment may also be affected). In the absence of accommodation, the recession will eventually reduce wages and prices or their rates of change, returning the economy to potential output.
- Increases in nominal aggregate demand and adverse supply shocks, if accommodated by increases in the money supply, result in a rise in the price level. A sustained inflation requires repeated increases in aggregate demand or repeated supply shocks (with monetary accommodation).
- Once expectations of a continuing inflation have been created, any rate of inflation can be maintained with the economy at potential output. For the inflation to continue, the price increases must be validated by increases in the money supply.

The Meaning of Full Employment

The increases in unemployment during the 1970s and 1980s have led some observers to question whether governments have given up on the commitment to full employment made in the early postwar period. Others have wondered whether the achievement of full employment is possible without steadily increasing inflation. Our review of the postwar experience and the evolution of understanding of macroeconomic behaviour suggest answers to these queries. Governments have revised their employment objectives in the light of evidence regarding the relationship between inflation and unemployment. In the past decade — in particular since 1979 — they have emphasized the need to bring inflation under control and have accepted temporarily abnormally high levels of unemployment as the cost of doing so.

The objectives of price stability and high levels of employment cannot be considered in isolation. When the relationship between the two is taken into account, the natural unemployment rate or NAIRU clearly emerges as a potential definition of full employment. Its key advantage in this respect is that it is feasible on a sustained basis. Higher levels of employment can only be achieved at the cost of steadily increasing inflation.

Although the NAIRU has much appeal as a definition of full employment, it does not necessarily coincide with alternative possible definitions of full employment — such as the level at which there is minimal hardship or no involuntary unemployment (Ashenfelter, 1983). Similarly, the natural unemployment rate, although it represents a state of macroeconomic equilibrium, is not necessarily socially optimal. These considerations suggest that although the NAIRU is a suitable definition of full employment for the purposes of macroeconomic policy, society should consider labour market and structural policies which may reduce the NAIRU and perhaps narrow the gap between the unemployment rate which is attainable on a sustained basis and that which society deems desirable. A number of these structural and labour market policies are examined in the studies in Riddell (1985a, 1985d).

Deviations from Full Employment

Discussions of the issue of full employment involve two distinct questions: What level of unemployment can and should be attained on average, or over the business cycle? And can large and prolonged deviations from this average or normal level be prevented or minimized? This latter question — the potential role of stabilization policy — raises many complex issues which are more properly dealt with elsewhere (see, in particular, the studies in Sargent, 1985). One important aspect of this question is, however, addressed in this study. The experience of the past two decades and developments in economic ideas have led to skepticism about the ability of governments to stabilize output and employment in the face of economic disturbances. Although it may be possible to offset or reduce large and extended deviations from potential output, the ability to "fine-tune" the economy is seriously open to question. This implies that deviations of output and employment and of wages and prices from their trend growth paths can be expected to continue to occur. A logical question is thus whether the nature or duration of such deviations from potential output can be influenced by institutional changes. The institutional arrangements that receive attention, largely because of their apparent significance, in chapter 6 of this study are those for wage determination.

Options for Controlling Inflation

Pursuing a full employment goal that is consistent with price stability (or stable inflation) may succeed in preventing the demand and supply shocks which do occur from once again creating an entrenched inflationary spiral. However, the experience of the past two decades suggests that this assessment may be overly optimistic. If an ongoing inflation does develop, the options available to policy makers will be those they faced in the late 1970s and early 1980s:

- Demand restraint, possibly combined with measures to enhance the credibility of the commitment to disinflation. This option is discussed in chapter 3.

- Wage and price controls, either of a voluntary or mandatory nature, possibly in conjunction with demand restraint. This option is discussed in chapter 4.
- Incentive-based incomes policies which employ taxes, subsidies, or other incentives for wage and price moderation, possibly in conjunction with demand restraint. This option is discussed in chapter 5.

The experience of the postwar period suggests that none of these options is particularly appealing. Perhaps it is inevitable that a choice must be made among unappealing alternatives. However, there may be institutional reforms which would, by increasing the flexibility of wages and prices, make disinflation through demand restraint less costly. Reforms of this nature are examined in chapter 6.

Chapter 2

Wage Inflation in Canada

Wage changes play a significant role in the inflationary process. Labour costs are an important component of total cost and reductions in the rate of price increase cannot be expected to occur, other than temporarily, without accompanying reductions in the rate of change of wages. For this reason, attempts to reduce inflation are typically directed to achieving reductions in wage as well as price increases. In addition, as noted in chapter 1, the belief that wage increases would respond only slowly to reductions in aggregate demand (or its rate of growth) has frequently been cited as a reason for not employing demand restraint or for supplementing it with other policies such as direct controls.

The purpose of this chapter is to summarize briefly what is known about the determinants of wage changes in Canada. This involves elaborating the basic expectations-augmented Phillips Curve or natural rate framework sketched in chapter 1 and assessing the extent to which the observed behaviour of wage inflation is consistent with that framework.

The Determinants of Wage Changes

Because of the importance of the topic, there has been a large amount of research into the determinants of wage changes. Much of this research follows the seminal papers of Phillips (1958) and Lipsey (1960) in relating the rate of change of wages to the unemployment rate or some other measure of the state of the labour market, and of Phelps (1968) and Friedman (1968) in including as an explanatory variable the expected rate of inflation. While there are important differences among the various studies discussed here, all employ this basic "expectations-augmented Phillips Curve" specification. Thus it appears that there is, in these studies, a substantial amount of agreement about the fundamental determinants of wage inflation. Of course, this apparent agreement reflects the view common to these studies that causation runs from changes in aggregate demand (or supply) to changes in output and employment to changes in wages and prices.[1]

Following the contributions of Phelps and Friedman, it was pointed out by Turnovsky (1972) and Turnovsky and Wachter (1972) that a third variable — commonly called a "catch-up" variable — should be included as a determinant of wage changes. In addition, although the dependent variable is the rate of change of nominal wages, the growth in real wages must also be explained. Indeed, this was the central point made by Phelps and Friedman: although firms and unions may negotiate over nominal wages, what ultimately matters is the real wage.

This brief discussion thus suggests the following specification for empirical work:

$$w_t = a_t + b\,(U_t - U_t^n) + c\,pe_t + d\,(P_{t-1} - pe_{t-1}) + \beta X_t \quad (1)$$

where

- w_t is the rate of change of wages
- a_t is the (anticipated) growth in real wages
- U_t is the unemployment rate
- U_t^n is the natural unemployment rate or NAIRU
- $U_t - U_t^n$ is the amount of excess demand or supply in the labour market at time t
- pe_t is the expected inflation rate at time t
- p_{t-1} is the actual inflation rate between time $t-1$ and time t
- $p_{t-1} - pe_{t-1}$ is the amount of unanticipated inflation at time t
- X_t is a vector of additional variables affecting wage changes
- b, c, d and β are parameters (or vectors of parameters).

The first four explanatory variables in equation (1) are common to most of the empirical studies of wage settlements. A brief non-technical discussion follows of the theoretical underpinnings of these four factors. An important point which emerges from this discussion is that this specification is appropriate for both the union and non-union sectors.

Excess Demand or Supply

The original derivation of the Phillips Curve due to Lipsey (1960), which assumed competitive labour markets, was based on two relationships: a positive relation between wage changes and excess demand for labour (the "law of demand"), and an inverse relation between excess demand for labour and the unemployment rate. The latter can be derived by expressing excess labour demand as the difference between the number of unfilled job vacancies and the number of unemployed workers, and assuming a stable (inverse) relation between unemployment and vacancies. The assumption of a stable relationship between the vacancy rate V and the unemployment rate U implies that there is a one-to-one relationship between excess demand and the unemployment rate.

Missing is an explanation of why excess demand or supply arises in the first place. Implicit in the theory behind the Phillips Curve is the assumption — one which is empirically well founded — that wages are set periodically, or at least not adjusted continuously. Between these intervals, excess demand or supply may arise. I will refer to the period within which wages are not adjusted as the contract period.[2]

There appear to be several reasons why wages do not adjust continuously to clear the labour market.[3] Transactions and negotiation costs are two obvious factors. It would be costly to adjust wages frequently. In the organized sector this would involve frequent costly firm-union negotiations and the possibility of a strike or lockout. More subtle explanations share two general features. First, they stress the long-term nature of attachments between employers and employees. Wages may clear the labour market over extended periods but not on a daily, weekly, or even monthly basis. Second, they involve the wage playing a role such as risk-sharing or providing incentives which is additional to the market-clearing role. Fulfilling more than one function means that the market-clearing role is not fulfilled continuously.

According to the natural-rate hypothesis, wages and prices will increase (decrease) relative to expectations when the economy is above (below) potential output. Thus the appropriate measure of excess demand or supply is the difference between actual and potential output, or between the actual and natural unemployment rates. Much of the early empirical research used the unemployment rate as the measure of excess demand, usually in a non-linear form. This is fine if the natural rate is constant over time (although it does affect the interpretation of the constant term a_t in equation 1), but is inappropriate otherwise.

As noted previously, because of demographic trends, changes in social legislation, and possibly other developments, the unemployment rate has not remained a consistent indicator of the "tightness" of the labour market through the postwar period (i.e., U^n has changed). There are two ways to deal with this situation. A number of authors (e.g., Fortin and Phaneuf, 1979) have constructed adjusted unemployment-rate series which are intended to provide a consistent measure of excess demand. The usual way this is done is to assume that the unemployment rate for males aged 25–44 has been (approximately) unaffected by these developments and so has remained a consistent measure of labour market tightness for that group. With this as a "benchmark," the unemployment rates for other age-sex groups are adjusted. The overall adjusted series is then a weighted average of these individual adjusted unemployment rates. Alternatively, some authors (e.g., Christofides et al., 1980b; Christofides and Wilton, 1985) use a measure of job vacancies (the help-wanted index) on the assumption that the developments that raised the natural unemployment rate did not significantly alter the natural vacancy rate.

An alternative procedure, used for example by Riddell and Smith (1982), is to measure excess demand in the labour market as the difference between the actual unemployment rate and the natural unemployment rate. A second equation is added to account for changes in U^n directly in terms of the demographic, legislative and other changes.

The notion of excess demand or supply is well defined for competitive labour markets. In the union sector, labour market tightness influences wage settlements by affecting the bargaining power of the firm relative to the union. This relative bargaining power depends primarily on the cost of a strike or lockout to the firm relative to the cost to the union and its members. When labour and product markets are tight (i.e., when U is less than U^n) the cost of a strike to the firm is high and the cost to workers low (to the extent that they can work elsewhere, possibly on a part-time basis, during the strike). The opposite holds when there is considerable slack in labour and product markets. Thus the "excess demand" variable $U - U^n$ is appropriate in both the organized and unorganized sectors.

Expected Inflation

If wages were adjusted simply to eliminate the current amount of excess demand or supply, then the unemployment rate or some other measure of excess demand would be the sole determinant of wage changes. This was Phillips's original specification, except that he also included the change in the unemployment rate to account for the "loops" around the curve.[4] However, with wages being set or negotiated periodically, we would expect that employers and employees would look not only at current conditions, but at the conditions expected to prevail during the remainder of the wage contract (whether an explicit contract as in the organized sector or implicit as in the non-union sector). This gives wage changes a "forward-looking" aspect, and is the rationale for including the expected inflation variable.

Expected inflation is a general term which includes several components: changes in the firm's product price, in wages in similar firms and industries, and in the cost of living. These reflect the fact that what matters to employers and employees are *relative wages* and *real wages*. To workers, what is important are wages relative to those received by comparable workers in other firms and industries (relative wages) and relative to the cost of living (real wages). Thus, expectations about wage changes elsewhere and about changes in the cost of living will be important factors in wage determination, especially when wages are not renegotiated frequently. To firms, what is important are wages relative to wages elsewhere (which affects the firm's ability to attract and keep workers) and relative to the prices that the firm can charge for its products (which affects the firm's ability to pay). Thus, expectations about product price increases should also be an important factor in wage determination. A fundamental difficulty with these expected inflation variables is that they are not directly observed or measured. Estimating the parameters in equation (1) thus requires constructing some proxy for expected inflation.

Most of the empirical studies have focussed on the expected increase in the Consumer Price Index (CPI). If all prices are rising at approximately the same rate, there is evidently no need to distinguish between (expected) product price inflation and consumer price inflation. However, there were some periods when product and consumer price changes differed considerably, although much of the difference may have been unanticipated.

Even if the average rate of product price inflation coincides with that of the CPI, there will be some variation in the rate across industries. Industries with product prices rising faster than average typically will be expanding output and employment and will have above average wage increases. The opposite will hold in declining industries. Most empirical studies do not incorporate the industry or firm level detail that would account for this variation.

The natural-rate hypothesis predicts not only that expected inflation will influence wage settlements, but that an increase in expected inflation of, say, x percent will increase the rate of change of wages by x percent at each level of excess demand. This prediction of a unit coefficient on the expected inflation variable implies that there is no long-run tradeoff between inflation and unemployment, a point which is discussed further below. Much of the empirical literature has been concerned with testing this once controversial prediction.

The prediction of a unit coefficient applies to the expected inflation variables as a group. Thus, if there are separate measures of expected product price, consumer price and wage inflation, a higher weight on one variable implies a lower weight on others. An economy in which there is a high weight on expected wage inflation (and therefore a low weight on expected price inflation) is sometimes referred to as being characterized by "wage-wage feedback." Similarly, an economy with a high weight on expected price inflation and a low weight on expected wage inflation is described as being characterized by "wage-price feedback." Clearly, these are matters of degree; an economy with wages 100 percent indexed to the cost of living is characterized by strong wage-price feedback. The extent to which an economy is characterized by wage-wage or wage-price feedback may be important in determining the short-run dynamics of adjustment to various economic shocks.

Catch-Up for Unanticipated Inflation

With wages being renegotiated infrequently, it is quite possible that the actual rate of wage or price inflation will turn out to differ from the expected rate. That is, the real wage and/or the relative wage at the end of the (implicit or explicit) contract will typically not equal the real or relative wage that was expected to prevail when the agreement was reached. If real or relative wages are lower than anticipated, there will be pressure from workers to "catch up." If real or relative wages are higher than expected, there will be pressure from firms to adjust wages downward, or to have them increase less quickly in the future. This suggests that some measure of the difference between the actual rate of wage and/or inflation over the previous contract and the expected inflation rate at the time the previous contract was signed should be included as an explanatory variable. Even if expectations are forward-looking, this catch-up variable gives a "backward-looking" aspect to wage determination.

Anyone who has read newspaper accounts of firm-union bargaining will have seen references to the need to "catch-up," and will not demand any further justification of this factor. Economists, trained that "bygones are forever bygones," sometimes are less easily convinced. Thus, it is important to note that the catch-up variable is a measure of excess demand specific to the individual bargaining situation; that is, it measures the extent to which the actual wage at the end of the contract differs from the equilibrium wage.[5] It therefore supplements the more general measures of excess demand discussed earlier.

The catch-up factor could go further and attempt to adjust for "bygones." For example, if actual inflation was greater than anticipated, not only is the end of contract wage below its equilibrium level but real wages were "too low" throughout the previous contract. Given the long-term nature of the relationship between firms and their employees, some compensation for these apparent bygones may be appropriate.

The catch-up variable creates additional difficulties for empirical research as it depends on expected inflation which is not directly observed. Any error in the measurement of expected inflation will lead to error in the catch-up variable.

Real Wage Growth

Although the dependent variable in equation (1) is the rate of change of nominal wages, the equation implicitly explains real wage growth. This can be most easily seen when $c = 1$ (i.e., the natural-rate hypothesis is correct) and unanticipated inflation is zero (for simplicity). Then (1) becomes:

$$w_t - pe_t = a_t + b\,(U_t - U_t^n) + \beta X_t \qquad (2)$$

Thus a_t is the anticipated growth in real wages, after allowing for the cyclical effect $b(U_t - U_t^n)$ and any additional determinants of wage growth X_t.

The primary determinant of real wage growth is the trend rate of productivity growth. Real wages will tend to grow at the rate of productivity growth, whether wages are determined by demand and supply or by firm-union bargaining, when the income shares going to labour, capital and other inputs are constant. Much of the empirical literature has proceeded on the assumption that the trend rate of productivity growth is a constant; that is, the studies have assumed $a_t = a$. This procedure is obviously questionable for data sets which include pre- and post-1973 data.

In negotiating wages, what presumably matters is the anticipated productivity growth over the life of the contract. There may therefore be a lag between changes in the trend rate of productivity growth and changes in (planned) growth in real wages. Labour market participants, like researchers, observe alterations in the trend some time after the change occurred. The significance of this point becomes clearer when we add the price equation.

The Price Equation

A common specification for the rate of price change is:[6]

$$P_t = w_t - q_t \qquad (3)$$

where q_t is the rate of productivity growth. Substituting (1) into (3) gives

$$P_t = (a_t - q_t) + b\,(U_t - U_t^n) + c\,pe_t + d\,(P_{t-1} - pe_{t-1}) \qquad (4)$$

Thus, if $c = 1$,

$$P_t - pe_t = (a_t - q_t) + b\,(U_t - U_t^n) + d\,(P_{t-1} - pe_{t-1}) + \beta X_t \quad (5)$$

The natural-rate hypothesis states that $U_t = U_t^n$ is consistent with any steady inflation rate $P_t = pe_t$. That is, at the natural rate U^n the rate of inflation should not tend to increase or decrease. Note, however, that if planned real wage growth a_t differs from productivity growth q_t or if there was unanticipated inflation in the previous period, then this prediction of a steady inflation rate does not hold. Of course, these outcomes may not persist. However, at any point in time a decline in productivity growth relative to planned real wage growth or unanticipated inflation inherited from the past can result in an increase in price inflation relative to expectations. These developments can therefore be confused with changes in the natural unemployment rate.

Other Determinants

A number of other factors have been investigated. Tax changes may affect labour demand (e.g., payroll taxes) or labour supply (e.g., income taxes). Shocks to the relative wage structure (e.g., union/non-union or public-private sector) may result in additional wage push until equilibrium is restored. Similarly, supply shocks may affect the growth of real wages. Other special events — such as wage control programs — may also affect the rate of wage inflation.

This brief description of the determinants of wage inflation sets the stage for a discussion of the empirical research on the subject. Perhaps the most obvious point to be made at this stage is that several of the key determinants — the natural unemployment rate, expected inflation, anticipated real wage growth — are not directly observed by the researcher, so proxies for each must be constructed. This creates considerable opportunity for diversity in the empirical research. It also implies that a certain degree of agnosticism with respect to the state of knowledge is appropriate.

Measurement of Wage Changes

Several measurement issues are worth noting. An important distinction is between wage rates and earnings. The latter depends not only on the hourly wage rate but on factors such as overtime pay and bonuses. Average wage or earnings indexes may also be affected by changes in the composition of employment; for example, if firms lay off mainly junior, low-wage employees in a cyclical downturn and rehire these employees in the upturn, the average wage or earnings index will vary countercyclically even if wage rates and earnings for each type of employee do not. For this reason, it would be preferable to use indexes based on fixed employment weights. Unfortunately, the average earnings indexes available in Canada do not have this feature.

Another important distinction is between current and deferred wage changes. In the postwar period there has been a marked trend toward the use of multi-year contracts in the unionized sector, a development discussed in chapter 6. Multi-year contracts often contain deferred increases. The magnitude of these may be predetermined (i.e., fixed at the time the contract is signed) or indexed to changes in the Consumer Price Index (referred to as a cost-of-living-allowance or COLA clause) or other variables. The observed change in wages or earnings at any point in time is thus a mixture of current and deferred changes. Yet the determinants of these two types of wage change clearly differ.

TABLE 2–1 Percentage Wage Changes in Canada, Annual and Quarterly

Year	All Major Collective Agreements in Force	New Non-COLA Settlements in Major Collective Agreements				
		Annual	Q1	Q2	Q3	Q4
1967	—	8.4	8.9	8.8	7.7	8.2
1968	8.0	7.5	7.5	7.8	7.7	7.3
1969	9.1	7.6	7.0	7.4	7.7	8.3
1970	8.5	8.7	8.8	8.2	9.0	8.7
1971	7.8	7.9	8.2	7.8	8.5	7.4
1972	7.4	8.8	9.3	7.9	9.3	8.8
1973	8.3	11.0	10.5	10.1	10.8	12.2
1974	12.3	14.7	12.4	13.5	15.9	19.8
1975	14.2	19.2	19.0	21.7	19.9	14.9
1976	14.3	10.9	14.6	11.1	10.0	8.8
1977	11.2	7.9	8.6	8.4	7.5	6.9
1978	6.8	7.1	6.9	6.4	7.3	8.1
1979	7.8	8.8	8.1	8.4	9.1	9.7
1980	9.7	11.1	9.5	11.2	11.6	11.6
1981	11.5	13.3	13.8	12.6	13.8	13.9
1982	—	10.0	12.9	12.5	10.2	7.2
1983	—	5.6	6.7	5.8	5.7	4.1
1984	—	3.5	3.9	2.9	3.1	4.5
1985	—	—	3.6	—	—	—

Source: Canada, Department of Labour, *Wage Developments*, various issues.
Note: Major collective agreements refer to bargaining units with 500 or more employees, excluding construction. Wage increases are measured as the compound average annual rate of increase in the base wage rate over the life of the agreement. Contracts containing cost-of-living allowance clauses are excluded.

Table 2-1 shows that the differences can be large. The first column shows the percentage change in base wage rates which occurred during the year; that is, it contains both current and deferred increases in all major collective agreements. The second shows the percentage change in base wage rates in new non-COLA settlements reached during the period. These are calculated on a life-of-the-contract basis; that is, they show the compound annual average increase in wages (both current and deferred) to take place over the duration of the agreement. Contracts containing COLA clauses are excluded because the value of these increases is not known at the time the contract is signed. The difference between the two series is at times as much as 5 percent. New settlements exhibit more variation and are a "leading indicator" for broader measures of wage change. (This is most evident over the 1974–78 period.) Most of the recent empirical studies use the data on new wage settlements as the dependent variable because of its evident advantages as a measure of wage change to be explained by current and expected future economic conditions.

Another implication of the move to multi-year contracts is that the fraction of the labour force negotiating a new agreement varies from year to year. In some years as few as 30 percent of major collective agreements are renegotiated while in other years more than 60 percent are renegotiated.[7] Thus, some of the variation in aggregate earnings (or wage) indexes is simply due to the timing of the "bargaining calendar." This is another reason for preferring the new settlements series over annual or quarterly changes in aggregate earnings.

In view of these difficulties associated with aggregate index data, researchers have increasingly turned to data on individual contracts. This approach treats each negotiated settlement as an observation and to a considerable extent circumvents the two problems discussed above. In particular, deferred increases are not so problematic in that all the increases to take effect during the contract are included in calculating the percentage change in wages, which is then explained in terms of economic conditions prevailing at the time the contract was signed. Similarly, variations in the proportion of the labour force bargaining in each period are evidently less of a problem in that one observes the underlying rate of change of wages. In addition to lessening the measurement difficulties associated with analyzing the determinants of wage changes, the use of contract data also provides considerably more micro detail and therefore permits the testing of some hypotheses which would simply not be feasible with more aggregative data.

Not all of the recent studies treat each individual contract as an observation. Reid (1979) and Riddell and Smith (1982) use more aggregative measures by employing as the dependent variable a weighted (by number of employees) average of the individual wage changes negotiated during the period; that is, a series such as that shown in Tables 2-1 and 2-2. It is important to note that use of these aggregate measures of the rate of change of wages does not raise the problems which are associated with aggregate measures obtained from wage index data.

In addition, not all of the recent research uses individual contract data or averaged contract data. Given the limitations of the Major Collective Agreements data (in particular, the use of the base wage and the limited coverage of the labour force), it is useful to have studies based on aggregate earnings indexes — despite the qualifications that attach to the use of these data — because the measure of wage change confounds both current and deferred increases and is sensitive to variations in the bargaining calendar.

Both earnings and wage rates do not include "fringe" or non-wage benefits. This omission implies that the observed hourly wage understates both the hourly cost of labour to the employer and the benefit received by the employee. Fringe benefits have become an increasingly large fraction of total benefits so that the true rate of wage change (i.e., that which includes the monetary equivalent of non-wage benefits) is also understated. There are no good time-series data on the monetary value of fringe benefits; surveys of large firms conducted by Thorne Riddell Ltd. suggest that non-wage benefits have increased from under 15 percent of total benefits in the 1950s to over 35 percent today.

Observed Behaviour

Table 1-2 shows the annual rate of wage change over the 1961–84 period, using the new settlements series. Tables 2-1 and 2-2 provide more detailed data. Inspection of the quarterly data in Table 2-1 indicates the substantial persistence exhibited by new settlements. (The inertia in the rate of wage change in all agreements is even larger, as a comparison of the two columns of annual data will verify.) Several developments stand out: the rise in wage settlements from 7–8 percent in the late 1960s to about 20 percent in the first three quarters of 1975; the steady decline in wage increases during the Anti-Inflation Program (which began in October 1975) from about 20 percent to 6–7 percent; the resurgence in wage increases in the late 1970s and early 1980s; and the dramatic decline beginning in 1982.

Table 2-2 shows current wage settlements for the private and the three components of the public sector. The largest differences across these sectors occurred in the period immediately prior to the AIP (1974/75) and during the disinflation of 1982–84.

TABLE 2–2 Wage Settlements in Major Collective Agreements, 1972–84

	Federal Administration	Local Administration	Provincial Administration	Private Sector
1972	8.8	7.6	7.2	9.7
1973	12.0	9.8	10.3	11.6
1974	11.2	12.6	14.2	16.8
1975	13.9	16.5	25.1	17.8
1976	11.9	10.4	11.2	10.5
1977	9.5	7.9	7.5	7.9
1978	6.7	6.5	7.3	8.2
1979	8.3	8.7	8.3	9.9
1980	10.8	10.4	11.2	11.8
1981	12.6	13.2	13.6	13.5
1982	8.3	12.9	11.3	10.8
1983	8.4	5.7	5.8	5.2
1984	5.0	3.2	5.4	2.8

Source: Canada, Department of Labour, *Wage Developments*, various issues, and Labour Data Branch (Ottawa: The Department).

Note: Major collective agreements refer to bargaining units with 500 or more employees, excluding construction. Wage settlements are measured as the compound annual rate of increase in the base rate over the life of the agreement. Contracts containing cost-of-living allowance clauses are excluded.

Empirical Results

A large number of studies of wage inflation have been carried out in Canada. Many of these use individual contract data (e.g., Christofides, Swidinsky and Wilton, 1980a, 1980b; Christofides and Wilton, 1979, 1985; Cousineau and Lacroix, 1977; Lacroix and Dussault, 1984; Riddell, 1979) or monthly or quarterly averages of individual settlements (e.g., Reid, 1979; Riddell and Smith, 1982). In addition, some researchers have employed aggregate earnings indexes (Fortin and Newton, 1981; Fortin and Prud'homme, 1984). These various studies will not be described in any detail here; rather, we will focus on the general nature of the findings common to this body of research and any important differences among the studies.[8]

Each of the studies includes a measure of labour market tightness and finds that excess demand is a significant determinant of wage changes; that is, there is a short-run Phillips Curve. A variety of measures of labour market tightness are used. If the unemployment rate alone is used, it is generally insignificant or perversely signed (Christofides et al., 1980a). Some allowance for variation in the natural unemployment rate is evidently needed to identify the short-run Phillips Curve. This is not surprising given the substantial shift in the U-V relationship shown in Figure 1-4. Riddell and Smith (1982) explicitly model the natural rate in terms of demographic and legislative changes, while Fortin and Newton (1981) and Fortin and Prud'homme (1984) use a measure of labour market tightness constructed originally by Fortin and Phaneuf (1979) which adjusts for these changes. Periods of excess labour demand and supply identified by these different methods are shown in Table 2-3. There is substantial agreement between the two measures; only 1972, a year of very slight excess supply according to Fortin and Phaneuf (1979), is classified differently. The other studies use measures of job vacancies — the job vacancy rate or the help-wanted index — as the labour market tightness variable. Most do not allow for possible changes in the natural vacancy rate (a concept analogous to the natural unemployment rate), although Christofides et al. (1980a) find that changes in the unemployment insurance system shifted the relationship between wage changes and the help-wanted index and altered its slope. This suggests that the factors to which Reid and Meltz (1979) attribute the shift in the U-V relationship also raised the natural job-vacancy rate.

A common finding of these studies is that the response of wage changes to variations in unemployment (or other measures of excess demand) is not large. The short-run Phillips Curve is fairly flat — a slope of 0.5 is a rough estimate (evaluated at the natural unemployment rate), although one study (Riddell and Smith, 1982) obtains a slope closer to one.

Both expected inflation and catch-up for previously unanticipated

TABLE 2–3 Periods of Excess Demand or Supply

	Excess Demand	Excess Supply
Fortin and Phaneuf (1979)	1966–69 1973–74	1970–72 1975–78
Riddell and Smith (1982)	1966–69 1972–74	1970–71 1975–80

inflation appear to play significant roles in wage determination. The studies indicate that the rise in inflation expectations and catch-up were responsible for most of the upward shift of the short-run Phillips Curve. Because the length of wage contracts varies considerably across bargaining units, it is difficult adequately to incorporate the influence of unanticipated inflation with aggregate data. The studies which use individual contract data (e.g., Christofides et al., 1980a, 1980b; Christofides and Wilton, 1985; Riddell, 1979) have important advantages in this respect.

However expectations of future inflation are formed, they will often turn out to be incorrect. The catch-up variable is intended to capture the effects of over or under prediction of inflation; that is to restore the real wage to its equilibrium level. The specification of the catch-up variable in equation (1) is appropriate when the prediction of a unit coefficient on the expected inflation variable holds (i.e., $c = 1$). However, if for some reason the wage contract does not fully incorporate expected inflation, then adjusting the wage in a subsequent contract for the difference between actual and expected inflation will not be adequate. In this context, Christofides, Swidinsky and Wilton (1980a) have introduced the distinction between unanticipated and uncompensated inflation. The latter is the difference between the actual rate of inflation over the previous contract and the amount of expected inflation incorporated in the previous contract; that is, uncompensated inflation $= p_{t-1} - cpe_{t-1}$. When $c = 1$, the two are equal. Christofides, Swidinsky and Wilton (1980a) argue, however, that employers and employees may prefer wage contracts in which expected inflation is not fully incorporated ex ante (i.e., c is less than unity), leaving the remainder to be adjusted ex post. Clearly the firm would prefer this arrangement; it is less clear why the employees would agree to it on a continuous basis, since it implies that real wages are understated even when there are no errors in forecasting inflation. Nonetheless, in their study of individual wage settlements over the 1966 to 1975 period, Christofides et al. (1980a) do find that the expectation parameter c is systematically less than unity. Indeed, they find that the uncompensated inflation component is somewhat more important than the expected inflation component. These findings are also supported by Riddell and Smith (1982) using more aggregate data. While these results do contradict the prediction of a unit coefficient on the expected inflation variable, they do not necessarily contradict the natural-rate hypothesis. In particular, the issue becomes whether the combined ex ante and ex post adjustment for inflation is equal to unity. Both Christofides et al. (1980a) and Riddell and Smith (1982) find that the combined effect is not significantly different from one.

The fact that inflationary expectations are not directly observed makes it difficult to distinguish between wage adjustments which are ex ante versus ex post responses to inflation. Expected inflation is usually measured as a distributed lag of past inflation, while the catch-up variable also contains past inflation. Studies such as Reid (1979) and Fortin and Newton (1982) which do not include separate expected inflation and catch-up variables will thus estimate the combined effect of these two aspects of wage determination. These studies also support the natural-rate hypothesis.

Although the Christofides et al. (1980a) result that c is systematically less than unity is consistent with the proposition that there is no long-run tradeoff between inflation and unemployment, the extent to which wages adjust to expected inflation on an ex ante versus ex post basis is clearly important for the short-run dynamics of output and inflation. Even with full ex ante compensation for expected inflation, the existence of a catch-up adjustment for forecast errors implies that unanticipated disturbances will have effects that will persist for several years. The smaller the ex ante compensation and thus the larger the ex post compensation, the more significant are the delayed responses to economic shocks. Even if expectations are forward-looking, there is therefore an important backward-looking aspect to wage determination. The implication of the Canadian studies is that this aspect is quantitatively significant.

Another potential source of inertia in wage inflation is the spillover effects of some wage settlements on others. This effect may arise because relative wages are important to both employees and employers. The combination of long-term overlapping wage contracts and relative wage effects can result in substantial persistence in wage inflation, an issue discussed in more detail in chapter 6. Several studies (including Christofides, Swidinsky and Wilton, 1980b; Fortin and Newton, 1982; Lacroix and Dussault, 1984; and Ford 1985) have examined the role of spillover effects in wage determination in Canada. One aspect which has been investigated in a number of studies is the effect of public sector wage settlements on those in the private sector. Wilton (1985) provides a detailed survey of this literature. The main finding is that there does not appear to be any pervasive spillover from public to private sector wage changes, but there is evidence of such effects in particular labour markets. Within the private sector, however, spillover effects, especially those within the same industry, do appear to be an important determinant of wage inflation (Christofides et al., 1980b; Ford, 1985).

The spillover effects estimated in the above studies are treated as a continuing aspect of wage determination. There may also be one-time or special factors which disturb the relative wage structure. The effects of these non-continuing shocks may persist for several years until equilibrium in the relative wage structure is restored. One occurrence of this nature is suggested by an examination of Table 2-1, which shows unusually high wage settlements in the public sector, particularly in provincial administration, during the early 1970s. As noted earlier, these may have largely reflected the substantial spurt in unionization in that sector which occurred during this period. Such special factors can result in wage settlements being unusually high given the other variables which affect wage changes. Empirical studies tend to support this assessment in that they typically underpredict wage inflation during the 1973 to 1975 period (see, for example, Reid, 1982).

Policy Implications

The empirical studies generally support the basic framework outlined in the previous chapter; that is, there is a short-run but apparently no long-run relationship between inflation and unemployment. They are relatively uninformative about the nature of expectations formation. However, they do point to several important sources of inertia in wage inflation, even in the context of forward-looking expectations: the short-run response of wage changes to variations in unemployment is small; catch-up for unanticipated or uncompensated inflation implies that the effects of economic disturbances persist for several years given the length of wage contracts; and spillovers among wage settlements, especially within the same industry, also imply that the effects of disturbances persist for several periods.

Chapter 3

Controlling Inflation by Demand Restraint

This chapter discusses the role of demand restraint in controlling inflation. Debate centres not on the ultimate success of a non-accommodative policy in ending or preventing inflation but on what damage such an approach would leave in its wake.

Alternative Views

There have been important changes in the views of economists and other analysts regarding the costs of reducing inflation via monetary and fiscal restraint. With the advent of the Phillips Curve the view emerged that these costs were very high because the estimated slope of the Phillips Curve was fairly flat, especially at higher levels of unemployment given the generally assumed non-linear nature of the relationship. This view played a major role in public policy in Canada. For example, the creation in 1968 of the Prices and Incomes Commission to examine alternative policies for combatting inflation and unemployment, the rejection in 1974 of monetary and fiscal restraint as "a cure worse than the disease" (Canada, Department of Finance, 1974, p. 6), and the adoption in 1975 of wage and price controls were based on this premise. The policy statement introducing controls stated in part (Canada, Department of Finance, 1975, p. 4): "The government has repeatedly emphasized its rejection of the use of severe monetary and fiscal restraint to stop inflation at heavy immediate cost in terms of unemployment and foregone output."

The natural-rate hypothesis did not alter the view that the costs of reducing inflation by monetary and fiscal restraint are very high. Its main implication in this regard was that these costs are temporary, occurring during the transition from high to low inflation rates. However, with the development of the hypothesis of rational expectations, a new perspective on the potential for these policies emerged. Sargent (1981, pp. 1–2) summarizes this perspective and contrasts it with the more traditional view:

> In the last fifteen years, many western economies have experienced persistent and growing rates of inflation. Some prominent economists and statesmen have become convinced that this inflation has a stubborn, self-sustaining momentum, and that either it simply is not susceptible to cure by conventional measures of monetary and fiscal restraint, or else that in terms of the consequent widespread and sustained unemployment, the cost of eradicating inflation by monetary and fiscal restraint would be prohibitively high. . . .
>
> An alternative "rational expectations" view denies that there is any inherent momentum in the present process of inflation. On this view, it is acknowledged that firms and workers have come to expect high rates of inflation in the future, and that they strike inflationary bargains in the light of these expectations. However, it is held that people expect high rates of inflation in the future precisely because the government's current and prospective monetary and fiscal policies warrant these expectations. Further, the current rate of inflation and people's expectations about future rates of inflation may well seem slow to respond to isolated *actions* of restrictive monetary and fiscal policy that are viewed as temporary departures from what is perceived as a long-term government *policy* involving high average rates of government deficits and monetary expansion in the future. Thus inflation only *seems* to have a momentum of its own, while it is actually the long-term government policy of persistently running large deficits and creating money at high rates which imparts the momentum to the inflation rate. An implication of this view is that inflation can be stopped much more quickly than advocates of the "momentum view" have indicated, and that their estimates of the length of time and the costs of stopping inflation in terms of foregone output . . . are erroneous.

According to this perspective, the costs of disinflation would be much less than is suggested by estimated expectations-augmented Phillips Curves if the monetary and fiscal authorities were to make a credible commitment to a non-accommodative policy stance.

This viewpoint appears to have had an important impact on demand management policy in the past decade — particularly that followed in the United States and the United Kingdom since 1979. Although the monetary and fiscal authorities may well have been skeptical that disinflation could be achieved at little cost, they have increasingly emphasized their commitment to a non-accommodative stance. In Canada, the attempt to establish a commitment to a policy of non-accommodation of inflation began with the introduction by the federal government of the Anti-Inflation Program in October 1975 and the adoption by the Bank of

Canada of monetary targetting in November 1975. Toward the end of the AIP, the governor of the Bank of Canada stated in his annual report for 1977:

> Before much longer we shall face yet another test, the phasing out of the mandatory income guidelines administered by the Anti-Inflation Board. For the first time in quite a while decisions on incomes and prices for large segments of the economy will have to be made solely on the joint responsibility of those directly involved. These decisions will be made in a market environment that is not going to be strong enough to absorb anything more than modest increases in incomes and prices without the loss of potential jobs and output. It is therefore very important that wage- and price-setting decisions should not be distorted by a resurgence of inflationary expectations. Since monetary policy has some influence on expectations I have been at pains to emphasize that no one should look to monetary policy to accommodate inflationary increases in costs and prices through excessive monetary expansion. (Bank of Canada, 1977, p. 7)

As noted in chapter 1, the hope that monetary gradualism and other policies would result in a continued decline in inflation following the end of the AIP was not met. By 1980, rates of inflation had returned to double-digit levels. The Bank's determination to pursue a disinflationary policy was stated clearly by the governor in his annual report for 1981:

> It seems to me that Canadians in general are not yet convinced that public policy in Canada will be firm enough and persistent enough to bring about a major reduction of the rate of inflation in Canada. Only the fact of firmness and persistence will convince them. If, instead, they see weakness of will on the part of the authorities, they will react quickly to protect themselves against accelerating inflation in whatever ways are available to them. People's confidence in the future value of money has been severely shaken, and central banks and governments no longer get the benefit of any doubt about their will to protect the value of their currencies. It would not take too much evidence of weakness of will on the part of the authorities to generate another wave of inflation in this country.
>
> In these circumstances the Bank of Canada has no responsible option but to continue to restrain the rate of monetary expansion in Canada. In these circumstances it cannot back off from that policy. (Bank of Canada, 1981, pp. 9–10)

The switch to a disinflationary policy stance by the monetary authorities was most dramatic in the United States beginning in October 1979. A similar policy was adopted in the United Kingdom following the election of the Thatcher government in the same year.[1] The recent experience, particularly that of the United States and the United Kingdom, provides, from the perspective of economic science, a critical experiment in the reduction of inflation by a determined policy of demand restraint. The results of that experiment are thus of considerable interest.

Impacts of Changes in Policy Stance

A large number of studies have examined the U.S. experience to determine if the disinflation of the 1980s was more rapid than would have been predicted on the basis of historical experience (Cagan and Fellner, 1983; Perry, 1983; Vroman, 1983; Blanchard, 1984; Eckstein, 1984; Fischer, 1984; Friedman, 1984; Taylor, 1984a). The results are mixed, with some studies finding no significant impact and others finding that disinflation occurred somewhat more rapidly than would have been expected on the basis of previous experience.

The price equations estimated by Friedman (1984) and Perry (1983) actually predict a more rapid disinflation than occurred, although Fischer (1984) calculates that the costs of this disinflation were at the lower end of the range predicted by Okun (1978). Studies based on wage equations (Blanchard, 1984; Cagan and Fellner, 1983; Eckstein, 1984; Perry, 1983; Vroman, 1983) generally find that wage settlements declined more rapidly than predicted, although there are important differences among the studies in the magnitude and timing of the prediction errors. Taylor (1984a) uses time-series analysis and finds weak evidence of an increase in wage flexibility. Because the unemployment rate attained during the 1981–83 period was outside the range of previous postwar experience, the tests based on estimated Phillips Curves are quite sensitive to the assumptions made about the non-linear nature of the relationship. Interpretation of the results is further confounded by the various special factors that may also have played a role. The monetary-fiscal mix in the United States produced a more dramatic increase in real interest rates and appreciation of the dollar than would have occurred if the two policies had been in concert; this may have reduced wage settlements (through greater threat of bankruptcies) and price increases (through import competition). Deregulation, increased competition from newly industrialized countries, and the decline in world oil prices may also have played a role.[2]

Buiter and Miller (1981b, 1983) examine the U.K. experience. Their results are also equivocal with respect to the independent contribution of the change in the policy stance. McCallum (1964) conducts multicountry tests (18 OECD countries) using both estimated Phillips Curves and time-series methods. He finds no significant evidence of an increased degree of wage responsiveness in these countries after 1980. Nor do the results for the United Kingdom and the United States — the countries with the most evident change in the policy regime — differ in the manner predicted by the credibility effect from those of the remaining countries.

The empirical evidence thus provides little support for the view that major gains in wage and price flexibility — and thus major reductions in the costs of disinflation — can be achieved by announcing and carrying out a policy of severe demand restraint. These results are consistent with two alternative views: the potential gains from a credible commitment to disinflation are large but the public did not believe that the authorities would persist with the policy; and the potential gains are small because of wage and price rigidities associated with implicit and explicit contracts and slowly adjusting expectations.

Enhancing Credibility

If expectations have a significant forward-looking dimension, there may be benefits to making the commitment to a non-accommodative policy more credible. The focus of policy thus switches to the problem of establishing or enhancing credibility. How best can the authorities convince the public of their commitment to the policy of not accommodating inflation in the future?

Achieving greater credibility is not a simple matter. Simply announcing the intention to pursue a non-accommodative policy is unlikely to be effective. Assuming the public is aware of the importance of wage and price rigidities in the economy, they will recognize that, unless everyone's expectations are affected, a non-accommodative stance will be a costly strategy and there will therefore be considerable pressure on the authorities to abandon it. Thus the public may be very skeptical about the willingness of the authorities to carry out the announced policy and to continue with the policy even after it has been in operation for some time and is having the predicted effect. An extended learning period may be required to establish the commitment to the non-accommodation of inflation.

If, as seems to be the case, the public is imperfectly aware of the structure of the economy and there is a distribution of views across the population about the way the economy works, the problem of achieving credibility is more difficult. As Schelling (1982) has emphasized, the government can commit itself to policy inputs but not to outputs. If everyone believes that limiting the growth of M1 (an example of a statement about policy input) will reduce the rate of inflation below what it would otherwise have been, then the inability to control the policy output will not be so important. The central difficulty will remain that of achieving credibility with respect to the stated plan for the inputs. However, when there is uncertainty about the effects of the policy in addition to the authorities' commitment to it, the effect of the announcement on expectations will be reduced.

In this connection an obstacle to establishing the credibility of disinflationary or non-accommodative policy is the reluctance of government authorities to detail the consequences of the policy they intend to pursue. This point is stated well by Schelling (1982, p. 80):

> I have never read a clear statement from any administration that unemployment itself had a key role to play in getting inflation under control. I have never read a clear statement from any administration that high interest rates

> had a key role to play in driving down the prices of buildings and equipment and consumer durables, and in depressing the labor markets in steel, automobiles, and housing. The money supply is a popular target of policy, because the money supply is an aggregate that nobody experiences personally. Tight money and low interest rates, or quick recovery and lower prices, are promised as compatible objectives. Budget deficits, despite doctrinal reversals that already had my head spinning twelve months ago, are treated as instruments of sympathetic magic rather than as means to increase or reduce current spending for goods and services by taxpayers, governments, or investors. I do not see any sign that anybody who is president, or wants to be, is able to come clean on what it is, in fighting inflation, he wants us to believe.

In Canada, as both Courchene (1983) and Lipsey (1983) point out, the recent recession may have been more effective in restraining inflation if the government had made clear at an early stage the nature and consequences of the policy, rather than suggesting throughout the first six months of the downturn that a recovery was soon to begin. Courchene suggests that the actions and predictions of the fiscal authorities were in some respects contradictory to those of the Bank of Canada, so that the commitment of the government to the anti-inflation policy was in doubt. Further, the record of the Canadian government may have contributed to skepticism, in contrast to the newer regimes in the United States and the United Kingdom.

It is difficult to determine how much more effective the demand restraint policy would have been if the government had, from the outset, "come clean" about the probable effects of the policy and appeared more supportive of the Bank of Canada. Certainly, when these changes did occur (in the June 1982 budget), the subsequent effects on wage and price increases were dramatic. But the extent to which these effects were due to the public sector wage controls included in that budget, the apparent increased commitment of the government to disinflation, and the severe recession is less clear. Those who support the use of incomes policies will point to the wage controls, while those who support the use of demand restraint will point to the commitment to disinflation contained in that budget. If the implementation of public sector wage controls was an important factor contributing to credibility, both groups are not far apart.

With respect to the future, demand restraint could possibly be made more effective, although I believe major gains are unlikely. Governments fail to "come clean" or continue to emit contradictory signals for their own reasons. Spelling out the intent to follow a disinflationary policy and detailing its consequences are politically dangerous.

The process of moving to a less accommodative monetary policy appears to be occurring now, especially in the United States and the United Kingdom. The authorities are investing in a "reputation for toughness," and like most investments, the current costs are high in relation to the current returns. Under the hypothesis of rational expectations, in order for the investment to have the intended effect, the switch to a less accommodative policy must itself be credible. As Taylor (1982) notes, the switch satisfies a necessary condition for credibility — the new policy rule is an improvement over the previous rule, at least in the context of a particular model of the economy. Specifically, the less accommodative policy is predicted by Taylor (1982) to lead to increased price stability without altering the average levels of output and employment. Increased fluctuations in output and employment would result, although these increases would be small relative to the gains in price stability.

If becoming less willing to validate increases in prices and wages is a policy improvement, why has the change not been made earlier? This is an important question, for, again, if the current switch to a new policy is to be credible, those involved in wage and price setting must believe the authorities are now committed to a change that they have not made in the past. The evolution of ideas sketched in chapter 1 suggests that there is a good answer to this question. Prior to the widespread acceptance of the natural-rate hypothesis, the wisdom of following a less accommodative policy was not widely recognized.

However, there remains some doubt about the superiority of pursuing a non-accommodative policy even in the natural-rate context. As Baily (1978) and McCallum (1983b) have pointed out, making credible the commitment to this policy stance may have some destabilizing effects. The benefits from the increased wage and price flexibility induced by this policy might be offset by greater fluctuations in consumption and investment demand. The latter effects may occur because firms and workers recognize that recessions will be somewhat more pronounced and prolonged.

Another observation on the current change in policy rule is that the reputation for toughness which is being acquired at such high cost may not attach itself to the monetary institutions but rather to the individuals currently in charge of those institutions. This seems to have been the case in the United States with respect to Paul Volker, and apparently played an important role in his reappointment as chairman of the Federal Reserve. However, because institutions generally outlive individuals, the initial costs of acquiring a reputation may have to be incurred too frequently to make the investment worthwhile. More generally, because in a democracy governments cannot commit future governments, the public may remain skeptical about the willingness of the authorities to adhere to a policy of non-accommodation of inflation.

Doubts about the willingness of monetary authorities to switch to and continue with a less accommodative policy have led to proposals for monetary reform which would remove discretion and constrain the authorities in a manner that would be clear to, and therefore taken into account by, those involved in wage and price setting. Some analysts have even advocated monetary reform such as the adoption of a gold or other commodity standard. The case for such reforms appears to be weak.[3] In the Canadian setting the simplest way to tie the hands of the monetary authorities would be to return to a fixed exchange rate. However, there are important advantages to the flexible exchange rate, so this approach would have significant costs. The benefits would also be uncertain in that Canada would be accepting the U.S. inflation rate.

Long-Run Impacts of Demand Restraint

In addition to the transitional costs discussed above, demand restraint appears to have important longer-run effects. These effects occur because of high real interest rates; thus they are most significant when monetary policy is the primary restraint instrument, as was the case in Canada and the United States during the disinflation of the early 1980s. High real interest rates not only reduce current aggregate demand (the intended effect) but also — because they reduce current investment expenditure — the future capital stock. Thus, after the economy has recovered from the recession, potential output will be lower than it would otherwise have been and the natural unemployment rate may be higher.

An additional longer-term consequence is particularly important in a small open economy such as Canada's. Unless other countries are also pursuing disinflation, the high real interest rates will cause an exchange-rate appreciation, reducing the country's competitive position. Because of the dynamics of exchange-rate movements (in particular, their tendency to "overshoot"), this reduction in competitiveness (and thus reduced output and employment) lasts for an extended period, thus raising the costs of disinflation by monetary restraint (Buiter and Miller, 1981a).

Conclusions

There is widespread agreement that demand restraint must play a role in reducing an entrenched inflation and that a non-accommodative monetary policy would contribute to price stability in the future. Views differ, however, on the costs of reducing inflation by demand restraint alone and on the wisdom of following a non-accommodation policy in the face of demand and supply shocks. The recent experience has confirmed that inflation can be significantly reduced through a determined policy of demand restraint but that the costs of that policy are extremely high. One might hope that this experience would enhance wage and price flexibility in future efforts at inflation reduction, but there is little basis for believing that this will occur. Evidently there is a need to examine alternative methods of bringing about a disinflation. These methods are examined in the next three chapters.

Chapter 4

Incomes Policies:
Can Wage and Price Controls Help?

The term "incomes policies" will be used to refer to policies which intervene in wage and price setting in order to influence the overall rate of wage and price inflation.[1] This definition covers a wide range of policy initiatives, including exhortation or "jawboning," the setting of guidelines or attempting to reach agreement on norms for wage and price increases, statutory wage and price (or profit) controls, and incentive-based incomes policies. Incentive-based incomes policies provide incentives for wage and/or price restraint through taxes or subsidies or by requiring firms to purchase "permits" to raise prices or wages, and are dealt with in the next chapter. This chapter examines various forms of direct wage and price control, both voluntary and mandatory.

Incomes policies are typically administered by government agencies set up, often on a temporary basis, for that purpose. This description applies to Canada, the United States and the United Kingdom — countries with decentralized collective bargaining and a non-union sector not covered by collective agreements. However, in some European countries, especially those with centralized bargaining between national labour and business organizations, the incomes policies are largely administered by private organizations. Although some discussion of the experience of these countries is contained in this chapter, most of the discussion is carried out in the context of the Canadian institutional setting.

In the postwar period governments have experimented with a variety of incomes policies. In Canada, these experiments included a number of attempts at voluntary restraint; perhaps the most formal and notable experiment was that of the late 1960s and early 1970s. As noted in chapter 1, this involved the creation of a special agency — the Prices and Incomes Commission. In addition, mandatory wage and profit controls were a key part of the Anti-Inflation Program of 1975–78. Wage controls were applied to public sector employees in the federal "6-and-5" program and associated provincial programs which began in 1982 and some of which, such as the B.C. Compensation Stabilization Program, are still in effect at the present time (1985). Similarly, in the United States, incomes policies were employed during the Korean War period (the Wage Stabilization Board of 1950–53), during the Kennedy and Johnson administrations (the guideposts of 1962–66), during the Nixon administration (the wage-price controls of 1971–74), and during the Carter administration (1977–81). In many European countries, periods without incomes policies of some form were less common than periods with such policies. There is thus a rich history of experience with incomes policies from which we may be able to infer their advantages and disadvantages.

A great deal has been written about incomes policies, and the subject is a controversial one. A wide range of views can be found in the literature. Some of these views are based more on strongly held a priori opinions than on a careful examination of the empirical literature. Nonetheless, even among those who have examined the evidence there are a variety of opinions on the advisability of using such policies. To some extent this situation reflects the assignment of different weights to difficult-to-measure factors. However, it also reflects the rather mixed record of these policies.

In what follows I attempt to give a balanced assessment of these policies. The underlying rationale is examined first. Subsequent sections examine the prospects for voluntary or negotiated wage and price restraint in Canada, the evidence on the effects of control programs, and the costs associated with these policies.

The Rationale for Incomes Policies

A variety of proposals for incomes policies have appeared. One useful distinction is between those which suggest permanent rather than temporary incomes policies, for the underlying rationale is very different. Since most advocates of a permanent incomes policy propose an incentive-based scheme, the rationale for permanent incomes policies is discussed in chapter 5. Here we examine the rationale for a temporary incomes policy.

The observation that reducing inflation by demand restraint policies alone involves very substantial costs provides the fundamental rationale for incomes policies. Direct wage and price controls attempt to achieve by fiat what the various causes of inflation inertia make difficult to obtain otherwise — a reduction in the actual rate of inflation without a substantial increase in unemployment. If the public can be convinced that the reduction in inflation is not simply temporary, then expectations of future inflation will decline, thus permitting less inflation at each unemployment rate. After expectations have declined to the target rate of inflation, the controls can be removed and the economy returned to the level of potential output (if not already there).[2] Monetary growth and fiscal policy must then be appropriate for the target rate of inflation.

This policy option thus involves temporary wage and price controls designed to move the economy to the desired equilibrium position (potential output, target inflation rate) at lower cost in terms of lost output and high unemployment. Its potential success does not rely on fooling the public in any way, providing growth in nominal aggregate demand is reduced in accordance with the lower rate of inflation permitted by controls.

A more precise statement of the rationale for a temporary incomes policy is worth spelling out. This also indicates the strong similarity between arguments for credible demand restraint and for a temporary incomes policy. There are two cases to consider. First, for conceptual purposes, we examine the situation in which wages and prices are flexible. Subsequently, the consequences of (temporarily) fixed wages and prices and staggered wage and price setting are discussed.

In both cases it is convenient to begin with the economy at potential output, though this is not essential to the argument. Suppose there is a steady state inflation rate of x percent, and the objective is to lower this to y percent. This will require reducing the rate of growth of nominal aggregate demand from x to y percent. Once the economy has adjusted to the lower rate of growth of nominal aggregate demand, it can be maintained at potential output and the lower steady state inflation rate.

In the case of flexible wages and prices the incomes policy could simply impose a norm for wage and price increases designed to reduce the average rate of inflation to y percent[3] and, at the same time, reduce the rate of growth of aggregate demand to y percent. If the wage and price controls were enforced, the economy would move immediately to the new equilibrium position. Thus the wage and price controls play the same role as a credible program of demand restraint. In principle at least, an increase in unemployment above the natural rate is not required for the policy to be effective.

Since the new steady state is preferred by both wage and price setters and the government authorities, there is no incentive for either to deviate from it once the controls are lifted. Thus, if expectations are rational the new steady state inflation of y percent will be maintained after the expiry of controls. If expectations are adaptive, the controls program will have to be maintained long enough to reduce expectations accordingly. Again, once this is accomplished, there would be no reason for inflation to increase in the post-controls period.

These predictions of no "post-controls bubble" will not hold if the wage and price control program is not accompanied by the necessary reduction in the rate of growth of aggregate demand (in this case to y percent). This is true however expectations are formed, though the nature of the post-controls wage and price bubble will depend on the extent to which expectations are adaptive rather than rational. Thus it is critical to the long-term and quite possibly short-term success of the temporary wage and price control program that it be accompanied by appropriate reductions in the growth in aggregate demand.

Two potential difficulties with this rationale should be noted. (More general difficulties with and objections to incomes policies are discussed later.) The first accepts this "economic" rationale for a temporary incomes policy, but argues that it is of little practical relevance because politically the temptation not to follow through with the appropriate reduction in the growth of aggregate demand is too strong. According to this "failure of the policy process" view, the initial success of the controls program convinces politicians that inflation is under control; they then proceed to expand the economy to reduce unemployment.[4] This results in excess demand in many goods and factor markets. The controls program either collapses under this pressure, and/or a wage and price explosion occurs at the end of the program.

This objection should certainly be taken seriously. As will be seen below, there is some evidence which appears consistent with this view. However, it is worth noting that the combination of a temporary incomes policy and reduced growth in aggregate demand does not necessarily require increases in unemployment above the natural rate in order to be successful. Thus the "failure of the policy process" view relies on political pressure to maintain or reduce unemployment below the NAIRU.

The second potential difficulty arises from the fact that any incomes policy which involves a ceiling on wage and/or price increases will distort relative wages and prices to some degree. Even if there is zero excess demand overall at the end of the controls program, there may be a need for relative prices and wages to adjust. If there is more upward than downward flexibility in prices and wages, this process will result in inflationary pressures.[5] This is an important qualification, not only because some evidence supports it (as discussed below) but also because it is relevant to the appropriate design of an incomes policy. Ideally, the policy will reduce the average rate of inflation but allow relative wage and price adjustments to occur.

Now let us turn to the case in which there are nominal wage and price rigidities and wage and price setting is not synchronized. For simplicity I will deal with non-synchronized wage setting, empirically the most relevant case.[6] Here it is again possible for a controls program, combined with the appropriate reductions in the rate of growth of nominal aggregate demand, to bring about a reduction in the steady state inflation rate without an increase in unemployment above the natural rate (Phelps, 1978a, 1979). However, in this case the incomes policy must be rather more cleverly designed.

The central problem is to ensure that relative wages are in equilibrium by the end of the controls period. As noted above, even with fully flexible wages and prices there is a need to be concerned about both the wage structure and the wage level (or its rate of change). However, non-synchronized wage setting introduces an additional consideration that complicates matters. To illustrate, take the simplest overlapping contracts case with two groups (A and B) negotiating annual contracts at six-month intervals. Without loss of generality, the equilibrium relative wage is assumed to be unity ($W^A = W^B$). If inflation is running at 10 percent, the two groups will be (in a steady state) leapfrogging each other, first one being 5 percent higher and then the other (see Figure 4-1). The difficulty with this situation is that $W^A \neq W^B$ at any time. Thus, a wage freeze, whenever it is imposed, will be unsuccessful in that the wage structure will be out of equilibrium whenever the controls are lifted. In this simple example, there are two workable options which approximate a wage freeze. If controls are imposed at t = 1 (i.e., $W^A = W^A{}_1$, $W^B = W^B{}_0$), the authorities could lower W^A to $W^B{}_0$ (at t = 1.5 if existing contracts are not allowed to be abrogated; at t = 1 otherwise) or allow W^B to increase to $W^A{}_1$ at t = 1 (i.e., a 5 percent increase), maintaining the freeze thereafter.

Of course, this is a particularly simple example. In general there are numerous groups with contracts of various lengths that overlap to varying degrees. Phelps (1978a) shows that in more complex cases there is a wage control system (i.e., a wage path) that, combined with the appropriate aggregate demand policy, will wind down the wage inflation, maintain the economy at the natural rate, and yield an equilibrium wage structure at the end of the controls period. However, approximating this wage path will not be a simple matter. As in the example above, there are two alternative paths in general. The first involves cutting wages as contracts expire. The case that is more likely to be attempted in practice allows smaller and smaller increases as contracts expire, reaching a zero allowed increase for the contract negotiated just prior to the imposition of controls.

Thus, with overlapping wage contracts, the ideal wage path for winding down an imbedded inflation involves gradual reductions in the allowed rate of wage increase, with accompanying reductions in the rate of monetary expansion just sufficient to maintain the economy at potential output. The control ceilings in each period are designed to yield an equilibrium relative wage structure at the end of the program. These wage control programs assume that existing collective agreements are not to be abrogated. If one is willing to do away with existing contracts, then a less gradual reduction in wage increases can take place. Even

FIGURE 4–1 Wage Paths with Overlapping Contracts

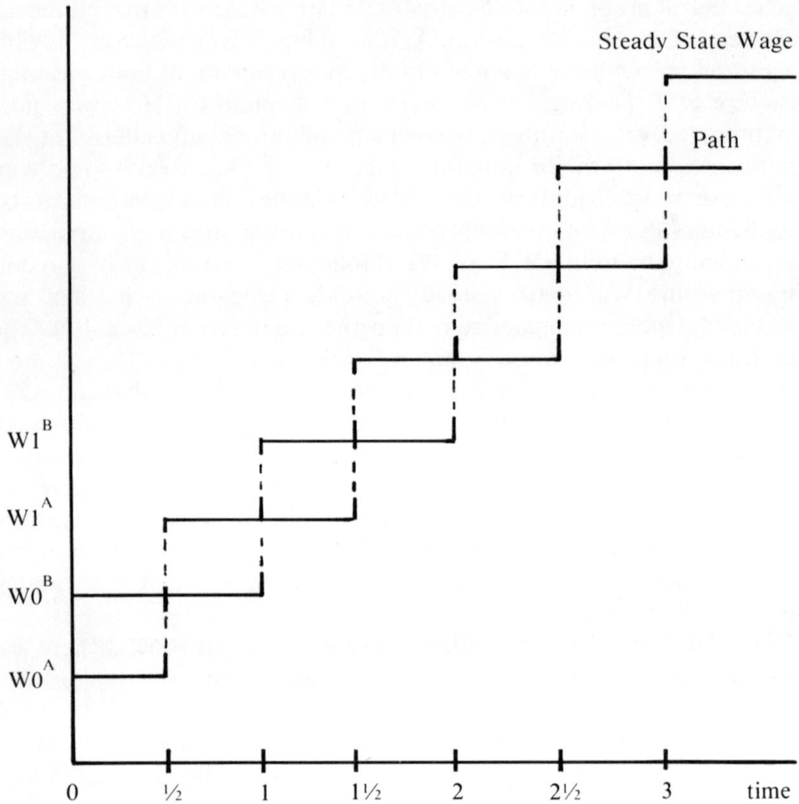

here, though, the same general principle holds — that the relative wage structure should be in equilibrium at the end of the controls period.

In summary, there is a theoretical rationale for a temporary controls program. In principle such a policy can contribute to a reduction in inflation without incurring substantial costs in terms of unemployment and reduced output. If properly carried out, the reduction in inflation can be permanent. Whether these desirable results can be achieved in practice is, of course, an empirical question.

The view that a temporary incomes policy can be successful in aiding the transition to a lower inflation rate appears to be widely held in Canada (but less so elsewhere) at the present time. Indeed, one knowledgeable observer, Vanderkamp (1982, p. 2), terms it "a middle-of-the-spectrum view, which may perhaps by now be seen as the conventional Canadian wisdom." The fact that econometric studies indicate that the

1975–78 Anti-Inflation Program had a significant independent effect on wage settlements has undoubtedly contributed to this "conventional wisdom." (The empirical evidence on the effectiveness of incomes policies is discussed below.)

An important part of this rather sanguine view is the proposition that the incomes policy needs to be carefully coordinated with a program of monetary and fiscal restraint. To maintain the economy at existing levels of output and employment, the rate of growth of aggregate demand should be reduced by the expected reduction in price inflation. Otherwise, the aggregate demand and incomes policies are working at cross purposes and the commitment to reduce inflation will lack credibility. One of the apparent mistakes of several previous control programs has been the belief — or perhaps hope — that the incomes policy will by itself reduce inflation so that expansionary monetary and fiscal policies can be followed.

This section has suggested that a temporary incomes policy can be a useful component of a package designed to make the transition from a high to a low inflation rate. However, little has been said about the costs of these policies or about the effectiveness of alternative forms of incomes policies. These issues are examined next, beginning with voluntary mechanisms and proceeding to mandatory wage and price controls.

The Scope for Voluntary Mechanisms[7]

One possibility would be to attempt to establish a broad national agreement among business, labour and government on the rate of change in wages and prices. Such an agreement would take the form of a norm or set of norms which all three parties would respect in the general process of wage and price determination. Clearly a system of voluntary restraint along these lines would have tremendous advantages. It would avoid the conflicts and tensions often generated by mandatory controls, and would accord with a general desire to avoid extending state intervention into the most detailed aspects of economic life.

Other countries have been able to rely for lengthy periods on voluntary mechanisms. During the postwar period a number of European countries devoted considerable effort to developing institutions and decision processes which encouraged an ongoing collaboration between government and major economic interests. Countries such as Austria, Sweden, Norway, Denmark and, for briefer periods, West Germany and the Netherlands established tripartite systems which, while different in important details, share the common element of centralized negotiations and accommodation among the three "social partners" — government, business and labour — over a wide range of economic policies. But the heart of these systems is the development of a voluntary incomes policy, and the apparent success of their economies during the 1970s in particular has often been attributed in substantial measure to the effectiveness of these mechanisms of social consensus. This section therefore examines the European experience with incomes policies and examines the prospects for such voluntary cooperation in Canada.

The Tripartite Experience

In examining the European experience, it is important to focus on two basic issues. An understanding of the first issue, the economic and political conditions under which voluntary incomes policies have been established and have flourished, is critical to any discussion of moving toward tripartism in Canada, where economic and political relationships are very different. The second issue, the actual impact of such incomes policies on the economic performance of the countries which have relied on them, must be analyzed to assess whether this cooperative behaviour has had an important, independent impact on the achievement of economic goals.

Virtually every student of European tripartism has stressed the extent to which such mechanisms depend on key features of the economic and political structures of the societies which rely on them. One factor which facilitated the emergence of tripartite relations was the concentration of both economic and political authority. Strong national employer and trade union federations which cover the great majority of enterprises and the work force must be capable of negotiating on behalf of their sector and concluding agreements which commit their memberships. Similarly, government leaders must possess the authority to fulfil understandings reached concerning public policy. Any fragmentation of political authority over economic policy, whether among different bodies at the national level or among different levels of government, can erode the capacity to make credible commitments. Centralization of economic and political authority is thus a precondition of a close integration of the three "social partners."

Certainly the countries with the most experience with tripartite voluntary incomes policies are centralized societies. Politically, they are either unitary states or, as in Austria and Germany, centralized federations in which authority over economic policy is heavily concentrated at the national level. Economically, they are also centralized, especially in the domain of collective bargaining. Strong central employer federations were well established in the Scandinavian countries in the 1940s; and in Austria a similar concentration was established by compulsory membership in the Chamber of Business. A parallel pattern has developed within organized labour. Countries such as Austria, Sweden, Norway and Denmark have high levels of unionization and the most highly centralized trade union movements in the Western world in terms of the financial resources and authority of the national federations over their affiliates and members. This framework generates a highly centralized process of wage formation, with direct or indirect government involvement in the negotiations a recurring feature of the system. Centralization of economic and political authority is thus a key feature of tripartite systems, producing elitist processes of decision making in important spheres of national life. This centralization derives in part from the fact that these are small countries with relatively homogeneous societies — a common language and culture and few serious regional divisions.

A second factor which facilitated the emergence of consensus mechanisms in these countries was the pattern of political alliances among the governing parties and the major economic interests. For the most part, modern tripartism was the creation of social democratic parties which were closely allied with organized labour. Social democratic governments or coalitions of which they were part gave a high priority to high levels of employment and expansion of the welfare state. In addition, they brought to power a faith in economic planning and a determination that labour should participate along with business and government in the processes of policy formation on the basis of greater equality. Indeed, social democrats often appealed to the electorate on the basis that their special relationship with labour made them uniquely able to deal with trade unions, to generate a wider social consensus, and to minimize social conflict over economic affairs. While conservative parties were often sympathetic to tripartite initiatives, social democrats adopted tripartism as a central element in their political philosophy in the postwar period. As Panitch (1985) observes, "the political and industrial wings of the social democratic labour movement are in many ways the authors of modern tripartism."

Even when these institutional and political factors are most conducive to tripartite decision making, consensus has been neither painless nor permanent. Rather, such voluntary collaboration is subject to continuing internal strains and occasional collapse. In general terms, tripartism reduces the autonomy of all three of the parties, and can generate severe tensions between the peak organizations representing the major economic interests and their memberships, especially if the leadership is seen to be cooperating in unpopular measures. These dangers appear to be greatest for organized labour. Leaders of even the most centralized federations can discover that the price of cooperative behaviour is the erosion of their membership levels and/or serious challenges from below.

As a result, since 1945 participatory processes have gone through a number of phases, each characterized, in the words of Panitch (1985), by an "active search for consensus around an incomes policy so as to facilitate full employment, price stability and balance of payments equilibrium, and each punctuated at its close by instability or breakdown of tripartite arrangements." The first phase covered the period of postwar reconstruction. The second phase, which began in the mid-1950s, eroded and in some cases collapsed in the late 1960s as the impact of wage restraint was felt. The policies of this period, in the words of Flanagan, Soskice and Ulman (1983, p. 4):

> [F]ailed to provide significant rewards for cooperation. In particular, the distributional implications of most of the policies were not advantageous to labour, and efforts by national union officials to cooperate with the incomes policy objectives of their governments eroded the institutional authority of the officials over the rank-and-file membership. In fact, cooperation . . . in several countries brought about reductions in real wage growth that were followed by grass-roots revolts, wildcat strikes, and the wage explosions of the 1960s.

The third phase of tripartism began in the very different economic circumstances of the 1970s, and was often a complement, rather than an alternative, to deflationary policies. In this context, negotiations broadened beyond simple wage policy to a wider "social contract" in which government offered unions various forms of compensation for their cooperation (wage indexation, price controls, tax reductions or increased social benefits, participation in management, and/or improved legal protection for unions). Yet again, these relations have been unable to contain all of the tensions involved, and breakdowns have occurred in several countries, including Sweden, Germany, and most recently Denmark. The underlying predisposition toward consensus forms of decision making may indeed be stronger in parts of Europe than in North America. But even there, success is not guaranteed.

Nevertheless, no system of economic management has avoided periodic crises over the last 20 years, and the question remains whether the voluntary approach, with all of its internal strains, still represents a better approach to managing a modern economy. An answer to this question requires a judgment of the economic record of tripartite countries. Unfortunately, a systematic examination of the performance of countries relying on voluntary incomes policies is a difficult task. Cross-country studies by political scientists, surveyed in Martin (1985), examine the correlation between the extent of tripartism and various measures of economic performance. These studies tend to conclude that tripartism is associated with lower unemployment, inflation, and strike activity and higher social spending.

Panitch (1985) compares the performance of Austria, Sweden, Norway, and Germany over the last 20 years with that of OECD nations generally. While there are important differences among tripartite countries, as a group they do seem to have performed better on the two dimensions central to this discussion — inflation and unemployment. However, these descriptive comparisons do not allow for other differences among these groups of countries, nor do they attempt to estimate the marginal contribution of tripartite incomes policies.

Empirical analyses (McCallum, 1983a, 1985a; Bruno and Sachs, 1984) which attempt to control for other factors and thus isolate the contribution of tripartite arrangements provide modest and tentative support for the view that inflation and unemployment performance since 1973 has been more favourable in "corporatist" economies with a high degree of centralization than in other countries. However, several unresolved questions remain and more research needs to be done on this issue (Calmfors, 1985).

Perhaps the most decisive impact of tripartism in these countries has been on the levels of industrial and social conflict. The decline in strike activity in countries such as Sweden, Norway, Denmark and Germany between the interwar and postwar periods was truly spectacular. Given their previous histories of high levels of conflict, it is possible that tripartism's major contribution has been in reducing the level of industrial disputes. In addition, several authors have argued that tripartite nations achieved greater social and political harmony during the 1960s and 1970s (Banting, 1985).

The Consultative Context in Canada

Clearly the distinctive set of factors which have facilitated tripartite incomes policies in parts of Europe is not replicated in Canada. Canadian institutions are characterized not by the concentration of power but by its fragmentation. In both economic and political institutions, authority is dispersed in ways which inhibit the centralized interaction which is the heart of tripartite systems.

In the political realm, federalism divides authority over economic matters between the two orders of government, and economic policy evolves through the independent and often competitive actions of 11 governments. This constitutional division does not preclude federal authorities from entering into discussions with business and labour about a voluntary restraint program, but it does limit the prospects for the kind of comprehensive agreement that business and labour might require. The federal government could not, for example, enter into any commitment concerning the salaries of provincial employees, who constitute a significant component of the membership of public sector unions, or concerning the wide array of provincially regulated prices. A fully comprehensive agreement would therefore require discussions among business, labour, and the 11 senior governments. But the history of federal-provincial conferences does not encourage high expectations of such deliberations.

Fragmentation of authority also characterizes the institutions representing both business and labour. Certainly Canadian business does not lack for spokesmen. There are some 480 nationally relevant associations in operation today, together with another 102 in the agricultural sector

(Coleman, 1985). In contrast to the European pattern, however, the Canadian system of associations is fragmented, pluralistic and competitive. The vast majority of groups represent special product interests which are not integrated into broader organizations and, in particular, into a single "peak" association representing business as a whole. General associations such as the Business Council on National Issues, the Canadian Chamber of Commerce, the Canadian Federation of Independent Business, and the Canadian Organization of Small Business clearly represent different elements of the business community. They are also direct membership associations with no formal relationship with sectoral organizations such as the Canadian Manufacturers' Association or the many subsectoral associations and, therefore, do not speak authoritatively for all business groups. The closest Canada comes to such peak organizations is at the provincial level with the Employers' Council of British Columbia and the Conseil du Patronat in Quebec. More importantly, as voluntary organizations themselves, these organizations would be hard pressed to bind their individual members to specific norms or commit the business community as a whole to a general course of action. Business associations do have an important role to play in consultations over economic policy, but in the case of a voluntary incomes policy they could only encourage their members to adopt certain guidelines for salaries and prices.

This pattern of dispersed authority is repeated in organized labour. Canada lacks the comprehensive and centralized labour structures which sustain tripartism in Europe. In the first place, unionization levels are substantially lower in Canada, and the problem of how to represent the interests of unorganized labour in any negotiations is more controversial. More important, however, is the pluralistic nature of the Canadian labour movement. Whereas the West German labour movement, for example, consists of a total of 16 unions, the Canadian movement is highly fragmented, reflecting the preponderance of small unions. In 1980 the labour movement consisted of 734 unions, two-thirds of which had fewer than 10,000 members and many of which had fewer than 500 members. This fragmentation in the organization of labour is the counterpart of decentralization in the system of collective bargaining. While varying somewhat from industry to industry and region to region, the bargaining system is highly decentralized. Rather than negotiations being conducted on an industry, provincial or national basis, most bargaining is between a single union and a single employer in a single location (see Davies, 1985, for a further discussion of the structure of collective bargaining). Even when account is taken of informal linkages among units, the system still ranks as among the most decentralized of any country. Certainly, as summarized by Davies, the contrast with tripartite nations is stark:

> [Centralization] is minimal when compared to the nations of Scandinavia and continental Europe, where multi-employer structures are the rule. In Canada, only about 8 percent of units and 25 percent of workers are covered by multi-employer structures. Moreover, a significant portion of these units are local in scope. Again this contrasts with Scandinavia and continental Europe where industry-wide or even national units are common. Only the United States and the United Kingdom exhibit comparable levels of decentralization.

This fragmented structure generates a parallel pattern at the national level. The Canadian Labour Congress is certainly the predominant central federation, and the one best positioned to engage in broad national discussions. However, there are several separate federations, and the CLC cannot claim to speak for all organized labour. More important, however, is the distribution of power within the federations. The real economic power of unions, the power to bargain collectively, rests firmly with the union locals, and is exercised within a tradition of considerable local autonomy. The central federation remains a voluntary association of unions, which regulates relations among affiliates and represents their collective interests to governments. Neither the executive of the CLC, nor indeed the executives of affiliated unions, has much ability to commit locals to movement-wide courses of action.

The limitations which result from dispersed authority were seen clearly in the consultations over a voluntary incomes policy in the 1970s. The "consensus consultations" in 1974–75 and the "post-controls" discussions of 1976–77 floundered in part on the fact that in Canada the locus of union decision making is the local. As Waldie (1985) observes concerning the post-controls consultations:

> There was not then, as there still is not, any precedent in Canada for a union central adopting a wage negotiating guideline. The CLC does not have the internal machinery for assessing any such standard or for generating consensus around it. Thus, even if the CLC leadership had seen such a standard as being in the interest of its members, they would have been making a radical change in the purpose and practices of the Congress in endorsing it. They would have done so at very considerable risk to themselves. They had no mandate from the 1976 Convention to engage in this kind of activity, and would have been held accountable for their actions at the 1978 Convention.

In contrast to the European pattern, then, the fragmented nature of our political and economic institutions constrains the prospects for developing a voluntary incomes policy. In addition, the underlying political relationships among business, labour and government are different here as well. As noted earlier, a key factor in the emergence of tripartism in Europe was the governing role of social democratic parties which were closely allied with organized labour. In such a situation, labour leaders tended to be in broad agreement with the overall direction of economic and social policy, which facilitated their cooperation in the risky business of incomes restraint. In the Canadian case, the political links lead in different directions. The close relationship between organized labour and the New Democratic Party complicates the process. In effect, organized labour faces an enduring tension between cooperation with the government of the day and its longer-term political objectives, a tension which contributes to considerable ambivalence about the value of consultative arrangements generally. Indeed, within the labour movement as a whole, there remains considerable skepticism about anything other than collective bargaining as a means of promoting the interests of its members.

Given this institutional and political context, it is perhaps not surprising that previous attempts to develop an incomes policy on a voluntary basis have been unsuccessful. In 1969 the federal government appointed the Prices and Incomes Commission which attempted to negotiate a package of commitments to restraint among business, labour and governments. After a series of exploratory meetings, however, the Canadian Labour Congress and the Confederation of National Trade Unions jointly rejected the call for voluntary guidelines. The commission did continue its effort, holding a National Conference on Price Stability in February 1970 at which it managed to secure the broad agreement of the business community to restrain price increases. But a subsequent attempt to develop a guideline of 6 percent for wage and salary increases failed to take hold in the face of the continued opposition of organized labour and the federal government's acceptance of several settlements which exceeded the guideline in its own public sector. Without meaningful commitments on wages and salaries, the program of price restraint expired at the end of 1970, and the commission was wound down.

In response to another acceleration in inflation in 1974, Finance Minister John Turner initiated a round of discussions with business and labour in the hope of achieving consensus on the necessity of exercising voluntary restraint. The discussions extended into a series of 20 meetings and later came to be known as the "consensus talks." The exercise took place at two levels. At the political level it involved the minister, officers of the Canadian Labour Congress, and businessmen selected by the minister. Underpinning these contacts was a series of meetings at the technical level, involving staff from the government, the CLC, and several of the corporations. The intent, on the government's side at least, was to reach a common understanding of Canada's economic situation as a foundation for an agreement on appropriate measures of restraint. However, when in April 1975 the government proposed a voluntary guideline for wage increases of 12 percent (up to a maximum of $2,400), with similar limitations on prices and profits, the proposal was quickly rejected by the CLC. The following October the government imposed a mandatory controls program.

Another round of consultations, known as the "post-controls talks," took place in 1976–77. Starting in September 1976, at the government's initiative, a series of high-level meetings was held to explore the possibilities of an early exit from controls and of agreement on post-controls policy. On the government side, the meetings involved the prime minister, several ministers, and a very few senior officials. At the outset, business and labour met separately with the government, but in early 1977 business and labour leaders discovered they had shared interests in an early end to controls and an improved system of consultation with government. Thereafter, meetings with the government proceeded on a tripartite basis. The process ended, however, at a last tripartite meeting on June 29, 1977, at which the government made specific proposals: controls would end in 1977, one year ahead of schedule, if business and labour would make certain commitments on wages and prices; but if there was no response within two weeks, controls would run their course. The CLC found the proposals unacceptable, rejected them outright, and effectively terminated the process.

The Canadian approach to consultation has traditionally been fragmented and informal. Furthermore, it has typically involved the separate representation of business and labour interests (Banting, 1985). However, in the past decade greater emphasis has been given to bringing together representatives of business, labour and government in an attempt to develop a common understanding of important economic issues, a trend examined in more detail in Crispo (1984), Adams (1985), Fournier (1985), and Waldie (1985). Probably the most significant recent example of this trend was the formation in 1984 of the bipartite (but government-financed) Canadian Labour Market and Productivity Centre. In addition, the Progressive Conservative government elected in 1984 has stressed the importance of consultation and consensus, and held a National Economic Conference in March 1985. There have also been similar developments in several provinces.

Whether these developments mark the beginning of a new era of consultative processes is unclear. At this stage the existing institutional structures are fragile, and it appears unlikely that governments would risk their continuation by attempting to tackle the contentious issue of incomes policy. For example, the National Economic Conference, unlike its Australian counterpart (the 1983 National Economic Summit), did not discuss the possibility of wage and price restraint in exchange for a more expansionary aggregate demand policy.

Summary and Conclusions

Despite the undeniable attractions of relying on voluntary agreement in developing an incomes policy, major constraints limit the prospects for such mechanisms in the Canadian context. The structure of our institutions and the complexities inherent in our political relationships limit the applicability of the tripartite model here. There is undoubtedly scope for consensus-building mechanisms, especially ones which encourage a continuing national dialogue about our economic problems and prospects. But when attention turns to incomes policies, our expectations must be conditioned by our experience. The desirability of consensus in a democratic society suggests that a voluntary program should always be the first preference of Canadian governments. Moreover, there is a possibility that the experience of the 1982–83 recession could lead to a reconsideration of traditional attitudes toward incomes policies.[8] If Canada once again faced serious inflationary pressures, voluntary incomes restraint might receive more sympathetic consideration. Nevertheless, the prospects of developing an incomes policy on a voluntary basis remain uncertain at best. Though attempting to reach such an agreement is probably a necessary precondition to the statutory approach, such an attempt is not likely to be successful.

Statutory Wage and Price Controls: Can They Work in Practice?

The potential benefits of statutory wage and price controls were explained above. The purpose of this section is to examine how well these programs have worked in practice.

Attempts to control rising prices by government fiat have been made since biblical days. The majority of these attempts were largely unsuccessful because the underlying source of inflationary pressures, the increase in the quantity of money, was not removed. Here we are discussing a much more sophisticated form of incomes policy, one in which the stipulation of norms for wage and price increases is accompanied by appropriate reductions in the rate of growth in the money supply, and other relevant components of nominal aggregate demand.

The focus here is primarily on the Canadian and U.S. experience. Both countries share several important institutional features affecting wage determination: a similar system with respect to union certification,[9] a decentralized structure of collective bargaining, the use of long-term overlapping nominal wage contracts in the union sector, and a non-union sector not formally covered by collective agreements negotiated in the union sector. In addition, although both countries have attempted various forms of exhortation and persuasion, they have also ended up with programs imposed by government and administered by a specially created agency.

The U.K. experience is also relevant, and is briefly discussed. There are a number of important institutional differences between the United Kingdom and North America. Though the U.K. structure of collective bargaining is decentralized compared to most other European countries, it is less decentralized than in North America. There have also been more varied attempts at incomes policies in the

United Kingdom, several of which have involved "social contracts" in various degrees. Another important difference is that wage contracts in the United Kingdom do not have fixed durations; indeed, they do not have the legal status of contracts in North America.

Measuring the Effects of Incomes Policies

Assessing the impact of a controls program is not a trivial task. Even if inflation moderated during the period of controls, this may have been due to other causes. Alternatively, even if inflation did not decline it may be that prices would have increased more in the absence of controls. In other words, in order to establish the effects of the controls it is necessary to determine what would have happened in the absence of the incomes policy but under otherwise identical circumstances.

This need to provide a counterfactural account occurs in any attempt at policy evaluation. The difficulties with estimating the effects of incomes policies are, in principle, not different from most other policies. Thus the results should receive no less or no more weight than those given to most other econometric policy evaluations. Nonetheless, it is worthwhile mentioning a number of the difficulties which arise in (although are not necessarily unique to) this particular application.

First, the procedure obviously relies on having a good understanding of the determinants of wage and price behaviour in the absence of controls. Any deficiencies in our model of the inflationary process will affect the predictions of what would have occurred in the absence of the incomes policy. This holds even if the deficiency (e.g., omitted variables) only applies during the period in which the controls were not in effect. A closely related point is that we are examining important aspects of the overall behaviour of the economy. A wide variety of other factors could provide alternative explanations of the observed behaviour of wages and prices during both the "controls on" and "controls off" periods. Although this is always true in policy evaluation, the scope for alternative explanations in this case may be somewhat greater than in many other applications.

Second, most of the empirical studies are based on a wage-price subsector of the type discussed in chapter 2. While this has proved to be a useful framework for empirical work, there are, as discussed earlier, alternative views of the appropriate way to model the inflationary process.

Third, most studies are based only on the wage-price subsector rather than on a more complete model of macroeconomic behaviour. This has certain advantages. The wage-price sectors of complete macromodels are generally quite crude compared to those used in empirical work on wage and price determination. Nonetheless, an obvious potential disadvantage is that certain aspects are largely ignored (e.g., exchange-rate movements).

There is also the view that macroeconomic models in general have been overspecified, and that they are consequently not a good tool for describing the behaviour of the economy and therefore for policy evaluation. This criticism of using too much a priori specification could certainly be applied to the wage-price sectors used to evaluate incomes policies. This suggests the use of alternative methods (in particular, "measurement without theory" methods) to check the conclusions reached through tightly specified models.

Nonetheless, the expectations-augmented Phillips Curve specification for the wage equation and an accompanying mark-up price equation (as well as an equation explaining movements in the natural unemployment rate) remains the primary workhorse of empirical work on the inflationary process. Thus the main difficulties that arise with this framework should be discussed. Some of these difficulties were noted previously; others are peculiar to the incomes policy application. Three difficulties noted earlier are modelling the time series behaviour of the natural unemployment rate; allowing for variable rates of productivity growth; and explaining the response of real wages to supply shocks and possibly other developments. Each of these can affect the conclusions reached with respect to the effects of periods of wage and price control.

There are also some difficulties associated more directly with the incomes policy intervention. Clearly, it is necessary to distinguish between periods when an incomes policy is in effect and not in effect. However, a simple on-off dichotomy is too crude to capture the variety of incomes policy experience, even in North America. Most policies have gone through various phases, sometimes including a decontrol phase. The separate policies, and the phases within them, have varied in their coverage with respect to both wages and prices, their degree of enforcement, and the tightness of their standards. Most studies are not able to deal with these complexities.

Many studies use a dummy variable in the wage and/or price equations to distinguish "policy on" from "policy off" periods. This procedure assumes that the policy shifts down the equation without affecting its slope; that is, it reduces the rate of wage or price change by the same amount at each level of expected inflation, unemployment, and so on. A more general procedure is to allow the slope coefficients as well as the intercept to be affected by the policy. With respect to the excess demand variable, this procedure was given some theoretical justification by Lipsey and Parkin (1970), whose work has been extended by Reid (1979). However, the procedure can also be justified more generally (and simply) by the hypothesis that an incomes policy alters the effect of expectations, excess demand, and other explanatory variables on the wage determination process. Hagens and Russell (1985) have explored this hypothesis with U.S. data.

Allowing the possibility of a completely different structure raises a further issue. The hypothesis that the same underlying structure applies during all incomes policies in a given country may be implausible. For reasons noted above, differences between policies (or even between phases within a policy) are quite possibly as large as the differences between "policy on" and "policy off" periods. Thus one may wish to allow not only the underlying structure to differ between "policy on" and "policy off" periods but also to differ across "policy on" periods. Because of their more extensive use of income policies, this aspect is more relevant to the United Kingdom and the United States than to Canada.

A final observation is that it will generally be important to examine wage and price behaviour in the post-controls period in order to determine whether any reductions in inflation achieved during the incomes policy were permanent or merely temporary.

The U.S. Experience[10]

In the post-World War II period, incomes policies were employed in the United States during the Korean War (1950–53), the Kennedy and Johnson administrations (1962–66), the Nixon administration (1971–74), and the Carter administration (1977–81). The policies varied considerably. The last three are the most relevant to the question of the probable effectiveness of such programs in peacetime, and this section will therefore focus on these periods.[11]

The Kennedy-Johnson program involved voluntary guidelines with respect to wage and price increases. These guidelines were introduced at a time when the administration was pursuing an expansionary aggregate demand policy and was concerned about the inflationary consequences. Compliance with the guidelines was monitored by the Council of Economic Advisors, a body with a professional staff of about 20 who had numerous other duties. Thus only conspicuous contraventions of the guidelines were noticed. There were no legal penalties for non-compliance; rather, the program relied on presidential "jawboning" and ad hoc penalties (e.g., by diverting defence contracts) in particular cases. President Johnson's decision to finance the Vietnam War by printing money rather than raising taxes appears to have led to the program's end. The tight labour market conditions resulted in a dramatic wage settlement in excess of the guidelines, and subsequently to their abandonment.

The Nixon administration's Economic Stabilization Program was the first peacetime use of mandatory wage and price controls in the United States. The program was introduced in August 1971, at a time when the economy was expanding. The purpose was to allow the expansion to continue without the inflationary consequences. There were several phases, beginning with a 90-day wage-price freeze. Phase II introduced more flexible controls, established a Price Commission to oversee prices and rents, and a Pay Board to deal with wage settlements. Guidelines were established (e.g., 5.5 percent for wage increases); increases in excess of these guides could be approved by the board. In phase III the controls became voluntary, beginning the process of decontrol. Phase IV reinstituted mandatory controls.

The Carter administration introduced an anti-inflation program in October 1978 at a time when inflation was increasing. The program involved formal standards for wage and price increases. These standards were administered by the Council on Wage and Price Stability and were intended to be accompanied by a compliance mechanism, called "real wage insurance," but the legislation for the latter was never passed by Congress. (Real wage insurance is discussed further in chapter 5.) Thus the program was largely voluntary.[12] There were two main phases, each lasting about one year. The second phase, the beginning of decontrol, involved the creation of a tripartite Pay Advisory Committee which relaxed the wage standard and blocked enforcement efforts by the Council on Wage and Price Stability.

A large number of econometric studies have examined the effects of these incomes policies.[13] Although there are some differences in conclusions among these studies, enough similarities emerge to make a summary feasible.

The guideposts of 1962–66 are generally found to have had a significant restraining effect on wage and price increases (see Sheahan, 1967; Perry, 1970, 1980; Gordon, 1975a; Reid, 1981), although recent research by Hagens and Russell (1985) suggests these estimates may be overstated. An effect of 1 percent on wage increases is an average estimate, whereas the guidepost was 3.2 percent.

There appears fairly substantial agreement that the mandatory controls of 1971–74 had, at best, no permanent effect on wage and price levels, though they did affect the timing of wage and price movements. The temporary restraining effects were offset by wage and price bubbles in the last two phases of the program and subsequent to its termination. Studies differ somewhat on the timing of these catch-up effects (compare Gordon, 1975a; Blinder and Newton, 1981; Reid, 1981; Hagens and Russell, 1985), but not on their occurrence. Indeed, most studies find this program was perverse; that is, the price level was higher after the program than it would otherwise have been.

Russell (1983) and Hagens and Russell (1985) conclude that the Carter Pay and Price Standards program had a significant restraining effect on wage settlements. The estimated effect is 1.3 percent over the program, and was as high as 2 percent during the period of maximum impact. However, as they note, these estimates could also have been produced by a change in wage behaviour. In particular, the energy price increase in 1979–80 was not passed on into wages and thus into prices in the manner implied by the wage equation; this could be a real wage response to a one-time supply shock rather than an impact of the controls.

Lessons of the U.S. Experience

The gains from these three programs of wage and price restraint have been modest at best. The most elaborate program, the mandatory controls of 1971–74, altered the time path of wages and prices but had, if anything, a perverse effect on the equilibrium wage and price level re-established following controls. In addition, this program involved the greatest costs in terms of allocative inefficiencies and administration. At the same time, the two attempts at voluntary restraint appear to have achieved some modest gains at relatively little direct cost in terms of induced inefficiencies and administration. There is some uncertainty, however, about the magnitude of these benefits, especially with respect to the most recent program. Those with strongly held views about the advisability of incomes policies are unlikely to be affected by this evidence. The estimated impacts are sufficiently uncertain to enable both proponents and opponents to appeal to the experience with these policies (see, e.g., Mayer, 1984, and Tobin, 1984).

Perhaps the clearest lesson of the U.S. experience is the importance of combining the incomes policy with appropriate fiscal and monetary restraint. All three of the policies introduced in the last two decades were combined with monetary and fiscal policies which were too expansionary. This clearly contributed to the downfall of each policy, and to the perverse impact of the 1971–74 mandatory controls.

This apparent tendency to combine programs of wage and price restraint with expansionary aggregate demand policies provides some support for the "failure of the policy process" view discussed above. The support is strongest in the case of the 1971–74 Nixon controls; however, this appears to be one of the few observations which supports the notion of a "political business cycle" upon which this failure of the policy process view depends.

The U.K. Experience

A bewildering array of incomes policies has been attempted in the United Kingdom, and the interested reader will find useful summaries in Fallick and Elliott (1981, Appendix) and Henry and Ormerod (1978). The wide range of programs and the limited number of periods during which no program was in effect combine to create formidable problems for econometric work attempting to estimate the programs' effects.

Parkin, Sumner and Jones (1972) surveyed early econometric research on the effects of U.K. incomes policies. They concluded that, with the exception of the immediate postwar experiment, the policies had little effect. More recent research (e.g., Henry and Ormerod, 1978; Henry, 1981; Sumner and Ward, 1983) typically finds that the programs reduced wage inflation during the period in which the programs were in effect. However, these effects were largely temporary; following the end of the programs, wages rebounded to levels close to those they would have reached in the absence of the policy.

A recent study by Pencavel (1982) has pointed to one possible explanation for this behaviour. Wage contracts in the United Kingdom do not have fixed terms. A wage claim can be entered at any time, although annual claims are the norm. Incomes policies have often attempted to operate not only on the size of wage settlements as in North America, but also on the duration of the agreement. Thus the policies act mainly to postpone the wage and price increases, especially if the incomes policy is not combined with the appropriate monetary and fiscal restraint.

Whatever the explanation, the general conclusion that incomes policies have only temporary restraining effects that are largely offset by wage and price "bubbles" at the end of the controls program is clearly not very favourable to the use of these policies. For this reason, many U.K. advocates of incomes policies have turned to the incentive-based schemes discussed in chapter 5.

The Canadian Experience

The United States and the United Kingdom have employed a variety of incomes policies in the postwar period, but their experience has not been overwhelmingly favourable to the argument for these policies. In some cases the policy appears to have had little effect. In others the effect was only temporary, restraint being followed by a post-controls wage and/or price bubble. However, in many of these cases the incomes policy was not combined with the monetary and fiscal restraint needed to convert temporary into lasting gains.

The 1975–78 Anti-Inflation Program (AIP) is probably the best example to date of a statutory incomes policy introduced as part of a package which attempted to include the appropriate restraint in the growth of aggregate demand. The case for wage and price controls as a means of aiding the transition from high to low inflation rates thus rests, to a considerable extent, on the AIP experience.

The AIP was introduced in October 1975 at a time when both wage and price inflation (particularly wage inflation) had accelerated rapidly. Price inflation had increased to over 10 percent in 1974 and remained at that level in the first three quarters of 1975. Wage settlements had risen dramatically through 1974 and 1975, exceeding 20 percent in the second and third quarters of 1975. Some of the largest increases were in the public sector, particularly in provincial administration. There was concern that a dangerous wage-price spiral was underway.

The AIP had four components:[14]

- fiscal and monetary policies aimed at increasing aggregate demand at a rate consistent with declining inflation;
- a temporary wage and price (or profit) control program;
- a commitment to limit the rate of growth of government spending to or below the trend growth in GNP;
- structural policies to increase competition, deal with problems in particular sectors (energy, food and housing), and improve labour-management relations.

The details of the mandatory wage and price controls component are described well elsewhere (see, e.g., Maslove and Swimmer, 1980; Reid, 1982). The salient features were as follows:

- A ceiling for compensation increases (wages and benefits) was set at 10, 8 and 6 percent, respectively, in the three years of the program. The announced goals for price increases were 8, 6 and 4 percent, respectively. The additional compensation increase of 2 percent per year was allowed for productivity (and thus expected real wage) growth. A further adjustment of −2 to +2 percent was permitted, depending on a group's experience relative to the CPI over the previous two or three years.
- Existing contracts were not abrogated; the ceilings applied to new settlements.
- Although all Canadians were expected to comply with the guidelines, the ceilings were binding on firms with 500 or more employees, construction firms with 20 or more employees, professionals, and all employees of the federal, participating provincial and municipal governments and their agencies.
- Price increases were not controlled directly, but indirectly by the limits on wage increases and the requirement that profit margins be held to specified levels (based on historical averages).
- The operation of the program was to be overseen by the Anti-Inflation Board. If the AIB was unable to obtain compliance with the guidelines, the act provided for an administrator who could enforce the board's decision or a modification of it. Decisions of the administrator could be appealed to an appeal tribunal.

Two features of the AIP were particularly relevant to the issue of the potential effectiveness of incomes policies: the combination of temporary wage and price controls with appropriate reductions in the growth in aggregate demand; and the fact that wage and price increases were to be gradually reduced in a series of phases. The design of the AIP thus corresponded closely to the theoretical rationale for temporary incomes policies outlined previously. The statements of relevant authorities made this clear. In the words of the governor of the Bank of Canada:[15] "It is useful to supplement financial discipline by direct action to restrain increases in incomes and prices — this approach can bring about the needed adjustment at less cost in terms of unemployment and lost output, and with less serious inequities, than would result from sole reliance on monetary and fiscal polices." As noted previously, in November 1975 the Bank of Canada announced the adoption of targets for the growth in monetary aggregates. These provided for gradual reductions in the rate of monetary expansion. The second feature — gradually declining norms for wage and price increases — received less emphasis. However, as discussed earlier, recent theoretical research suggests that this aspect is important in an economy with overlapping wage contracts, given the decision not to abrogate existing agreements. Thus the AIP is an example of a temporary incomes policy with desirable design features, and considerable attention should focus on the program's effectiveness.

A number of empirical studies have addressed this issue, and are summarized in Table 4-1. The studies are divided into two groups. The top part of the table contains studies of the impact on current wage settlements while the studies in the bottom part are based on average earnings which are affected by both new settlements and agreements reached prior to the controls program. For this reason the estimated impacts are expected to be larger in the first group, especially in the early phases of the controls program. Indeed, because of long-term contracts, the effects of controls (if any) on average earnings will extend beyond the end of the program even in the absence of other lagged or feedback effects. For purposes of comparability, estimated AIB effects are expressed as an average over the three years of the program, although several studies find the impacts were larger toward the end of the program than at the beginning (see, e.g., Christofides and Wilton, 1985). With the exception of Letourneau (1979), all estimated effects reported in Table 4-1 are based on a single equation methodology; they therefore do not include feedback effects between wages, prices and other variables.

Looking first at the top group of studies, all find that the AIB had a significant impact on negotiated wage changes with estimates of the average impact in the 2.0 to 4.5 percent per year range. Only the Riddell and Smith (1982) study estimates the impact to be below 3 percent per year. Their comparatively low estimate appears due to a relatively high estimated slope of the short-run Phillips Curve (i.e., coefficient on the excess labour market demand variable); relative to other studies, this causes them to attribute more of the reduction in wage inflation to the rise in unemployment which occurred during the AIP, and therefore less to the controls program. Reid's (1979) relatively high estimate of 4.5 percent appears due largely to the absence of a catch-up variable in his specification. Thus, most of the studies indicate that the AIB reduced current wage settlements by 3 to 4 percent per year over the three years

TABLE 4–1 Empirical Studies of the Impact of the AIB

Author	Sample Period	Dependent Variable	Estimated AIB Impact (annual average reduction in percentage wage changes)
Cousineau and Lacroix (1978)	1967–77	Individual contracts	3.3
Christofides and Wilton (1979)	1967–78	Individual contracts	3.2
Reid (1979)	1967–78	Quarterly averages of individual settlements in manufacturing	4.5
Riddell and Smith (1982)	1967–81	Monthly averages of individual contracts	2.0
Christofides and Wilton (1985)	1967–81	Individual contracts	3.2
Letourneau (1979)	1963–78	Average weekly earnings, industrial composite	2.5
Fortin and Newton (1982)	1957–78	Annual, hourly compensation	2.0
Helliwell (1983)	1954–80	Average annual earnings, industrial composite	2.5

of the policy. This is a very large impact. Assuming the slope of the short-run Phillips Curve to be approximately 0.5, the same direct effect on wage inflation would have required unemployment rates of approximately 13 to 14 percent throughout the three-year period rather than the 7 to 8 percent unemployment rates actually experienced.[16]

The studies in the bottom group also conclude that the AIB had a significant impact — a reduction of 2 to 2½ percent per year in the overall rate of wage inflation. These studies typically find — as would be expected given the nature of the dependent variable — that most of the impact on aggregate wage change occurred in the second and third years of the program. Helliwell (1983), for example, finds no impact in the first year but estimated impacts of 3.0 and 2.9 percent in 1977 and 1978. By not allowing for the effects of settlements reached during the AIP but which affect average earnings in subsequent years, these studies may understate the impact of the program.[17] Even if this is not the case, such large estimated effects on aggregate earnings suggest that the impact of the AIB extended beyond the controlled groups.

Under the controls program, compensation agreements were to be submitted to the AIB for approval. If the settlement was found to be above the guideline, the AIB could order a rollback. Most of the studies in Table 4-1 estimate the combined effect of AIB rollbacks and the "counterfactual impact" — the difference between the settlement submitted to the AIB (or, in the case of organizations not covered by the guidelines, the observed wage increase) and that which would have occurred in the absence of the program. Some of the studies (e.g., Christofides and Wilton, 1979) employ data on wage settlements prior to any AIB rollback, and thus estimate only the counterfactual effect. Because only a few settlements were rolled back, this difference has only a small effect on the estimated impact of the program.[18]

Incorporating feedback effects among wages, prices and other variables will tend to raise the estimated impact of the program on wage inflation. Lower wage settlements in the first year of the program, for example, imply less price inflation than would otherwise have occurred, thus reducing wage settlements in subsequent years. Inflationary expectations may also decline, reducing subsequent wage increases. These feedback effects are not taken into account in the single equation studies which treat the actual (and expected) price change as exogenously determined. In a simulation study using a wage-price sector, Wilton (1984) finds the average reduction in wage inflation to be 4.3 percent when feedback effects are included, compared with 3.2 percent otherwise. Simulations with the MACE macroeconomic model produce even larger estimated impacts of about 5 percent per year over the 1977–80 period (Helliwell, 1983).

The AIB's effect on price increases has received less attention but the studies that have been carried out, such as those by Letourneau (1979), Helliwell (1983), and Wilton (1984), conclude that the program had a significant restraining effect on price inflation.[19] In assessing the program's effect on price inflation it is important to note that only about 60 percent of the commodities which make up the Consumer Price Index (CPI) were subject to controls, and these were controlled indirectly via restraints on profits. The annual rate of change in the CPI declined from about 11 percent in the two years prior to the AIP to 6.2 percent in the first year of the program and 8.8 and 8.7 percent, respectively, in the second and third years of the program (Table 1-2). The substantial decline in inflation in the first year appears to have been primarily due to a reduction in food prices, and to have had little to do with controls. In the second and third years of the program, in contrast, there were substantial increases in the uncontrolled food, energy and import prices which offset the downward pressure on price inflation associated with controls (see the data on the CPI less food and energy in Table 1-2). These unanticipated inflationary shocks in 1977–78 meant that the program did not achieve its objectives with respect to price inflation. Of course, these shocks would have tended to raise the inflation rate in any event; the issue addressed by the econometric studies is how much higher price inflation would have been in the absence of the program. Because the

AIB was concerned with current wage settlements, many of which involved contracts of two years or more, its impact on prices would be expected to be low early in the program but to continue well beyond the end of the program. Letourneau (1979) estimated the impact on the rate of inflation at 1.3 percent in 1978, the final year of controls, with smaller impacts in earlier years. However, because his sample ended in 1978, these estimates may well understate the program's impact on prices. Wilton's (1984) estimates indicate that price inflation would have been 1–2 percent higher in each of 1977, 1978 and 1979 in the absence of controls. There was little independent effect on prices in the first year of the program because existing wage contracts were not abrogated. The effect on price inflation became larger as the AIP proceeded, and indeed peaked in 1979, the year following the end of the program. Helliwell's (1983) analysis — which employs a full econometric model of the economy (as compared to Wilton's (1984) analysis which is based on the wage-price sector alone) and which includes two years of post-controls data (unlike Letourneau, 1979) — produces the largest estimated impacts on both wage and price inflation. The average rate of increase in consumer prices is estimated to be 3 percent higher over the period 1977–80 in the absence of the AIP. The effects on other key variables, such as real GNP growth and the exchange rate, depend on the monetary and fiscal stance adopted in the absence of controls.

In summary, there is substantial agreement that the AIP had a significant impact on wage settlements, and that this in turn resulted in reduced price inflation. There are some differences in the effects estimated by different researchers but the similarities are more evident than the differences. In particular, the estimated effects on both wage and price inflation (especially the former) are larger than would have been predicted on the basis of the previous experience of other countries.[20] Although it is possible that subsequent research will discover an alternative explanation for the dramatic decline in wage inflation and the moderation in price inflation over the 1975–78 period, it is equally possible that research will cause the estimated impacts to be re-evaluated upward.[21]

As discussed earlier in the context of the U.S. and U.K. experience, a fundamental issue is whether any reductions in wage and price inflation achieved during an incomes policy are merely temporary or in fact permanent in nature. Several of the empirical studies summarized in Table 4-1 have included data from the post-AIP period (Riddell and Smith, 1982; Helliwell, 1983; Christofides and Wilton, 1985). All find no evidence of a post-controls wage or price bubble.[22] Thus the AIP experience supports the view that direct wage and price controls can aid the transition from high to low inflation rates, the "conventional Canadian wisdom" referred to above.

Estimating the impact of controls necessarily involves a counterfactual exercise. However, it is not clear that the general public thinks in these terms.[23] The increases in the uncontrolled prices in the last two years of the AIP, although they would have increased the rate of inflation in any event, may have contributed to a perception that the controls program was unsuccessful. Whether or not this was the cause, public opinion polls suggest that support for wage and price controls, which was high in the 1970s, waned in the 1980s (Johnston, 1985).

More recently, in July 1982, a program of wage controls affecting public sector employees was introduced as a complement to the policy of severe monetary restraint that began in the early 1980s. At this point in time there are no published studies of the effectiveness of these selective wage controls, which involved ceilings of 6 and 5 percent in the first and second years of the program in the federal jurisdiction and various norms in the participating provincial jurisdictions. There is no doubt that wage settlements in the public sector declined markedly in 1982, as did those in the private sector (see Tables 2-1 and 2-2). The difficulty is determining how much of the decline was associated with the severe recession and how much with the controls. While a complete answer awaits careful econometric research, it does appear from a simple inspection of the data in that the 6 percent ceiling in the first year of the program had some independent effect on public sector wage settlements. The 5 percent ceiling in the second year of the federal program was in retrospect probably too high, resulting in public sector settlements that were quite possibly higher than they would have been in the absence of the program. This illustrates one of the problems with setting norms for wage and/or price increases in advance — they may turn out to be inappropriate for the economic conditions at the time they take effect.

The Costs of Mandatory Wage and Price Controls

As stated earlier, virtually every Western industrialized country has implemented incomes policies of one form or another. Thus there is experience not only with the effects of these policies, but also with the associated problems and other costs.

The costs associated with direct wage and price controls are by no means trivial. The program requires a bureaucracy to monitor wage and price or profit increases and ensure compliance with the guidelines. Reporting procedures are also required, adding a burden on the private sector.

The magnitude of these administrative and compliance costs will depend on the nature of the program. Costs will be low if the program is largely voluntary, with little monitoring and enforcement of the guidelines. The impact of this type of program may be equally small, although the Kennedy-Johnson guidelines in the United States — which relied primarily on self-enforcement by employers — appear to have been surprisingly effective. However, as the policy moves along the spectrum from voluntary to mandatory, the need for an elaborate set of rules and regulations grows. These are needed not only for the policy to have its intended effect of restraining cost and price increases but to make the program appear equitable.

There are a wide variety of pricing and compensation practices which, if the program is to be credible, its rules and regulations must encompass. Furthermore, if the program is to be effective it must not be easily circumvented by wage and price increases in disguised forms. The extraordinarily wide variety of pricing practices and the opportunity for changing various dimensions of product quality — not only the physical nature of the product but the associated servicing, financing, speed of delivery, and so on — is often cited as indicating the futility of price controls. Certainly these aspects make price controls costly to administer. They are more likely to enable firms to undermine the program's impact if there is excess demand for goods while the program is in place. These various methods — or potential methods — of undermining the intended effect of the controls program also become more significant the longer the duration of the policy.

Because labour is less heterogeneous and compensation practices less diverse, wage control programs are easier to administer than price controls. Even in this case, however, there are a variety of complications with which to contend. Among the most important are fringe benefits and other forms of non-wage compensation, incentive-pay plans (bonuses, profit-sharing, piece rates, and so on), and compensation whose value is not known at the time of the wage change (COLA clauses, stock options, and so on). These aspects are either of sufficient quantitative significance — as in the case of fringe benefits and COLA payments — to prevent a wage control program from ignoring them, or they need to be covered by the regulations in order to maintain equity of treatment. The implications of these complications are similar to those for price controls. If the controls program is in effect during a state of overall excess demand for labour, these various complexities become a means of circumventing the allowed rates of wage increase. Furthermore, the longer the program lasts, the more complex the required set of regulations.

The need for a controls program to be perceived as being equitable adds to the administrative burden. Although on a cost-benefit analysis (measured in terms of the objective of restraining inflation) it might make sense to exclude from coverage certain groups of individuals or forms of compensation, this would undermine public support for the program. As stated by McMenamin and Russell (1983, p. 444):

> An irony of an ambitious controls program is that an inordinate amount of effort is expended on the design of measurement rules for types of compensation which have but a trivial effect on inflation. . . . This is an implication

of the paramount need to promote the appearance of equity — an impression that appears . . . to be as essential in a mandatory program as in a voluntary one for building and maintaining public support.

The costs of administering the 1975–78 wage and price controls were probably less than $100 million per year (Wilton, 1982). The annual budget of the AIB was less than $20 million, and the costs borne by the private sector and the provincial and municipal governments were likely under $80 million per year. Compared to the estimated benefits of the program, these costs are very small.

Although perhaps not large, the administrative costs should not be ignored. In this respect it is important to note that the features of the controls program which are desirable on the grounds of reducing the required degree of administrative complexity — namely, that the program be temporary and that it be accompanied by restraint in aggregate demand — coincide with those which economic theory predicts are most desirable for the program to be effective in achieving a permanent reduction in the rate of inflation.

In addition to the direct administrative burden, there are the costs due to distortions associated with setting general wage and price change guidelines or limits. Normal market forces would have produced distributions of wage and price changes, with some changes being below average and others above average. An ideal incomes policy would scale down all wage and price increases by some common amount, thus preserving the planned changes in relative wages and prices. This would ensure that the policy would have no adverse effects on resource allocation. The control norms or limits cut off the upper tail of the distribution, and may cause some of those wage and price changes that would have been below the ceiling in the absence of controls to rise to the ceiling; that is, the control limit may become a floor as well as a ceiling. Thus, some of the changes in relative wages and prices that would otherwise have occurred are prevented. The program may be designed to allow for exceptions but doing so adds considerably to the administrative burden.

In any given year there is considerable variation in negotiated wage settlements.[24] A controls program which sets upper limits, even with allowance for exceptions, is bound to alter this distribution in undesirable ways. In addition, application of the ceilings to all wage settlements is bound to be inequitable in some cases. These inequities can undermine support for the program.

The two desirable design factors stressed in the discussion of administrative costs — temporary controls and the absence of overall excess demand during the program — are also likely to minimize the resource allocation costs. Nonetheless, having zero excess demand overall (or perhaps excess supply as in the AIP) will generally imply excess demand in some markets. These cases can be dealt with by allowing exceptions in clear cases of market shortages. Although the administrative burden is thereby increased, such provisions can contribute to the lasting effect of the policy (in addition to reducing the resource allocation costs during the program) by minimizing one potential source of a post-controls bubble.

The studies that have been carried out of the 1975–78 AIP have not documented any clear cases of resource misallocation (Wilton, 1982). Although this does not imply that there were no such costs, Tobin's observation that "it takes a heap of Harberger triangles to fill an Okun gap" certainly seems apt.

Possibly the largest potential costs of mandatory wage and price controls are those associated with the loss of "social capital" or goodwill among different groups in society and between citizens and the state. Controls obviously interfere with the freedom of individual firms, workers and their representatives to set or otherwise determine wages, prices and other conditions important to individuals' welfare. Removing or limiting this freedom runs the risk of destroying some of the goodwill which enables society to function smoothly and with minimal conflict. Furthermore, wage and price controls are bound to be inequitable in some cases, with the result that certain groups may feel that they are forced to make an unnecessarily large sacrifice for the common good. These "social capital" costs are obviously difficult to quantify; however, this does not imply that they are not substantial. In the case of the AIP, the organized labour movement bitterly protested against the program, launched a court challenge of the constitutional validity of the Anti-Inflation Act, and organized a one-day general strike to protest the policy. Relations between the federal government and organized labour were severely strained, and various channels for labour-government consultation and collaboration were, at least temporarily, closed (Waldie, 1985; Riddell, 1985b).

Two additional costs of a political nature should be mentioned. As Lipsey (1977) has noted, in implementing controls, governments may try to obtain the support of organized labour or other interest groups opposed to the policy by enacting legislation favourable to these groups but detrimental to society as a whole. He cites the enactment in the United Kingdom of universal closed-shop legislation as an example of this tendency. Another potential long-run cost of a temporary controls program results from the fact that it may be politically difficult to lift the controls from certain sectors. Rent controls still exist in some provinces as a legacy of the "temporary" Anti-Inflation Program.

Constitutional and Political Issues

There are various constitutional and/or political issues associated with statutory wage and price controls. The division of powers between the federal and provincial levels of government places important limits on the federal government's capacity alone to mount a statutory controls program. Under normal circumstances, the subject matter of prices and incomes falls largely within provincial jurisdiction pursuant to s. 92(13) of the Constitution Act, 1867, as a matter of "property and civil rights" within the province. The federal Parliament may legislate incomes policies in the federally regulated sector, which includes banks, airlines, railways, federal Crown corporations, and in the federal public sector.

In the 1976 Anti-Inflation Act Reference case, the Supreme Court of Canada held that the federal emergency power can be used to enact universal wage controls in peacetime. The Anti-Inflation Act, passed in 1975, gave the federal government regulatory authority over prices, profit margins, and wages in selected areas of the private sector; it applied directly to the federal public sector, and it authorized the government to enter into agreements with the provinces to apply the program to the provincial public sectors. Administered by a federal tribunal and federal officials, the act was to be temporary until 1978, unless terminated earlier.

Challenged by several trade unions, the Anti-Inflation Act was referred to the Supreme Court of Canada, which held in a seven-two decision that the act was valid within the federal power to make laws for the "peace, order and good government of Canada" in an emergency situation. Several key points flow from the case. First, the court will not ask whether, on the evidence, there is an emergency, but rather, whether there is a "rational basis" for the legislation. Second, extrinsic evidence — for example, economic briefs and government white papers — will be admissible in determining whether a rational basis exists. Third, the onus of proof is on the opponents of the legislation to show that there is no rational basis for emergency legislation. And, fourth, the court will not look at the wisdom or likely success of the legislation. Thus this case suggests that the federal Parliament may introduce a statutory wage and price control program under the "peace, order and good government" power providing there is a "rational basis" for the legislation. Further, the court is unlikely to question the government's assessment of emergency conditions.

One important limitation, however, is that emergency legislation is inherently temporary. A permanent system of federal wage and price controls is precluded by the division of powers; a permanent system would have to be the creation of both levels of government, or sustained through an amendment to the Constitution. Moreover, if the federal government resorted to a succession of "temporary" emergency programs, the nature of the emergency might become legally suspect.

The Canadian Charter of Rights and Freedoms may have some implications for the conduct of incomes policy. An incomes policy does not interfere with an individual's right to join or form a union but does restrict what can be achieved through collective bargaining. Thus temporary wage controls that restricted collective bargaining would not appear to be contrary to the freedom of association guaranteed in the charter. However, most incomes policies are selective in their coverage. For example, the AIB guidelines applied only to firms with 500 or more employees, firms whose employees bargained in an association with employees of other firms, construction firms with more than 20 employees, federal government and Crown corporation employees, employees of participating provincial and municipal governments, and professionals. A policy that covers only part of the labour force could be challenged under the equality provisions of the charter.

The nuances of the constitutionality of controls are reinforced by the political complications of such programs. Controls would be more likely to succeed if business and labour supported them, but this would raise the same set of constraints and tensions examined in the earlier discussion of voluntary mechanisms. Moreover, the fact that wages are easier to control than many prices may increase suspicions that the program is essentially anti-labour in nature. Even if it was not intended to slow the growth in real wages, the program might have this effect if there were unanticipated inflationary shocks in the uncontrolled prices sector, as occurred in the last two years of the AIP. Each occurrence of differential treatment of this kind would make it even more difficult to obtain the cooperation, and in the extreme, the compliance of labour in future anti-inflationary efforts. This fundamental logic underlay the extension of the "social contracts" negotiated in Europe to a wider and wider range of public policies during the 1970s.

More generally, incomes policies extend political authority over a wider range of private activity, dramatically reinforcing the state's involvement in — and perceived responsibility for — the fate of the economy. Furthermore, a "social contract" in effect transfers more of the distributional function of society into the public realm. Governments have long influenced income redistribution through the tax-benefit system, but an incomes policy makes the state much more clearly involved. An incomes policy places distributional questions at the very centre of the government agenda, and channels conflicts over them firmly into the political process. The danger is that the conflicts generated by the effort might seriously exacerbate political tensions in the wider society. These considerations suggest that, on political grounds, programs of wage and price control should be used infrequently — a conclusion also implied by economic and legal factors.

Summary and Conclusions

This chapter has examined both economic theory and empirical evidence relating to the use of various forms of wage and price control, with particular emphasis on the Canadian experience. The main conclusion that emerges from this assessment is that temporary controls programs can play a role in achieving permanent reductions in inflation, provided that they are part of a larger package incorporating the appropriate restraint in aggregate demand. This combination of policies appears to reduce the very substantial costs associated with disinflation via pure demand restraint, and thus can be interpreted as a more equitable way of spreading the costs of reducing inflation across the entire population.

Although voluntary mechanisms of wage and price restraint are highly desirable, the structure of Canada's political and economic institutions makes achieving agreement unlikely — a prediction confirmed by our experience. The recent severe recession, which has made the costs of reducing inflation by demand restraint more evident, may make labour and business more receptive to appeals for voluntary restraint should the need for these arise in the future. However, prospects of achieving agreement remain uncertain at best.

Experience with wage and price control programs in the United Kingdom and the United States has been mixed. In some cases the programs appear to have had little impact other than of a temporary nature. In other cases the policy appears to have achieved some moderation in inflation.

Robert Russell (1983, p. 132–33) summed up his discussion of U.S. incomes policies as follows:

> As I read the record of income policies, I believe they can be effective instruments of anti-inflation policies for very short periods of time. If intelligently designed and prudently administered, they can generate a small one-time downward shift in the Phillips curve, thus facilitating the implementation of restrictive macroeconomic policies. It is, however, a mistake to perceive them as long-term anti-inflation policies. The longer such policies are in effect, the more complicated and legalistic they become. Distortions and market disruptions, which may initially be of minimal proportions, gradually accumulate until the induced inefficiency costs of the program become onerous. In addition, the program inevitably becomes entangled in controversy over issues of equity. There are an untold number of design issues whose resolution will inevitably work to the benefit of some and the disadvantage of others. Important and powerful political-economic groups will have selfishly different views of what constitutes equity in the design and implementation of the incomes policies. Moreover, incomes policies are vulnerable to extraneous shocks (such as the world oil price explosion). Finally, the political temptation to relax fiscal and monetary policies, under the delusion that incomes policy alone can keep the lid on inflation, can generate inflationary pressures that torpedo the incomes policy.

This is, in my view, a balanced assessment of the U.S. record with incomes policies. The general principles enunciated by Russell are equally applicable in the Canadian setting.

The Canadian experience, in particular the Anti-Inflation Program of 1975–78, has been more favourable. Econometric studies generally conclude that the wage and price controls reduced new wage settlements by 3–4 percent in each of the three years of the program, and price inflation by 1–3 percent per year, with the reduction in price inflation concentrated in the second half of the program and continuing well beyond the end of the AIP. The somewhat greater success of Canada's 1975–78 controls program relative to the experience of the United States and the United Kingdom can probably be attributed to two key design features: the coordination of the wage and price controls with monetary and fiscal restraint, and the use of gradually declining norms for wage and price increases. The apparently moderate nature of the administrative and resource allocation costs associated with the AIP can probably be attributed to the temporary nature of the program and the fact that it was combined with moderate slack in product and labour markets.

Although both economic theory and empirical evidence indicate that the combination of wage and price guidelines and appropriate restraint in aggregate demand represent an attractive alternative to reliance on demand restraint alone to reduce inflation, it would be a mistake to resort to controls on a regular basis. The interference with individual freedom and the inevitable inequities associated with mandatory limits on wage and price increases result in a loss in good will between different groups in society and alter the relationship between the citizens and the state. For this reason and others, controls should be limited to situations in which there is widespread agreement on the need to reduce inflation to more acceptable levels. Constitutional considerations reinforce this point.

Because direct controls are a tool which should be used infrequently, and because the experience of some countries with their use has been disappointing, interest has recently shifted to alternative policies for restraining inflation. Many of these policies can be categorized under the heading of incentive-based incomes policies, the subject of the next chapter.

Chapter 5

Incentive-Based Incomes Policies: *Survey and Assessment*

The high cost of reducing inflation by restrictive monetary and fiscal policies has led to increased attention to the use of incomes policies. Yet the experience with the various wage and price control programs employed in Western economies has not been overwhelmingly favourable. For these reasons, some economists and policy analysts have turned to innovative forms of incomes policies. The central feature of these policies is that they involve the creation of incentives to reduce wage and price inflation. By utilizing rather than supplanting the price system these proposals hold out the promise of reducing inflation without incurring two of the main costs of direct wage and price controls — the administrative costs of overseeing and enforcing the program, and the allocative inefficiencies which result from interfering with market forces. Moreover, these schemes promise to interfere less with individual freedom than direct control programs.

The earliest of these innovative proposals works through the tax system; these are termed tax-based incomes policies or TIPs. More recent suggestions utilize artificial markets rather than taxes or subsidies; the wage increase permit plan (WIPP) and the market anti-inflation plan (MAP) are examples. Within each of these two groups there are a variety of proposals; for ease of exposition I will refer to schemes that employ taxes or subsidies as TIPs and schemes that involve the creation of artificial markets as MAPs. In addition, I will refer to TIPs and MAPs together as incentive-based incomes policies (IBIPs).

The purpose of this chapter is to summarize and assess these various schemes. The next section is devoted to a survey of the various TIP and MAP proposals that have been made, together with a sketch of the history of these ideas. Following sections assess each of these proposed incomes policies. They thus provide a critical analysis of the arguments made for and against TIPs and MAPs.

A Survey of Incentive-Based Incomes Policies

This section contains a detailed survey of IBIPs. It begins with a summary of the salient features of these schemes. The second subsection describes the various forms of TIPs and MAPs that have been proposed or implemented. The schemes are discussed in the order in which they were first proposed so that an historical perspective on the evolution of these ideas is provided. The third subsection examines the features of a "state of the art" TIP or MAP. A final subsection summarizes Canadian proposals. This first section is intended as a descriptive overview. The critical assessment of the various proposals is carried out later in the chapter.

Salient Features of IBIPs

IBIPs are schemes which create incentives for moderating wage and/or price increases without otherwise interfering with market forces. TIPs provide these incentives through taxes and/or subsidies. MAPs involve the creation of artificial markets in "rights" to increase wages and/or prices. Sometimes included as a third member of the family is the contract approval incomes policy (CAIP), which uses the government's role as a major purchaser to influence the price- and/or wage-setting behaviour of firms seeking to supply goods and services to the government. Relatively little will be said about CAIPs here; clearly they can be used with TIPs, MAPs or direct controls.

The distinction between direct controls (either mandatory, voluntary or negotiated) and incentive-based incomes policies is that the former impose certain limits, guidelines or norms on wage and price setters while the latter impose a set of rules, leaving firms and employees free to determine wages and prices subject to these rules. (The rules may, of course, involve a norm for wage or price increases.) Thus these schemes attempt to achieve the informational advantages of decentralized decision making in addition to permitting freedom of choice.

The reader will notice an analogy with methods to control pollution and other externalities. The general public and policy makers typically suggest direct controls (effluent standards, etc.) for dealing with these environmental problems. Economists have recommended either a system of taxes and subsidies or the creation of artificial markets in "pollution rights" as more effective methods of achieving the optimal levels of pollution. The latter is especially recommended, for markets in tradeable emissions permits have important theoretical advantages over direct regulations. These schemes are also being put into practice; for example, the transition to a system of air pollution controls based on marketable emissions permits has been underway in the United States since 1977. As stated by Roger Noll (1981): "the most widely supported direction of reform [of environmental regulation] is to introduce a greater measure of decentralized decision making, guided by economic incentives, as a substitute for regulatory rules promulgated by government."

Direct wage-price controls and TIPs are usually advocated as temporary incomes policies which would be abandoned once the underlying inflation rate was reduced to the target level. In contrast, MAPs are viewed as being permanent features of the economic system. The analogy to environmental control suggests the existence of an externality leading to market failure in wage and price setting. Establishing the existence of such an externality would imply that there is a fundamental economic rationale for permanent intervention in wage and price setting, as there is for the control of pollution. No one believes that environmental regulation, however implemented, should be abandoned once acceptable levels have been reached. This issue is discussed in the next section.

The main design features of TIPs and MAPs are described briefly here; the details will be filled in when specific proposals are examined. TIPs can involve taxes (stick approach), subsidies (carrot approach) or both. These may be based on wage increases, price increases, profit margins or combinations thereof. The taxes may be levied on firms through the corporate profit tax or through a payroll or value-added tax and/or on workers through the individual income tax or through a payroll tax.

Most TIPs have a norm or guideline for percentage increases in wages and/or prices. A discrete TIP applies the same penalty to all increases above the norm, or the same reward to all increases below the norm. A continuous TIP provides a schedule of tax or subsidy rates corresponding to each wage and/or price increase; an advantage of such a scheme is that it need not have a specific norm. Combinations of discrete and continuous schedules are possible; for example, the policy could provide for a schedule of tax rates for increases above the norm and a fixed subsidy or tax rate below the norm.

MAPs involve the creation of tradeable permits to increase wages or prices by some amount (e.g., 1 percent). Firms are issued a number of permits based on the target rate of inflation and the rate of productivity growth. Firms that wish to raise prices or wages more than their allocation allows may purchase permits from firms that wish to raise prices or wages by less than their allocation allows.

Historical Evolution of IBIP Proposals

The Scott Proposal

Perhaps the earliest TIP proposal was that of Scott (1961). He suggested a tax on price increases and discussed some of the advantages and disadvantages of this scheme. The tax was to be applied to corporate profits. Scott preferred a continuous scheme, and provided an illustrative list of tax rates (based on the U.K. corporate income tax) for various average percentage increases in the company's prices. The average increase would be a weighted average of the percentage increases in the various products produced by the firm, the weights being the quantity of each product produced or sold.

Scott also proposed that companies be allowed to opt out of the program, in which case they would pay a fixed tax rate on corporate profits. This rate would be "sufficiently high to ensure that enough firms would opt in for the scheme to be effective. On the other hand, it should not be so high as to cripple those firms which did opt out" (p. 353).

The reasons given by Scott for allowing firms to opt out point to some of the difficulties with this scheme for a tax on price increases. First, because of adjustment to economic change, some prices will increase more than others in the absence of a controls program. Scott did not feel that those firms whose prices would rise rapidly in the absence of the program should be heavily penalized as a result of the program. Second, there are the difficulties associated with measuring average price increases. These could be substantial for some firms, and Scott preferred to allow firms with large measurement problems to opt out of the program. Several variations on the opting out provision are also discussed by Scott; examples include opting to exclude 10 percent or less of sales from the program for firms with a large number of products, some of which do not make much contribution to total revenue; and allowing firms to opt out permanently rather than opting out for a portion of the program.

Scott's basic argument was that the tax on price increases would not only add to whatever incentives already exist for price restraint but would also make firms more resistant to increases in costs. He felt that the main effect of the tax would be on absolute levels of price increase, and there would be little effect on relative prices. This in an important aspect of any IBIP, and is discussed in detail later.

Scott concluded by considering some objections to the proposed tax. These include:

- possible increases in industrial disputes;
- the fact that the tax is unfair to those firms whose input prices, for reasons beyond the firms' control, rise much more than average (which Scott does not dispute, although his opting out provision does put an upper bound on this handicap);
- the difficulty of measuring price changes and of handling related problems such as new or "improved" products, quality changes, and services which have no readily identifiable quantity;
- administrative costs;

- the incentive created to lower quality rather than change price; and
- the use of accounting procedures ("tricks") through subsidiaries, etc., to affect the reported price changes.

The Steuer Proposal

Another early proposal was made by M.D. Steuer (1962). An interesting feature of Steuer's suggestion was a contingency arrangement similar to that later incorporated in the "real wage insurance" plan put forward by the Carter administration in the United States (discussed below). Specifically, Steuer suggested that the proceeds of wage increases in excess of the norm be paid into a central fund which would hold the money in accounts for each individual worker. The money would be repaid if prices did not rise in excess of the price norm. Price increases in excess of their norm would give rise to increases in the corporate profits tax. The level of disaggregation at which these arrangements would apply was left for further consideration.

The Wallich-Weintraub Proposal

Undoubtedly the best known early TIP proposal was that of H. Wallich and S. Weintraub. Indeed, many writers credit Wallich and Weintraub with originating the TIP idea. Their initial suggestions were made independently (Wallich, 1966, 1970; Weintraub, 1970). Subsequently, they collaborated on a more complete discussion (Wallich and Weintraub, 1971). Weintraub continued to write on the subject (see, e.g., Weintraub 1978, 1982) and remained one of the most vocal TIP proponents until his recent death.

The Wallich-Weintraub proposal involves a norm for wage increases, with firms permitting wage increases above the norm paying a higher rate of corporate tax. The intent is to restrain wage increases by increasing the costs of high settlements to employers. They argue that prices are based on a constant markup over wages (with allowance for productivity growth), so that controls over price increases are not necessary. They cite evidence that the economy-wide markup of prices over wages has been nearly constant over both the short run and the long run but do not cite evidence at more disaggregate levels. They also appear confident that adding incentives for wage moderation but not for price moderation will not alter the average markup.

Various ways of measuring wage increases are discussed by Wallich and Weintraub. Several involve average wage comparisons at two different points in time. This method raises a number of difficulties; for example, firms will have an incentive to hire low-wage workers to lower the average wage or firms may "fire" some high-wage workers at the appropriate time. The method they prefer involves calculating the percentage increase in wages for each group of employees (e.g., by skill or grade classification) and then obtaining the overall increase in wages as a weighted average of these individual increases. This method is somewhat more complex than the others but it does avoid some of the important flaws associated with comparisons of average wages.

Wallich and Weintraub discuss a number of additional problems which may be associated with their proposed TIP. Since price increases are not subject to the TIP, the possibility that firms will permit high wage increases and pass these on in the form of price increases is discussed. This concern with tax shifting is the main rationale for basing the TIP on the corporate income tax, which they argue is less likely than various alternatives (e.g., payroll tax) to be shifted forward. A second problem discussed is the possibility that the policy will cause an increase in strikes or strike length. Other problems include the fact that the choice of the corporate income tax raises the difficult issue of how to deal with the public and quasi-public sectors, and the issue of dealing with new firms.

Proposals of the Early 1970s in the United Kingdom and Ireland

A number of TIPs were proposed in the United Kindgom and Ireland in the early 1970s. Fogarty (1973, Appendix 1) provides a useful summary of these plans. Clearly the idea was beginning to be seriously debated at that time in the United Kingdom as well as in North America. Indeed, a tax on wage increases became part of the policy platform of the U.K. Liberal party in the early 1970s.

Hungarian Wage Control

Hungary is the only country to have actually implemented a TIP. Centrally controlled wages, in effect since 1957, were replaced in 1968 by a wage-increase TIP when the country moved to a more decentralized decision-making system (Fogarty, 1973; Portes, 1977). Initially the tax was based on wage increases in excess of a common norm (of zero). Subsequently, in 1971 the tax was amended to allow wage increases which reflected productivity increase.

An important part of the 1968 reforms was the introduction of profit sharing for all classes of employees (top management to rank and file). These bonuses are also important to the TIP, for excessive wage increases result in the profit shares of managers and workers being heavily taxed.

The Hungarian system, like the Wallich-Weintraub plan, was based on average wages for the enterprise. The accompanying incentive to hire low-paid workers led to labour shortages in these areas and subsequent amendments to the procedures for calculating wage increases.

Knowledgeable observers (e.g., Portes, 1977) conclude that the Hungarian wage-increase TIP has helped to moderate inflationary pressures. The implications of this conclusion for non-centrally planned economies are less evident.

The French Plan

While Hungary is the only country to have adopted a TIP, several countries have seriously considered implementing such a policy. Sumner (1975) and Malinvaud (1978) report that a price-increase TIP came close to implementation in 1974/75 in France. Indeed, the law had been placed in the statute book but was not applied because inflation began to moderate. The TIP was planned to be temporary in nature; indeed, the legislation provided that the levy would be withdrawn once price increases fell below an annual rate of 6 percent for three successive months.

The tax was to be based on the increase in value added after deduction of export transactions, of increases attributable to changes in factor inputs, and of a uniform allowance for anticipated price and productivity increases. Sumner (1975) notes that the levy may have had an impact on the firms' choice of factor proportions arising from the accounting rules specified for measuring input changes.

The Okun Proposal

Okun (1977) proposed a carrot TIP for wage and price restraint as part of a package for achieving prosperity and price stability. Firms pledging to hold their percentage increase in wages and prices below the respective norms would receive a tax reduction on corporate profits. The employees would receive an income tax rebate. The price increase norm would allow a dollar-for-dollar pass through of any increases in costs of materials and supplies.

In the valuable and insightful book written just before his death, Okun (1981, pp. 348 – 53) recommends that various forms of TIP be used, in conjunction with other policies, on a temporary rather than permanent basis. Examples include a reward tax credit for employees with wage increases below the norm used in conjunction with expansionary aggregate demand policy, and a reduction in the corporate income tax or an improved investment tax credit for corporations complying with norms for wage and/or price restraint.

The Seidman Proposal

In a series of articles, Seidman (1976a, 1976b, 1978a, 1978b, 1979a, 1979b, 1981) discusses various aspects of TIPs. While most of these articles are concerned with the assessment of different TIPs, he does advocate specific plans which are variants on the Wallich-Weintraub proposal. In Seidman (1976b) he suggests the addition of a reward for employees receiving wage increases below the norm in the Wallich-Weintraub plan (which imposes a penalty on firms granting wage increases above the norm). The reward would take the form of a payroll tax credit. Seidman recommends a tax credit which is continuous for wage increases below the norm; in particular, the tax credit is some multiple of the difference between the actual wage increase and the norm. The purpose of the employee carrot is two-fold: to make the program appeal more to labour, and to increase the effectiveness of the program. In addition, he suggests that the employee tax credit may reduce the incidence of industrial disputes.

Most previous authors suggested or implied that their proposed TIP be temporary in nature. Seidman is one of the first to advocate the implementation of a permanent TIP. This recommendation follows logically from his view, first expressed in Seidman (1976a), that decentralized wage and price setting by individual firms and workers is socially inefficient for the same reason that decentralized setting of pollution levels is socially inefficient. This point is of fundamental importance, and is discussed in the next section.

Subsequent proposals by Seidman have been primarily directed toward making TIPs more equitable and more acceptable to labour. In addition to the employee reward scheme discussed above, Seidman examines a price increase TIP on the large corporations subject to the wage increase TIP; a real wage insurance scheme similar to that proposed by the Carter administration (discussed below); and a profit restraint insurance scheme. The last scheme involves a uniform tax surcharge on all the large firms covered by the penalty TIP if their total profit increased abnormally in any given year.

Markets in Permits to Raise Prices or Wages

The analogy between wage and price setting and environmental pollution (or, more generally, externalities) immediately suggests an alternative to taxes and/or subsidies — the creation of markets in rights to raise wages and/or prices. In the literature on externalities, the use of market-type solutions is known to have important theoretical advantages over the use of taxes and subsidies as well as direct controls.

Early market-based schemes were suggested by von Weizsacker (1975) and Howard (1976). Von Weizsacker's proposal would require firms to purchase permits to increase prices and would create markets to facilitate trading of these permits. The supply of permits would be tied to the money supply. Howard's scheme would involve issuing to firms permits with a fixed value per person employed and would require firms to hold permits equal in value to the firm's total payments to its factors of production.

Neither of these schemes was fully worked out. They are best thought of as precursors to the more completely specified Market Anti-Inflation Plan which is discussed below.

The Wage Increase Permit Plan (WIPP)

The Wage Increase Permit Plan involves the creation of markets in permits to increase wages. It was first advocated by Lerner (1977a, 1977b,

1978), and would work as follows. Firms would be issued permits each period (e.g., each year) which would allow them to increase their wage bill by, say, 3 percent over the previous period. Firms wishing to increase their wage bill by more than 3 percent would have to purchase permits from firms willing to increase their wage bill by less than 3 percent. Thus, if each permit applies to $1,000 in wages, one permit would allow firms to raise wages by $30, and an employee earning $20,000 per year would result in 20 permits being issued to the firm. A market would be set up for trading in permits.

To prevent the WIPP from affecting employment, the employer would lose the permit when an employee leaves the company. When a new employee is hired a new permit is issued at the employee's previous salary. This latter stipulation removes the incentive to "fire" an employee and hire him or her back at a higher salary. Newly hired employees without previous employment experience would receive permits based on their starting salary. At the end of the period, each old permit held by the firm would be replaced by a new permit worth 1.03 times the old.

In Lerner's proposed WIPP the number of permits issued to a firm would depend on the earnings rather than wage rates of employees. In this case the WIPP could affect the firm's choice of hours versus employment in adjusting to temporary changes in demand. However, a WIPP based on nominal wage rates and normal hours could be designed.

Two features of the WIPP concerned Lerner: the appearance of being anti-labour because of the focus on wages, and the reliance on the link between wages and prices to reduce price inflation. For these reasons Lerner subsequently began to advocate the MAP rather than the WIPP.

Market Anti-Inflation Plan (MAP)

The Market Anti-Inflation Plan is analogous to the WIPP, except now the permits are based on value added rather than the wage bill. It can thus be called a price version of the WIPP. Variants of the MAP were outlined in a series of articles by Colander and Lerner. They have refined their proposal in their jointly authored book, Lerner and Colander (1980). It is this version which I will discuss here.

Firms would be issued permits based on their value added in the previous period. The central authority overseeing the MAP (which could be the country's central bank) would decide on an allotment of MAP credit. For example, if 2 percent growth is to be accommodated, each firm would be issued permits or MAP credit equal to 1.02 times their net sales in the previous period. Firms that want to increase their value added by more than 2 percent would purchase permits, and firms willing to increase their value added by less than the growth norm would sell permits.

The MAP is equivalent to having a second currency; in addition to the currency used for market transactions there is the "MAP credit" which firms maintain with the central authority. Firms are required to keep their net sales equal to their MAP credit. To ensure that firms accomplish this by adjusting prices and not outputs or inputs, a number of additional regulations are required. These focus on inputs rather than outputs. Hiring new employees gives the firm a permit worth the employee's salary in the previous job. For employees entering the labour force for the first time the value of the permit is equal to the worker's starting salary. New investment gives the firm a permit equal to the annual interest on the new investment.

The MAP, and its predecessor the WIPP, are intended as permanent features of the economic system.

Real Wage Insurance (RWI)

This proposal was made in the United States during the Carter administration. Proposed by the administration in January 1979, it died in Congress in April 1979. Mitchell (1980) provides an account of its brief life.

RWI was a reward TIP on wage increases below the norm of 7 percent. The novel feature was that the reward to workers accepting increases below the norm was not predetermined but rather depended on the realized inflation rate. Specifically, workers accepting an increase below the norm would receive a reward equal to the difference between the actual rate of inflation and the norm (to a maximum of 3 percent) times their base salary. Thus, workers agreeing to wage increases below the norm were "insured" against inflation rates of up to 10 percent.

Mitchell (1980) illustrates some of the anomalies associated with the scheme. Shortcuts, designed to reduce the administrative complexity, created inequities for various bargaining units and various individuals within a bargaining unit.

Request-Control Systems

Another form of incomes policy which combines aspects of incentive-based policies and direct controls is the request-control system advocated by Baily (1976) and Bellan (1983) and the closely related direct relativity bargaining advocated by Wood (1978). The basis for these schemes is the proposition that what matters for resource allocation are relative wages and relative prices; the absolute wage or price level is irrelevant. This neutrality principle follows from the property that demand and supply functions are homogeneous of degree zero in all prices and wages. The absence of a long-run tradeoff between inflation and unemployment also follows from this property.

The request-control system works as follows. At the beginning of each period each firm submits its planned wage or price increase to the control authority. The control authority calculates the average wage or price increase. Each request is then scaled down by the average so that the planned changes in relative prices are preserved but the overall rate of inflation is maintained at zero. In the case of a wage request-control system the proposed wage changes could be scaled down to average some positive amount (e.g., the underlying rate of productivity growth) to allow for price stability and growth in real wages.

In Wood's direct relativity bargaining scheme, existing collective bargaining or other wage-setting procedures would be used to determine relative wages while the overall wage level would be set by the central authorities. The scheme would make it obligatory for negotiators to tackle relative wages directly, within the firm, within the industry, and subsequently among industries. Failure to reach agreement on relativities would lead to an independent chairman, appointed by the government, settling the outcome. Employers could compensate other employers to achieve a particular outcome. When the relative wages are determined, the government would set one (and thus each) wage level. This process would be repeated annually to ensure no major distortions persisted.

Layard-Jackman Proposal

Layard (1982a, 1982b) and Jackman and Layard (1982b) proposed a permanent TIP for the United Kingdom. The TIP would involve a tax on the increase in the firm's average hourly earnings in excess of the economy-wide norm (to be declared annually). It is also recommended that the scheme be revenue-neutral. In order to achieve this, the proceeds of the tax would be rebated to all employers in proportion to their wage bill. This feature has several purposes: to ensure that the scheme provides no net fiscal stimulus (or contraction), whatever the magnitude of earnings increases; to avoid any net economy-wide passing-on of the tax into prices; and to avoid being unfair to employers.

An important contribution of Jackman and Layard is their analysis of the economic effects of a TIP on wage increases. Most earlier TIP proponents based their recommendations very loosely, if at all, on an underlying model of the behaviour of wages, prices, employment and output. The next section takes up the analysis of IBIPs.

Summary

This section has provided a summary of the main IBIPs in roughly the chronological order in which they have been discussed and proposed. The reader will have noted the considerable variety of these schemes. Not every contributor to the literature in IBIPs has been mentioned (although most have) since some proposed policies are minor variants on schemes proposed by others. Nonetheless, the reader will now have a good appreciation of the evolution of these ideas.

A "State of the Art" IBIP?

Discussions of incentive-based incomes policies have been appearing since the early 1970s. Has a consensus view about the most desirable form of such a policy, assuming one is to be adopted, emerged? The answer to this question would appear to be "No." A variety of TIP proposals continue to be advocated and the most recent contributions (e.g., Layard, 1982a, 1982b) add new twists. One point on which there is widespread agreement is that a TIP on price increases would be administratively infeasible. Thus a wage increase TIP, usually combined with some provision to make the policy appear less anti-labour, is reasonably described as a consensus view. However, there appears little agreement on other design features. With respect to market-based schemes, the consensus proposal, albeit among a fairly small number of authors advocating these schemes, is the Lerner-Colander MAP.

Canadian IBIP Proposals

A number of authors have discussed the use of a TIP as a component of Canadian anti-inflation policy. As far as I know, only Maslove (1982) has considered the adoption of a market-based scheme in Canada.

The Canadian TIP proposals are typically variants on the schemes described earlier. They are, however, of considerable interest here because they attempt to take into account the characteristics of the Canadian economy and its institutions.

The Donner and Peters TIP

Donner and Peters (1979), students of Weintraub at the University of Pennsylvania, have advocated a modified Wallich-Weintraub TIP. The tax would be on the size of wage and salary increases in excess of a single economy-wide norm. (They recommended 5 percent in 1979.) The corporate income tax would be used; they note that the corporate tax rate could be reduced to maintain the same average tax rate so that the net revenue of the tax would be zero.

They suggest that the TIP would apply to the 200 largest employers in the private sector. Federal and provincial civil servants would have the norm applied to their settlements. They proposed one modification to the Wallich-Weintraub plan: "A federal government commitment to the public that the augmented TIP plan would be administered fairly. If it could be determined that real wages or purchasing power were being curtailed unfairly, or that TIP were providing excess profits, then further tax measures would be introduced to remedy the situation." This feature could be termed a form of implicit real wage insurance.

One aspect of the Wallich-Weintraub proposal which concerned several TIP proponents is its possible anti-labour appearance. Numerous authors, notably Seidman, have recommended modifications to offset this appearance. Donner and Peters are unique in recommending that the TIP be accompanied by expansionary monetary and fiscal policies in order to make the program appeal to labour. Most economists, as discussed in the previous chapter, view the incomes policy as a complement to disinflationary demand management policy, and therefore would oppose the combination of a TIP with policies designed to expand output and employment.

Donner and Peters also recommend a government contract authorization incomes policy based on the wage norm as a supplement to the TIP.

The Bodkin Proposal

Bodkin (1981) addressed the question of whether Canada should adopt a TIP "in lieu of *any other incomes policy* and as part of a package which includes appropriate monetary and fiscal discipline (particularly the former)." He concluded that it was not clear that a TIP should be adopted. However, if a choice had to be made between direct controls of the Anti-Inflation Program variety and a TIP, Bodkin definitely would favour the latter.

Bodkin's preferred TIP is a variant on the Okun plan. There would be tax relief (in the form of a percentage of earnings) for employees who state their intention to stay within, and in fact do stay within, the guidelines. In addition, employers would receive a modest tax rebate if price increases and/or profit margins are within the guidelines. A simple national norm would apply to wage increases. The program would be universal but voluntary. On the employee side there would be no need to distinguish between employees in the private and public sectors.

The tax rebate to employers would be based on one of three criteria: profit margins no higher than the previous year, or an average of several previous years; determination that the firm has no appreciable power to set prices; or where the firm demonstrates that price increases reflect no more than a pass-through of costs with customary markups. The guidelines for firms are regarded as a nuisance but are felt necessary to make the program appeal to labour.

Bodkin's proposal is one of the few to offer a tax reduction to both employers and employees. This recommendation reflects Bodkin's view that a reward TIP is much less likely to lead to federal-provincial jurisdictional disputes. The estimated total cost (in 1980) was roughly $3 billion based on a 2 percent subsidy capped at $30,000 income.

A subsequent exchange between You (1982) and Bodkin (1982) added little in terms of concrete policy proposals. You was skeptical about the effectiveness of the proposed TIP and, indeed, felt that only a much more expensive plan would have an appreciable effect. An important source of You's skepticism appears to be his view that the TIP works (or does not work) by altering expectations. In fact, as Bodkin (1982) notes, the intent of TIPs is also to reduce actual wage and price increases below what they would otherwise have been given the level of expectations. Of course, the longer-run success of the policy does rely on reducing expectations but this reduction may occur only because of the decrease in actual inflation.

The Barber and McCallum Plan

Barber and McCallum (1982) advocated a temporary (three-year) program of direct controls similar to that employed in the Anti-Inflation Program. Since a TIP was one of the alternatives they considered, their recommendation implies a rejection of a TIP. However, their proposed package does incorporate either real wage insurance or "wage share insurance." The latter involves specifying a base ratio of total corporate profits to total wages, salaries, and supplementary labour income. If aggregate profits exceed this ratio there would be a surcharge on the corporate profit tax, the proceeds of which would be distributed to employees through reductions in personal income tax. The wage share insurance scheme ensures that the program does not favour profits over wages, at least at the aggregate level. Barber and McCallum also indicate that "a looser form of incomes policy, perhaps taking the form of wage-price guidelines or a tax-based incomes policy, will be needed in the immediate post-controls period" (p. 109).

In their discussion of TIPs, Barber and McCallum suggest a novel scheme for making a penalty TIP on wage increases less anti-labour and anti-collective bargaining in appearance. This would leave unions free to negotiate a lump-sum cash payment as a supplement to the wage increase allowed under the TIP. Barber and McCallum do not stipulate, but presumably non-union employers would be allowed to make these lump-sum payments as well. The argument for the lump-sum payment scheme is that it would "serve to prevent the bargaining process from having a pattern-setting inflationary effect while leaving the union free to gain additional benefits for its members" (p. 40).

Other Canadian Views

It may be useful to conclude this section by briefly summarizing other views expressed by economists and policy analysts regarding the desirability of adopting an IBIP in Canada. Maslove (1982) compares alternative incomes policies (direct controls, TIP and MAP are the main choices) on various criteria. His order of preference is MAP, TIP, and direct controls. Fortin (1983) warns against one form of TIP; a payroll tax on wage increases may result in both lower wage inflation and higher price inflation. Lipsey and Purvis (1982) recommend against the adoption of a TIP, primarily on the grounds that the inequities associated with the TIP could be blamed on the tax system in general rather than the anti-inflation policy, resulting in a loss of confidence in the rough justice of the tax system and ultimately a breakdown in voluntary compliance with the system.

In his analysis of TIPs, Scarth (1982) concludes that the benefits of an employer TIP on wage settlements in excess of the norm exceed the costs. The benefits are estimated with a small macro simulation model and an assumed degree of effectiveness of the TIP. The benefits are similar to those under a direct controls program. Scarth also concludes that both an employer penalty TIP and an employee penalty TIP, both based on excess price increases, worsen the dynamic adjustment of the economy to a lower inflation rate. Scarth also finds that "the single most effective policy for lessening the transitional unemployment costs of disinflation policy in our model is one of government incentives for shortening wage contract length" (p. 124), an issue discussed in the next chapter.

Cornwall and Maclean (1984) advocate a TIP as part of a framework for economic recovery. Other parts of the package include expansionary aggregate demand policy, measures to stimulate productivity growth, and an industrial strategy. They are unique in arguing for a TIP as part of a permanent voluntary incomes policy.

An Assessment of Incentive-Based Incomes Policies

This section will assess the probable benefits and costs of IBIPs. This is not a simple task, for experience with these programs is limited to the Hungarian case and many of the benefits and costs would be difficult to measure even if these programs had been implemented on a more widespread scale. Further, the variety of proposals makes evaluation difficult. Clearly it will not be possible to provide a separate assessment of each of the IBIPs outlined in the previous section. Rather, I will attempt a general assessment of TIPs and MAPs and then examine how specific design features will alter these general advantages and disadvantages.

Before beginning this assessment some more basic issues need to be addressed. To begin, the underlying rationales for incomes policies are outlined. These can usefully be dichotomized into those which argue, respectively, for a permanent and a temporary incomes policy. We then examine the case for a permanent incomes policy.

Even within proposals for a permanent IBIP there are two quite different approaches. One, for which the MAP is suggested, creates institutional arrangements intended to maintain a fairly constant average price level but otherwise to interfere as little as possible with output, employment and the allocation of resources. The second, for which a permanent TIP is proposed, sets out to alter the equilibrium levels of output and employment. For the former the intent is to shift down the entire distribution of wage and price changes, leaving relative wage and price changes unaltered.

Rationales for an Incomes Policy

Most advocates of incomes policy make explicit the rationale which provides the basis for their proposed approach. These various rationales reflect a variety of views about the inflationary process and the relationship between inflation and unemployment. The following list contains the main arguments that have been advanced:

(1) Decentralized individual wage and price setting is socially inefficient owing to an "inflation externality." According to this view a permanent incomes policy is required to deal with this externality.

(2) The economy is biased toward inflation owing to the market power of large corporations and unions. This bias results in price stability and full employment being incompatible, so that a permanent incomes policy is required if full employment is to be maintained.

(3) A primarily European view is that either the level or the structure of real wages in a highly unionized economy may result in an inefficiently high equilibrium level of unemployment, and that an incomes policy is required either to lower real wages or alter the structure of real wages. Typically this view leads to a call for a permanent incomes policy.[1]

(4) A temporary incentive-based incomes policy, possibly as part of a package including demand restraint, is an attractive alternative to pure demand restraint in making the transition from a high to low inflation rate. This is equivalent to the rationale discussed in chapter 4 for direct wage and price controls. Thus, a temporary TIP and direct wage and price controls should be thought of as alternative means of achieving the same objectives.

Because the rationale for a temporary incomes policy has already been discussed, the following subsection focusses on the case for a permanent incomes policy.

Is There a Case for a Permanent Incomes Policy?

One trend evident in the evolution of ideas is the increasing number of IBIPs proponents who advocate permanent incomes policies. This trend reflects, I believe, two factors. First, and most fundamental, is the view that decentralized individual wage and price setting involves an externality or divergence between private and social cost. Second is the view that it is possible to design an IBIP which would allow the relative wage and price changes needed for allocative efficiency to take place.

Possibly the first statement of the view that decentralized wage and price setting results in an "inflation externality" or excess of social over private cost is that of Seidman (1976a, p. 40):[2]

> [O]nly the traditional designation of inflation as a macroeconomic, rather than a microeconomic problem, can account for the neglect of this approach

thus far. From a microeconomic perspective, prices rise when the average business firm grants a wage and salary increase that exceeds the average growth rate of productivity in the economy. If the problem were regarded as micro-economic — the consequence of undesirable behavior by the average firm — economists would naturally propose a tax on the undesired activity in order to discourage it.

A comparison with the environmental pollution problem is instructive. Pollution is regarded by economists as a microeconomic problem. It arises because polluting firms are not charged for their use of a scarce resource-clean air or water. Economists almost unanimously recommend the use of effluent taxes (charges) to "internalize the externality," that is, to make polluting firms pay for the use of this valuable resource just as they must pay for any other. These traditional market incentives are generally regarded as the best method of controlling pollution. On the one hand, almost no one expects voluntary guideposts to be effective. In the microeconomic sphere, economists accept as an axiom that economic agents will behave according to their own self-interest, largely unaffected by what is best for society. On the other hand, most economists reject direct controls on polluters (except in extreme cases) because, in contrast to tax incentives and the market mechanism, controls are cumbersome, costly to administer, inflexible, and inefficient.

The microeconomic perspective, when applied to the traditionally macroeconomic problem of inflation, immediately reveals a similar "externality." When business firms grant wage and salary increases in excess of the average growth rate of productivity in the economy, they impose a cost on society by producing the public good ("bad") called inflation. Yet they are not charged for doing so, and therefore do not take this social cost into account when they make their wage-salary decision.

This view played an important role in the development of IBIP schemes. As Lerner (1977a, 1977b) points out, the analogy with pollution immediately suggests the use of markets in rights to raise wages and prices because of the attention given to marketable permits schemes in the environmental literature.

Much more important than its role in the development of the IBIP literature is the fact that this view appears to provide a fundamental economic rationale for intervention on a continuing basis in the wage- and price-setting process.[3] The form this intervention should take is not implied, but the objective of the intervention would be to equate private and social costs, just as the objective of environmental regulation is to achieve a social optimum by equating the private and social costs of polluting activities.

The view that decentralized wage and price setting involves an externality appears to have become widely accepted. No one, to my knowledge, has disputed it, although many have ignored it. At the same time, numerous writers have agreed with this view; Seidman (1976a, 1978a, 1979a), Lerner (1977a, 1977b, 1978), Lerner and Colander (1980), Maital and Benjamini (1980), and Scarth (1982) are examples.

I now wish to argue that this view is incorrect. The analogy to environmental pollution is inappropriate. There is some validity to the externality view in the sense that, with respect to reducing inflation, those involved in wage and price setting are caught in a prisoner's dilemma situation, or, more generally, a socially inefficient Nash equilibrium.[4] However, the existence of this socially inefficient outcome provides an economic rationale for a temporary rather than permanent incomes policy.

To begin, note that the analogy to environmental pollution is certainly not appropriate. Pollution activities — indeed, externalities in general — lead to an inefficient allocation of resources. They are remedied by expanding some activities and contracting others. Decentralized wage and price setting does not produce an inefficient allocation of resources. The inefficiency, if one exists, is a macro phenomenon — a rate of inflation different from the optimal rate of inflation. The use of an inappropriate analogy leads to an incorrect policy proposal — a permanent TIP or MAP.

A more accurate description of the inflationary process is that once expectations of a continuing inflation have been established, individual wage and price setters are trapped in an inefficient Nash equilibrium. Perhaps the best known such situation is the prisoner's dilemma game, shown in Figure 5-1. Two moves are available to each player. The first number in each box is the utility payoff to player A; the second is B's payoff. The number 1 represents the worst outcome, 4 the best outcome, and so on. The numbers themselves are arbitrary but the relationship between them is important.[5]

This game has the property that the optimal outcome for the two players as a group (i.e., the socially optimal outcome) is not to confess; however, when they act independently, each player's optimal strategy is to confess. That is, the Nash equilibrium of this game is for each prisoner to confess. This latter property follows from the fact that player A's best choice is to confess, whatever A thinks B will do (and thus is also the optimal choice if A is uncertain of what B will do). Because the situation is symmetric, the same is true for B. Thus, both players realize they would be better off by not confessing, yet both will confess if they must act independently.[6]

The description of the inflationary process as a prisoner's dilemma situation is suggested by the following quotation: "Inflation is like a crowd at a football game. No one is willing to be the first to sit down" (U.S. President J. Carter, October 25, 1978, televised address). Here the outcome "everyone sitting down" is preferred to the outcome "everyone standing up," yet the latter outcome obtains.

In fact, the prisoner's dilemma situation applies to the inflationary process, but in a restricted sense. The description is apt in an ongoing inflation with an underlying inflation rate different from the target or

FIGURE 5–1 The Prisoner's Dilemma

		Prisoner B	
		Don't Confess	Confess
Prisoner A	Don't Confess	3,3	1,4
	Confess	4,1	2,2

optimal rate.[7] Further, it only applies to the process of reducing inflation to the optimal rate. Individual wage and price setters are not permanently trapped in an inefficient Nash equilibrium.

To see this, examine first the simplest case in which all wages and prices are set at the same time and in which actual and expected inflation were equal in the previous period. Thus the underlying inflation rate is the expected inflation rate; there is no inflation inherited from the past due to "catch-up." Figure 5-2 shows the situation facing wage and price setters, treating each as a group. Of course, an additional "real world" complication here is that there are many players rather than two; the significance of this aspect is discussed below. The socially efficient outcome involves all wage and price setters practising moderation; that is not incorporating the expected rate of inflation so that the wage-price spiral ends and everyone becomes better off. This accounts for the (3,3) entry in the upper left cell compared to the (2,2) lower right cell. For example, if there were a common expected inflation rate of 10 percent and a target rate of zero, then those wishing to keep their relative wage or price constant would set the increase at zero rather than 10 percent, those wishing to raise the relative wage or price by 2 percent would choose an increase of 2 percent rather than 12 percent, and so on. However, if wage moderation is practised without price moderation, real wages will fall and profits rise, yielding the upper right (1,4) outcome. Similarly, price moderation without wage moderation yields the lower left cell outcome. In these circumstances decentralized wage and price setting will lead to the socially inefficient outcome in which the inflationary spiral continues.[8]

With many wage and price setters who act independently, a suboptimal outcome is more likely. No one union is likely to practise wage moderation, or firm practise price moderation, as their contribution

FIGURE 5–2 The Inflationary Spiral as a Prisoner's Dilemma

		Price Setters: Don't Incorporate Expected Inflation	Price Setters: Incorporate Expected Inflation
Wage Setters	Don't Incorporate Expected Inflation	3,3	1,4
	Incorporate Expected Inflation	4,1	2,2

alone will do little to lessen the inflationary spiral. Even if an agreement on wage and price moderation were reached, there may be incentives to cheat. However, in countries with highly centralized labour and business organizations, the socially optimal outcome may be attained through cooperative behaviour.

The observation that the socially inefficient outcome will obtain provides an economic rationale for controls — or some other mechanism for achieving the outcome best for society. Note, however, that the socially optimal and non-optimal outcomes coincide when the expected and target rates are equal. Thus there is a rationale for a temporary, but not a permanent, incomes policy. This argument remains valid when there is inherited inflation and staggered wage and price setting.

This analysis can also be carried out in the form of a game in which the central authorities and wage and price setters are the two players.[9] This game is shown in Figure 5-3. The size of the off-diagonal elements is less evident in this case, and the game is not necessarily of the prisoner's dilemma form. Nonetheless, the conclusion that the socially efficient outcome will not be achieved through decentralized wage and price setting remains. In this case there is a qualification; the efficient outcome would be achieved with decentralized wage and price setting if the authorities could make credible their intentions to end monetary growth.

In summary, the "inflation externality" argument does not justify a permanent incomes policy, though it does point to the potential benefits of a temporary incomes policy. What of the other arguments for permanent IBIPs?

The second rationale mentioned above for a permanent incomes policy is based on the view that the market power of large corporations and unions causes the economy to have a built-in inflationary bias which makes full employment and price stability incompatible. This rationale

FIGURE 5-3 The Inflationary Spiral and the Monetary Authorities

		Wage and Price Setters: End Wage and Price Inflation	Wage and Price Setters: Continue Wage and Price Inflation
Central Authorities	End Monetary Growth	4,4	1,1
	Continue Monetary Growth	3,1	2,2

is quite different from the inflation externality argument which is consistent with competitive wage and price setting. It is a view that has long been argued by Galbraith and typically is labelled neo-Keynesian. Lipsey (1984, p. 53) calls this the "theory of secular inflation."

Some versions of this view appear inconsistent with the natural-rate hypothesis. They also seem to fall victim to the "high vs. rising" confusion (Friedman, 1968): market power may well result in prices or wages being higher than otherwise, but will not result in their rising more rapidly than otherwise. As discussed previously, the natural-rate hypothesis is compatible with monopoly power in both product and labour markets.

Presumably, more sophisticated versions of the theory of secular inflation mean that, because of the market power of large firms and unions, the NAIRU is higher than what they regard as "full employment."[10] This, of course, may well be true, but it cannot constitute a theory without an operational definition of "full employment." The obvious candidate is the unemployment rate which yields the greatest net benefit to society according to some criterion (such as the Pareto criterion). The policy problem is then to remove the divergence between this socially optimal unemployment rate and the NAIRU, for only the latter is consistent with price stability.

This way of posing the issue implies that the second and third rationales listed above for a permanent incomes policy may be operationally equivalent. The level of real wages and/or the structure of wages are two potential sources of an inefficiently high NAIRU.

In order to evaluate these arguments, two questions need to be addressed. First, would an IBIP lower the NAIRU? Second, if the NAIRU is socially inefficient, is a permanent incomes policy the appropriate way to remove this inefficiency? These questions are examined in detail in a subsequent section.

Layard (1982a) also presents a separate case for a permanent incomes policy. His argument is based on the fact that an excess of the trend growth in real wages over productivity growth has the same effect on inflation-unemployment choices as an increase in the natural unemployment rate. Layard's view, supported by the empirical work of Grubb, Jackman and Layard (1982), is that an important cause of the current stagflation in OECD countries has been that the actual rate of growth of real wages has not declined as quickly as the feasible rate of growth of real wages (which depends on productivity growth). To prevent inflation from increasing, unemployment must be maintained above the NAIRU because of this failure in the wage-setting process. Rather than using high unemployment to restrain inflation, Layard recommends a permanent TIP.

A divergence between the actual and feasible rate of real wage increase may be an important factor in the recent stagflation. However, as Layard states: "One would of course expect in due course the target real-wage growth in the wage equation would change to reflect whatever changes had happened to the feasible rate of growth of real wages" (1982a, p. 223). Thus, it is not clear why this divergence should lead one to favour the adoption of a permanent incomes policy. To the extent that it is a sound argument, it is an argument for an incomes policy that would last as long as is required to restore the equality of actual and feasible real wage growth.

The analysis in this section may now be summarized. Various arguments have been put forth to justify the adoption of a permanent incomes policy. One such argument is based on the view that private wage and price setting is socially inefficient owing to an "inflation externality." The other arguments appear to be based on the view that the NAIRU is socially inefficient and that a permanent incomes policy is the appropriate way to remove this inefficiency. Upon closer scrutiny the first argument is found to be invalid. There is an inefficiency in wage and price setting in an ongoing inflationary spiral, but this inefficiency disappears when the underlying inflation rate equals the optimal inflation rate. Thus, a temporary incomes policy designed to facilitate the process of reducing the underlying inflation rate to the target rate may be warranted on these grounds but a permanent incomes policy is not.

The second argument is on firmer ground. Certainly there is no basis in economic theory to presume that the natural unemployment rate or NAIRU is socially optimal. In these circumstances, a permanent TIP is one of several policies which could, in principle, yield a socially preferred outcome. Thus, of the various rationales for a permanent IBIP, a TIP designed to reduce the NAIRU probably warrants the most serious attention. In addition, a temporary TIP to aid the transition from high to low inflation rates has considerable appeal. Both involve analyzing the effects of a TIP on wage and price setting, to which we now turn.

Analyzing the Economic Effects of a TIP

The most frequently recommended TIP is one in which firms are penalized (rewarded) for granting high (low) wage settlements. The penalty or reward could be administered through the corporate tax, a payroll tax, or through a direct levy. To analyze the effects of such a tax we need a model of wage determination into which a TIP can be introduced. Ideally such a model should be general equilibrium in nature, so that the macroeconomic effects of a TIP on wage changes, price changes, and unemployment can be assessed. Also, the model should recognize that in many of the firms that would be covered by the TIP, wages are determined by collective bargaining.

A number of theoretical analyses of a TIP on wage settlements have appeared. Some have been explicitly partial equilibrium in nature while others have attempted to capture general equilibrium effects. Some have employed models in which either the firm or the union unilaterally sets wages and employment while others have employed collective bargaining models. I will give a brief survey of this literature here, and indicate what I feel are the most useful contributions.

The earliest analyses of the economic effects of a TIP were partial equilibrium in nature. Wallich and Weintraub (1971) use a Hicksian-type bargaining model in which the outcome of negotiations is predicted to occur at the intersection of the (downward-sloping) union concession function and the (upward-sloping) firm concession function.[11] The TIP shifts down the firm's concession function; thus the model predicts a lower wage settlement. Isard (1978) uses an asymmetric bargaining model in which the firm knows the union's (or workers') concession function and chooses the wage offer and anticipated strike length that maximizes after-tax profit. This occurs where the firm's highest isoprofit curve (combinations of wage rates and strike length that yield equal profits) is tangent to the workers' concession function. The TIP changes the slope of the isoprofit curves, leading to the prediction of a lower wage increase and longer anticipated strike length.

Isard also examines the effect of a Wallich-Weintraub TIP on price increases, assuming the TIP will lower wage settlements. Under profit-maximizing behaviour, the TIP will lower prices as well as wages. This prediction arises because the lower wage leads to a lower profit-maximizing price. There is no attempt to offset the tax by raising prices because the profit-maximizing price is independent of a tax on (economic) profits. However, in practice the corporate profit tax applies to accounting, not economic profits. Thus some upward effect on prices is to be expected, as well as downward effect on the rate of return to capital.

Isard also shows that with naïve markup pricing the firm may attempt to pass on the tax in the form of higher prices.

Kotowitz and Portes (1974) analyze the effect of a Wallich-Weintraub TIP on a single market in which the union sets the wage and the firm chooses employment given that wage. Thus the union is constrained by the firm's labour-demand curve. The union's utility function is assumed to depend on the rate of growth of wages and the rate of growth of employment. The introduction of a TIP rotates the labour-demand curve, leading the union to choose a lower rate of growth of wages and a higher rate of growth of employment. Latham and Peel (1979) extended this analysis to the case in which the firm is a monopsonist. In this case a TIP reduces not only wage increases but also employment and output, and therefore may cause prices to rise.

Seidman (1978a) analyzes the effect of a TIP in both a bargaining model and a model in which the firm sets the wage. The bargaining model has the wage determined at the intersection of a "union push" function and a "firm resistance" function. Seidman's discussion reveals that these are essentially the same as the Hicksian concession functions discussed above. The TIP shifts the firm resistance function, leading to a lower negotiated settlement. Seidman's analysis of the wage-setting firm assumes that the firm is a monopsonistic competitor in the labour market and a monopolistic competitor in the product market. The TIP causes the firm to choose a lower wage and thus also employment. This case is analyzed by Nichols (1979), who compares the effect of a TIP to that of a wage subsidy and payroll tax in a static equilibrium model.[12]

When the firm faces an upward-sloping labour supply curve and a downward-sloping product demand curve, a TIP will lower the wage, reduce employment and output, and raise the price. Conversely, a wage subsidy raises the wage paid to employees, increases output and employment, and lowers the price. As Nichols notes, it is not clear which policy should be described as inflationary. What this does indicate is the danger of presuming that a TIP will have the same effect on prices as on wages.

A tax on wage (or price) *increases* creates an intertemporal decision problem for decision makers as the choice of a wage in this period affects the available opportunities in future periods. This feature of a TIP, which is ignored in the above studies, is taken into account in a recent paper by Oswald (1984a).[13] Oswald examines the effect of a tax on wage (or price) increases on the wage (or price) chosen by the firm or union under fairly general conditions. (Essentially all that is required is that the firm's or union's objective function be increasing in the wage or price and decreasing in the tax rate.) His analysis assumes a continuous tax schedule, and predicts that a TIP will lower the optimal (utility or profit maximizing) wage or price. He also shows that a tax on wage increases and a marginal employment subsidy are similar in their effects and equivalent under certain conditions. The reason is that a TIP encourages smaller wage increases and thus, if employment is determined according to a downward-sloping demand for labour curve, encourages larger increases in employment, which is what a marginal employment subsidy does.

Oswald's results are more general than others in the literature. However, they apply only to the choices made by individual economic agents — firms or unions — and do not incorporate subsequent adjustments made by the industry or economy.

These various partial equilibrium models predict that a TIP will lower wage increases whether wages are set unilaterally by the firm, by the union, or jointly through bargaining. A continuous tax schedule is predicted to lower all wage increases relative to what they would otherwise have been. The subsequent effects of the TIP will vary according to the market structure of the labour and product markets and other factors. There are typically offsetting effects on prices. By reducing wages and thus costs, the TIP tends to lower prices. However, pressures for price increases result when the firm has some monopsony power, when the TIP takes the form of a payroll tax, or when the corporate profits TIP applies to accounting rather than economic profits. All of these predictions are based on partial equilibrium models and therefore do not take into account subsequent effects on the industry or economy. In particular, if the proceeds of the tax are put back into the economy in a direct price or cost-reducing manner, as recommended in the Layard-Jackman proposal, concerns about perverse effects on prices may disappear.

General equilibrium models of the joint determination of wage and price changes and unemployment, especially models which incorporate collective bargaining, are at an early stage of development. Seidman (1978a) and Jackman and Layard (1982a) suggest that a TIP on wage increases would shift down the wage equation by an amount which is independent of the unemployment rate and which varies directly with the magnitude of the TIP tax rate. The implication is that a TIP can reduce the NAIRU and thus allow the economy permanently to attain a lower unemployment rate. This claim is now examined.

Seidman simply asserts this claim on the basis of his partial equilibrium analysis. The argument appears to be that since a TIP will cause a wage-setting firm to reduce its wage increase (or a firm and union to reach a lower settlement) below what it would otherwise have been, this must represent a downward shift of the wage equation. Although this appears to be a reasonable conjecture on the basis of the partial equilibrium results, as indicated below, it is not necessarily true in all cases.

Layard's claim is primarily based on the formal model outlined in Jackman and Layard (1982a). There are N essentially identical wholly unionized industries, and $L_i = L/N$ of the labour force is attached to industry i. In each industry the wage is assumed to be set by the union and the firm is assumed to choose employment given that wage. Thus the union is constrained by the firm's labour-demand function. The union is assumed to choose the wage which maximizes the wage bill. Let W^*_i be this wage (in industry i) and E^*_i the associated employment. Then there are $L_i - E^*_i$ unemployed workers in industry i and the equilibrium unemployment level is $L - E^*$ where E^* equals the sum of the E^*_i.

In this model the equilibrium unemployment consists of an excess supply of workers in each industry owing to the wage-setting policies of the union. The equilibrium level of unemployment, if positive, is socially inefficient. Thus any policy or event which lowers the real wage will also reduce the NAIRU and improve social welfare.

A TIP on wage increases (which they combine with a rebate or subsidy to make the overall program fiscally neutral) rotates the labour-demand curve, the rotation occurring at the wage norm. Thus the union chooses a lower wage increase and, consequently, equilibrium unemployment falls. The fiscal neutrality assumption is very important to this outcome.

There are two caveats concerning the Jackman-Layard prediction that a TIP will lower the NAIRU. First, recent literature on wage and employment determination in unionized industries suggests that efficient wage-employment outcomes (i.e., outcomes on the contract curve) may occur rather than inefficient outcomes (outcomes on the labour-demand curve). (See Macurdy and Pencavel, 1983; Martinello, 1984.) Chatterji (1984) shows that if an efficient bargaining model were used, the Jackman-Layard result may not hold. The more risk averse the union members are, the more likely that a wage inflation tax will reduce the equilibrium level of employment (i.e., increase the NAIRU) and the real wage. (The contract curve is positively sloped in this setting owing to risk aversion and thus equilibrium wages and employment will move in the same direction.)

A second difficulty arises from the attempt to make the inflation tax fiscally neutral. Chatterji also points out that if the union had rational expectations, it would realize that the subsidy was determined by the fiscal neutrality assumption and, given that all firms and unions are identical, it would not change its wage demand following imposition of the TIP.

A limitation of the Jackman-Layard analysis, at least in the North American setting, is the assumption that the economy is wholly unionized. This assumption implies that there is a one-to-one correspondence between the union-determined wage and the equilibrium unemployment rate, at least when the outcomes are on the labour-demand curve. It is in this sense that high real wages cause unemployment. However, the existence of a non-union sector implies that this simple correspondence disappears. Union-determined wages may still cause unemployment in this case, for some workers may "wait" for jobs to turn up in the higher paying organized sector, especially if there is frequent turnover or the possibility of an upturn in economic activity. This type of unemployment is associated more with the wage structure than with the level of real wages. We would expect that a TIP applied to the whole economy would be a very blunt instrument to deal with this type of unemployment. Recent analysis by Oswald (1984b), which employs a general equilibrium model with both a union and non-union sector, tends to support this view, although a TIP is not analyzed. Oswald finds that a general incomes policy which reduces wages across the economy as a whole may lower social welfare under some conditions, even when the administrative costs of such a scheme are ignored. The policy is more likely to raise welfare if the non-union sector is excluded.

The recent analysis of Pissarides (1985) adds support for the claim that a TIP can reduce the NAIRU. In Pissarides' model the equilibrium unemployment is due to imperfect information and search rather than union wage setting. A tax on wage increases above the norm has the effect of raising the equilibrium unemployment rate. However, when the proceeds of the tax are used to subsidize employment for wage increases below the norm, the overall effect is to lower equilibrium unemployment. Pissarides' results thus reinforce the importance noted above of the fiscal neutrality provision advocated by Jackman and Layard.

Pissarides does not examine whether the reduction in equilibrium unemployment associated with a fiscally neutral TIP leads to an improvement in social welfare. In general, the equilibrium level of unemployment in models of search and imperfect information is not necessarily socially efficient (Mortensen, 1984). Whether a TIP can be expected to improve welfare in these circumstances remains an interesting issue for future research.

The literature on the general equilibrium effects of a TIP is clearly at an early stage of development. At this stage it appears likely that a fiscally neutral TIP will lower the NAIRU in most but not all situations. Whether a permanent TIP is the best policy for achieving a reduction in unemployment is a more difficult question. Arguments for a permanent incomes policy designed to lower the NAIRU have appeared mainly in Europe where "classical" or "real wage" unemployment is much more of a policy concern than in North America (see, e.g., Malinvaud, 1978). In the North American setting the case for a permanent TIP to reduce the NAIRU is weaker than in Europe.

However, the various theoretical studies examined in this section generally do support the view that a temporary TIP on wage increases could form a part of a policy package designed to aid the transition from a high to low inflation rate.

The Resource Allocation Effects of an IBIP

An ideal incomes policy would scale down all wage and price increases by some common amount, thus preserving the planned changes in relative wages and prices. This would ensure that the policy would have no adverse effects on resource allocation. The request-control and direct relativity bargaining schemes attempt to achieve this result, although in practice they would limit their attention to wage changes and therefore attempt to preserve planned relative wage changes alone.

Most advocates of incomes policies, especially advocates of direct controls, recognize that the policy will distort relative wages and, if controlled, prices. Indeed, evidence suggests that wage control programs are often designed to narrow wage differentials in order to make the program more acceptable to organized labour and to workers.[14] Whether intended or not, the costs associated with these distortions need to be taken into account in assessing incomes policies.

A simple example will aid the exposition. Suppose the distribution of price increases that would occur in the absence of an incomes policy is as shown below. The rate of inflation would be 6 percent. An ideal incomes policy would scale these down by some common amount. The common amount would be 6 percent for a rapid deflation, but this is not essential. The important feature to aim for is equal downward pressure at all points of the distribution (see Table 5-1).

Designing a TIP that would preserve the planned changes in relative wages and prices would be difficult even if wage and price setting were fully synchronized. However, some TIPs are more likely to approximate this desired result than others. In particular, a continuous TIP will exert downward pressure at all points of the distribution, although equal downward pressure at each point will be difficult to achieve. An example of a linear continuous TIP schedule is shown in Table 5-2. This exerts downward pressure at each point in the distribution because all firms can lower their corporate profit tax rate by lowering their price increase. A linear schedule will exert equal downward pressure at all points in the distribution if the marginal effect on pretax profits of a 1 percent reduction in the rate of price increase is the same at all points in the distribution. However, this is not the end of the story; there is also the effect on expectations to consider.

In the above example I used the term "planned changes in relative wages and prices" to emphasize that individual firms and workers make wage and price changes based on their expectations about wage and price inflation elsewhere in the economy. Of course, expectations may vary across individuals so that some of the observed variation in wage and price changes is due to differing expectations.

While a continuous TIP schedule exerts downward pressure at all points in the distribution, the response of each wage or price setter depends on their beliefs about how others will respond. In order to preserve the planned changes in relative prices, the implementation of the TIP must alter each individual's expectations by the same amount. The way this moderation might be (approximately) achieved is discussed below.

TABLE 5–1 A Simple Distribution of Price Changes

Commodity	1	2	3	4	5
Proportion of GNP	1/5	1/5	1/5	1/5	1/5
Planned Percentage Increase in Price	2	4	6	8	10
Non-Inflationary Price Increase	−4	−2	0	2	4

TABLE 5–2 A Linear Continuous TIP Schedule

Observed Percentage Price Increase	Tax Rate on Corporate Profits
10	60
8	55
6	50
4	45
2	40
0	35
−2	30
−4	25

Most proposed TIPs involve a discrete rather than continuous schedule. Typically this involves stating a norm for wage or price increases with a (possibly continuous) schedule of tax rates for increases above the norm and a lower rate for increases below the norm. Such a scheme will not preserve the wage or price change distribution. There is no downward pressure exerted on increases that would have been below the norm in the absence of the TIP. If there is a single tax rate for increases above the norm (the simplest TIP), then there will be downward pressure on a portion of the distribution to the right of the norm (see Figure 5-4) but not on the upper tail of the distribution.

It is important to note that even a continuous TIP will have adverse effects on resource allocation. This also applies to the MAP as long as the price of MAP credit is non-zero. These effects may not be large enough to cause the costs of a temporary IBIP to exceed the benefits, but they could be a serious problem for a permanent IBIP.

The general nature of these resource allocation effects is clear. Since a TIP or MAP discourages price and wage increases and encourages decreases, the movement of resources into expanding sectors will be slowed down and the movement of resources out of contracting sectors will be increased. Of course, if the rate of adjustment was suboptimal to begin with (it is often suggested that the movement of resources out of contracting sectors occurs at too slow a pace owing to various rigidities), then the IBIP could possibly improve matters. However, the additional

FIGURE 5–4 The Effect of a TIP on the Distribution of Wage Changes

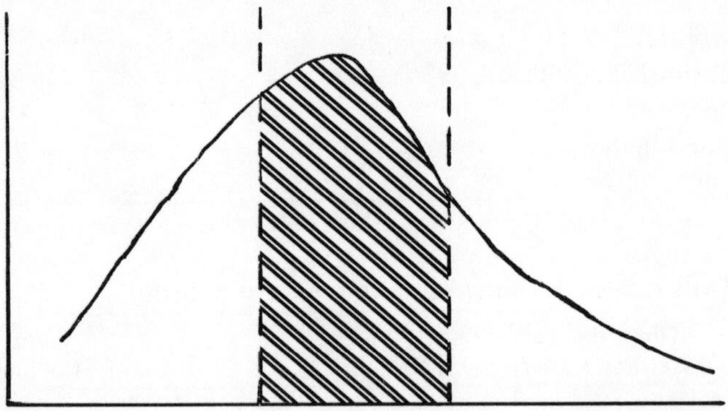

costs imposed on sectors whose relative price is increasing are not only unfair but also will, in general, impose some efficiency costs.

Lerner and Colander (1980, chap. 10) argue that the price of MAP credit would fall to zero (or close to zero) once the initial disinflation was completed. If this prediction were confirmed, the price of MAP credit would be socially optimal. (This follows from the analysis of the previous section which indicated that the socially efficient and inefficient solutions coincide when the underlying inflation rate equals zero.) As long as the price of MAP credit remained near zero, the MAP would not have any significant adverse effects on resource allocation. TIPs do not offer this (predicted) benefit of a decrease in allocative inefficiencies as the underlying inflation rate declines. Thus, a TIP should be designed to be temporary; that is, contain a sunset clause.

There are a number of factors that need to be taken into account in choosing between a discrete and continuous TIP (or combinations of the two). One advantage of a continuous TIP is that it is not necessary to choose a specific norm, eliminating the risk of setting too high or too low a norm. In addition, there is the danger that a specific norm will become a floor as well as a ceiling (the latter with respect to eligibility for the lower tax rate). That is, the wage changes that would otherwise have been below the norm may occur at the norm. At the same time, there may be an advantage to setting a norm in terms of altering expectations and reducing the variance of expectations.

It is difficult to weigh these various factors, given our limited knowledge. Probably a continuous TIP should be preferred to a discrete or discrete-continuous version, but predictions could also be made about the average rate of wage or price inflation expected to prevail during the program. The argument for a continuous TIP is that it adds little in terms of administrative complexity and exerts downward pressure at all points in the distribution. However, because there will be considerable uncertainty generated by a novel policy, there is a case for making informed predictions about the effects of the policy so that the variance of expectations is not increased. A tendency for the predicted average increase to become the minimum may be expected. There may be some advantage to predicting the expected decrease in the rate of inflation rather than the expected rate itself.

This concern about preserving the distribution of wage or price changes is misplaced if there is little variability in wage settlements or price changes. However, as inspection of Table 5-3 confirms, there is considerable variability in wage settlements in any given period. The coefficient of variation is rarely less than one-third and frequently between 0.4 and 0.5. (The last three years are exceptions.) The range is typically from a minimum of zero or close to zero to a maximum of over 30 percent.

Examination of the histograms (not shown) reveals that the distributions are skewed with a long tail at the upper end. Those settlements in the upper tail undoubtedly reflect a variety of special factors. One advantage of a TIP over direct wage and price controls is that the control authorities do not need to deal with the demand for exceptions due to these special circumstances. The length of the upper tail and the relatively small number of employees involved suggest that it is not worthwhile attempting to exert downward pressure at all points in the distribution through a fully continuous TIP schedule. That is, the TIP schedule could be "capped" at, say, two standard deviations above the (estimated) mean, with a common tax rate applicable above this point.

Would a TIP on Wage Settlements Increase Strike Activity?

Several authors have suggested that a TIP on wage increases could increase the frequency or duration of strikes. This claim, like others, can only be assessed on a priori grounds. Thus we need to know the causes of strikes and whether a TIP would affect these causes.

Isard (1978) appears to have been the only author to investigate the probable effects of a TIP on strike activity. His prediction that a TIP on wage increases would lead to an increase in the frequency and duration of strikes is based on a theory of strikes similar to that of Ashenfelter and Johnson (1969). In this model the firm is assumed to know the union's concession function and to choose the strike length which maximizes profits subject to this concession function. A TIP on wage increases shifts the firm's isoprofit curves in a way that makes the firm more resistant to wage increases but is presumed not to alter the workers' concession function. Thus the optimum strike length increases.

The Ashenfelter-Johnson theory of strikes is, however, seriously

TABLE 5–3 Summary of Wage Change Distributions

Year	Mean	Standard Deviation	Coefficient of Variation	Minimum	Maximum
1967	8.4	3.6	0.4	1.9	27.8
1968	8.9	5.3	0.6	0.0	36.8
1969	8.5	6.9	0.8	2.5	82.1
1970	8.8	4.1	0.5	1.2	47.6
1971	8.3	2.9	0.3	0.0	36.7
1972	8.9	3.0	0.3	0.4	36.5
1973	10.7	4.3	0.4	1.9	49.5
1974	15.3	6.6	0.4	1.5	100.4
1975[a]	20.2	8.6	0.4	2.4	74.5
1975[b]	15.8	6.9	0.4	6.2	52.0
1976	11.4	5.3	0.5	1.5	64.8
1977	8.0	2.8	0.4	0.0	55.8
1978	7.3	2.3	0.3	0.0	38.8
1979	8.8	2.1	0.2	0.8	32.6
1980	11.1	2.3	0.2	2.4	21.5
1981	13.6	3.2	0.2	0.0	32.8

Source: Calculations by the author using Labour Canada Major Collective Agreement data. For a description of these data see Department of Labour, Canada, *Wage Developments*, annual.

Notes: Each observation is the compound annual average percentage increase in the base wage rate over the length of the contract. COLA contracts are excluded. The data include all settlements involving 500 or more employees in Canada (excluding construction) and many settlements involving 200–499 employees.

a. Pre-AIB.

b. Post-AIB.

flawed on logical grounds (see, e.g., Lacroix, 1985). An alternative view is that strikes are primarily caused by miscalculations in bargaining and imperfect information. This is not a new argument; however, it has been more formally developed in recent contributions and has received some empirical support (Lacroix, 1985; Riddell, 1985c). While it may well be naïve to believe that there is a single cause of strikes, the view that strikes are primarily "accidents" due to mistakes, differing expectations about the future, and imperfect information appears most consistent with a priori reasoning and empirical evidence (Lacroix, 1985; Riddell, 1985c).

According to this view, the prediction that a TIP on wage increases would increase strikes because it would make firms more resistant to wage increases without changing the aspirations of workers or union leaders is incorrect. However, there may nonetheless be some increase in strike activity because the introduction of a novel policy will make the outcomes of collective bargaining more uncertain and will make miscalculations or mistakes more likely. Any such effect would be expected to be temporary.

A Comparison of TIPs *and Direct Controls*

A central conclusion of chapter 4 was that the combination of a temporary incomes policy and demand restraint may enable society to reduce an imbedded inflation at less cost than is the case with reliance on demand restraint alone. To determine what form of incomes policy may be most desirable requires examining both the benefits (i.e., probable effectiveness) and costs of direct controls and TIPs.

The impact of a TIP and direct controls on wage and price increases depends on very similar factors. Neither policy is likely to have much effect on the inertia in wage inflation unless it abrogates existing contracts. Both may reduce expectations, although there is little evidence to indicate that they will do so, and the reduction in expectations may be delayed until there is some demonstration that the program is having the intended effect. However, it appears unlikely that a TIP would achieve a rapid disinflation. Simulations of the effects of such a program that have appeared in the literature (e.g., Seidman, 1978a) appear much too optimistic. Because of the resource allocation effects and the inevitable unfairness of such a policy (even a continuous TIP which exerts downward pressure at all points in the wage change distribution will impose higher penalties on firms with higher wage settlements), it is important not to make the penalties too large. Thus it appears unlikely that one would want to impose a TIP that would reduce wage inflation by more than 1 to 2 percent per year. This is somewhat less effective than direct controls along the AIB lines but nonetheless would enable an ongoing inflation to be gradually wound down.

This argument suggests that the benefits of a TIP on wage increases would probably be somewhat less than those of direct controls (as well as being more uncertain). What about the costs? These can be discussed under three main headings: administrative, allocative inefficiency, and social capital costs.

One of the claims made by several advocates of TIPs is that the administrative costs would be much lower than those of direct controls because the program could be accommodated by the bureaucracy which administers the tax system. I do not claim expertise with respect to the administrative costs of either policy; the reader would want to examine the written assessments of those with expertise in this area (e.g., Dildine and Sunley, 1978). However, it appears likely that the costs of administering a TIP on wage increases would be very similar to those of direct controls. This prediction is based on the following factors. First, there is no reason to believe that the relationship between the number of firms covered and the effectiveness of the program is different for the two policies. Thus the degree of coverage which is appropriate on cost-benefit grounds will be quite similar for both policies. Second, both programs would involve monitoring the wage settlements of the covered firms and assessing their compliance with the guidelines or tax schedule. This is not an activity which the tax authorities currently carry out. Third, a difficult and expensive part of this activity — the valuation of non-wage benefits, incentive pay and future-value compensation — would be common to both agencies. For these reasons a TIP on wage increases may well involve a bureaucracy similar in size (and required skills and knowledge) to that of the AIB.

Turning to allocative efficiency costs, both policies alter the distribution of wage changes, direct controls cutting off the upper part of the distribution and a TIP cutting out a segment from the middle of the distribution. It is difficult to say which effect is more serious. Both will distort relative wages to some extent. The TIP has the advantage that it does permit large increases to occur so that serious shortages of labour or inequities in compensation can be dealt with by wage setters.

While price controls are well known to lead to serious allocative inefficiencies, the same does not appear to be true for temporary wage controls. This may result from the long-term nature of many contractual arrangements in the labour market. For the same reason, the distortions to the relative wage structure seem to lead more to problems of worker morale than to shortages or surpluses of labour. Indeed, because of the long-term overlapping nature of wage settlements, the relative wage structure becomes distorted, even in the absence of incomes policies, by various unanticipated shocks. This does not imply that the distortions caused by incomes policies do not impose some costs. Nonetheless, as discussed in the previous chapter, it does not seem to be the case that a temporary program such as the AIB does not lead to even moderately large allocative inefficiencies. This would probably also be true for a temporary TIP on wage increases.

The social capital costs are the most difficult to measure and assess, but possibly also the most important. These involve the general reduction in goodwill and cooperative spirit, the harm to the collective bargaining system, the animosity and distrust of labour, the direction of labour's effort and resources away from collective bargaining and toward the political arena, and the possible increased acceptance of intervention by government as a method of solving economic problems. Because of its "voluntary" nature, this is an area where a TIP may involve lower costs than direct controls. The main difference is that while a TIP complicates collective bargaining and individual decision making, it does not displace it.

A potentially important offsetting factor arises from the reliance of a TIP on the tax system (Lipsey and Purvis, 1982). There is a considerable concern that the tax system may already be too complex, and that it needs to be simplified and made more equitable. The social capital imbedded in the tax system is clearly very large in that it relies to a considerable extent on voluntary compliance. Whether a TIP would further erode confidience in the system is not clear, but it is a danger which should be kept in mind. With respect to the other dimensions of social capital, there does not appear to be any major difference between the two types of incomes policies.

The above leads to the conclusion that direct controls and a TIP on wage increases are similar in their probable benefits and costs. It is difficult to be precise, but our discussion suggests that the TIP would have slightly lower benefits and costs.

It is worth noting that this conclusion is similar to that reached by Scarth (1982) but differs markedly from that reached in recent analyses in the United States (see, e.g., Tobin, 1982; Nordhaus, 1983) and the United Kingdom (see Layard, 1982a, 1982b). This difference results not from differing views about the effectiveness of TIPs (although most authors do not give numerical estimates) but rather from differing views about the effectiveness of direct controls. In particular, U.S. and U.K. observers regard direct controls as ineffective and have turned to TIPs as an alternative. In Canada, however, the AIB experience has convinced most observers that direct controls can have a significant impact on wage increases without incurring substantial costs or a post-controls wage explosion.

Conclusions

This chapter has attempted to provide a detailed survey of the literature on incentive-based incomes policies together with a critical analysis of the arguments made for and against these policies. Special attention was given to the use of incentive-based incomes policies in the Canadian setting.

The conclusions have been summarized throughout, so they need only be listed here:

- Contrary to several claims in the IBIP literature, there is not a sound economic rationale for a permanent incomes policy to deal with an "inflation externality." Thus our analysis does not favour the use of the Market Anti-Inflation Plan or a permanent TIP as methods for dealing with inflation on a continuing basis.
- The argument that a permanent incomes policy may be needed because the economy has a built-in inflationary bias, the "theory of secular inflation," is indistinguishable from the view that the NAIRU is too high and should be lowered by a permanent incomes policy.
- The argument that a permanent TIP should be used to lower the natural unemployment rate runs into two difficulties. First, theoretical models do not predict that a TIP would necessarily lower the NAIRU.

Second, even if a TIP could be expected to lower the NAIRU in most circumstances, alternative policies may be preferable on cost-benefit grounds.

- Direct controls or a TIP on wage and price increases could be employed on a temporary basis in conjunction with demand restraint to reduce an ongoing inflation. A program of direct controls similar to the AIP appears likely to be more effective than a TIP. The two policies would require similar administrative machinery. The TIP would possibly result in fewer inefficiencies in resource allocation and less reduction in social goodwill, but would add to the complexity of the tax system. On balance, direct controls are probably a better choice.
- Direct controls or a TIP on wage increases appear attractive as methods for achieving a once-and-for-all disinflation. The costs and benefits of the two policies are similar, although there is more uncertainty regarding the TIP. Either policy should be coordinated with monetary and fiscal policy designed to maintain the economy at levels of output no greater than potential output.
- There is no considerable variation in wage changes in any given period. The variation creates difficulties for both direct controls (which tend to cut off the upper tail of the wage change distribution) and a TIP on wage settlements (which tends to remove a segment from the centre of the distribution). It is not clear which effect is more serious, or which leads to more relative wage catch-up in the post-incomes policy period.
- A continuous TIP has the advantage that it places downward pressure at all points in the wage change distribution and thus causes little distortion in the relative wage structure. However, it also penalizes firms with higher wage settlements even if they respond to the policy. Both from the point of view of fairness and allocative efficiency, there is therefore an argument against a substantial penalty. This implies that a continuous TIP should not attempt to achieve a rapid disinflation.

Chapter 6

Structural Changes in Wage-Setting Mechanisms

Demand restraint is a costly disinflationary policy because of the inertia or momentum in the inflationary process. What is the cause of this persistence? The answer to this question might suggest institutional or other changes that would reduce this inertia, making disinflation less costly to pursue. In his annual report for 1982 the governor of the Bank of Canada raises this question and indicates that there may not be a simple answer:

> [O]ur economic system has exhibited stubborn resistance to a reduction in the rate of cost and price inflation. Why has the resistance been so stubborn?
>
> Let me say first of all that I doubt that anybody is able to give a definite answer to this question. It involves an aspect of the functioning of Canadian society that has received far too little consideration. . . . I think it likely that a thorough examination of the question would point to policy initiatives of one kind and another that would improve appreciably the prospects for employment and output in Canada. (p. 10)

This chapter discusses the contribution which certain institutional features of our wage determination system may make to wage and price inertia and assesses structural changes in our wage determination system which might lead to improved economic performance, especially with respect to price stability and high levels of employment. As the previous discussion made clear, the menu of policy options in the absence of such reforms is not very appealing.

For conceptual purposes, it is helpful to divide long-term structural policies into two groups. The first group, the ones examined in this chapter, are structural changes which are intended to reduce the fluctuations in output and employment which result from any particular economic shock. These reforms may therefore enable the economy to be maintained closer to its natural unemployment rate and level of potential output. The second set of reforms are ones which would lower the natural unemployment rate, thus permitting the economy to operate with lower normal unemployment levels. These are examined by Kaliski (1985) and Riddell (1985a), among others.

The structural issues discussed in this chapter have a long-term time horizon. That is, our concern here is not with the short- to medium-term issue of how to return the economy to more normal levels of output and employment. While the structural changes considered here could perhaps have reduced the severity of the recent recession, they are not intended as a means of accelerating the current recovery. Reflecting this long-run focus, the discussion will often deal with an economy in an initial position of full employment or potential output.

Employment Stability and Price Stability

As noted in the first chapter, it is now generally accepted that in the long run there is no tradeoff between inflation and output or employment. This implies that there is little to gain from pursuing a goal other than price stability in the long run. Accepting somewhat higher inflation will not permit the attainment, other than temporarily, of lower levels of unemployment. In this sense, the natural unemployment rate is a realistic definition of full employment, one which can be reached on a sustained basis.

However, it is worthwhile recalling John Maynard Keynes's famous dictum, "In the long run we are all dead." To a considerable extent, what matters for economic performance is the sequence of short runs in which the economy can, and typically does, deviate from normal levels of employment. The magnitude and duration of these deviations from potential output must be another concern of employment policy.

The early postwar period was characterized by an increasing confidence in the ability of governments to stabilize output and employment and thus protect citizens from the vicissitudes of the business cycle. At least up to 1980 the postwar era compares very favourably to earlier periods in this regard. However, two points have emerged from our accumulated experience with Keynesian macroeconomic policy and from the events of the past two decades. First, there is now skepticism about our ability to stabilize the economy through discretionary monetary and fiscal policy.[1] It may certainly be possible to avoid serious recessions (especially if *not* faced with a need to reduce deeply embedded inflation without resorting to incomes policy), but the notion that governments will improve performance by attempting to smooth out cyclical fluctuations completely is seriously open to question. Second, the commitment to using discretionary aggregate demand policy to prevent even minor recessions may well have imparted an inflationary bias to the economy, as discussed earlier. Paul Samuelson noted this possibility in 1974:

> I believe that the present inflation is rooted deep in the nature of the mixed economy. . . . We live in the age after Keynes. Electorates all over the world have eaten of the fruit of the tree of modern economic knowledge and there is no going back to an earlier age. High employment or full employment is everywhere a goal insisted on by the electorate of all political persuasions. A half-century ago there was no comparable political sentiment effective against incurring prolonged depression or even stagnation; rather there was often a pre-occupation with the perils of inflation, of budget and foreign trade deficits. This shift in populist attitudes of governments necessarily shifts the odds against stable prices (and of course against falling prices). No longer can one expect half of the peace-time years to experience falling prices. If general price levels rarely stand still and often rise then the secular trend of prices must be upward on the average. (p. 802)

Recognition of these two factors has shifted attention away from activist stabilization policy toward the structural characteristics of the economy which may be associated with large and lengthy deviations from full employment. This very useful shift in focus has led to increased awareness of the fact that economies with different institutional characteristics have quite different performance in terms of the extent to which they deviate from normal levels of output and employment.

Stating this point in somewhat different terms, the increased recognition of the limited ability of governments to foresee and offset economic shocks in a manner which will stabilize cyclical fluctuations, as well as the possible inflationary consequences of doing so on a continuing basis, has led to the opinion that fiscal and monetary policies should be directed more toward longer-run goals and objectives. This in turn implies that it is desirable to consider structural changes to the economy such that the various shocks that cause cyclical fluctuations result in shorter and less severe deviations from full employment.

Change is the most pervasive feature of modern economic life; the economy is continually being affected by various shocks. In some cases these shocks are partially anticipated, while in others they are quite unexpected. How the economy reacts to these disturbances depends on the economy's institutional features and on a number of other factors. Initial reactions to shocks can give rise to subsequent effects which cumulate, causing cycles in overall economic activity.

Consider first the case of changes in aggregate demand. When there is a net increase or decrease in aggregate demand, the impact will fall partly on wages and prices and partly on employment. A decline in aggregate demand of, say, 10 percent can result in a 10 percent decline in output and the accompanying decline in employment with no change in prices, a decline in prices of 10 percent with no change in output and employment, or some combination of the two. The extent to which the impact falls on wages and prices (i.e., on nominal variables) on the one hand and output and employment (i.e., on real variables) on the other depends on a number of factors which are discussed in turn.

One factor is the current position of the economy relative to potential output or full employment. The effect of an increase in aggregate demand on output and employment will typically be larger if the initial position of the economy is below potential output than if above potential output. In terms of the model outlined earlier, the short-run aggregate supply curve is non-linear, and in particular has a convex shape. The remaining factors will be discussed in the context of a change in aggregate demand which occurs when the economy is initially operating at potential output.

The second factor is the extent to which the change in aggregate demand was anticipated. An important general proposition, though one about which there is considerable controversy, is that the more changes in aggregate demand are anticipated, the less effect they will have on output and employment and the greater effect on wages and prices.

The relative time horizon also affects the division between real and nominal effects. Starting at potential output, a permanent change in aggregate demand will alter wages and prices alone in the long run but may have real effects in the short run. This is simply a restatement of the proposition that there is no long-run tradeoff between inflation and unemployment.

As we learned (or were reminded) in the 1970s, supply shocks such as increases in energy or food prices can also lead to deviations of output and employment from their normal levels. These shocks are particularly troublesome in that they tend to raise prices and reduce output and employment. In addition, they may imply that a downward adjustment in real wages is needed to restore labour market equilibrium.

The response to these shocks depends in an important way on the nature of wage determination in the economy.[2] Thus we turn to an examination of the consequences of existing institutional mechanisms for wage setting.

Key Features of Wage Determination

This section discusses features of the North American system of collective bargaining, and the accompanying arrangements for wage setting that appear to impart considerable inertia to wages and consequently to prices. This persistence of wages and prices implies that the short-run impact of changes in aggregate demand falls primarily on output and employment. Thus, large and lengthy deviations from full employment can, and do, occur. Structural changes which led to greater wage and price responsiveness might therefore enable us to achieve greater stability in employment and output.

Three key features of wage setting are discussed: the length of wage contracts; the fact that wage contracts typically overlap (i.e., at any point in time some are being renegotiated while others are still in effect); and the fact that contracts typically fix the wage to be paid in advance. The way these features impart wage rigidity is described below. The potential structural reforms to deal with problems resulting from these features are threefold: shorter contracts, synchronized wage setting, and compensation arrangements which tie wages more closely to economic performance — often referred to as gain-sharing.

Contract Length and Synchronization

Recent research by macroeconomists (in particular Fischer, 1977, 1984; Phelps, 1978a; and Taylor, 1980a, 1980b, 1983) has pointed to long-term overlapping nominal wage contracts as an important source of inertia in wage inflation in North America. Wage contracts in the union sector in Canada and the United States are often two to three years in length. Table 6-1 shows the proportion of major collective agreements of different lengths and the average contract duration over the 1970–84 period. These agreements also typically specify nominal wage rates to be paid throughout the contract period; that is, the wages are not contingent on the economic conditions prevailing at the time the wage is paid. The main example of a contingent contract is the cost-of-living allowance (COLA) provision which makes wages contingent on movements in the CPI.[3] The table also summarizes the extent of COLA contracts in major collective agreements. In addition to their length and non-contingent nature, another important feature is that the contracts overlap each other; in an average year about half of all settlements are renegotiated. Although there is some seasonality in the "bargaining calendar," settlements are spread throughout the year.[4] For a number of reasons these features appear to be an important source of persistence in wage inflation.

First, an obvious factor in the sluggish response of the average wage to changes in economic conditions is that only a fraction of wages are renegotiated or reset each period. The observed change in the average wage in the economy is affected by the fraction of wages that do not change, by implementation of deferred increases (increases provided for under contracts negotiated in previous periods), by increases under COLA provisions, and by new settlements reached during the period. The magnitude of deferred increases was determined when the contract was negotiated. The size of such increases may have been based on anticipated economic conditions; however, it is not affected by the actual

TABLE 6–1 Percentage of Employees Covered by New Contracts

Year	1-Year Contracts	2-Year Contracts	3-Year Contracts	Average Duration of New Agreements	Percentage of Employees Covered by New Wage Settlements	Percentage of New Settlements Containing a COLA Clause
1970	12	52	36	26	41	14
1971	13	52	35	26	45	10
1972	13	43	44	31	52	36
1973	14	54	32	26	42	22
1974	35	58	7	21	56	40
1975	41	39	20	21	45	41
1976	48	25	26	23	79	38
1977	72	24	4	16	53	24
1978	50	42	8	19	65	20
1979	27	39	34	25	55	37
1980	26	41	33	26	59	43
1981	29	56	15	22	43	32
1982	46	45	9	19	51	28
1983	51	26	23	20	68	28
1984	46	32	22	21	54	15

Source: Canada, Department of Labour, *Wage Developments*, various issues, annually to 1982. Information since 1982 is calculated from Canada, Department of Labour, *Major Wage Settlements*.

Note: One-year contracts are those with a term less than 18 months; two-year contracts are those with a term of 18–29 months; three-year contracts are those with a term of 30 months or more.

conditions prevailing at the time such increases go into effect. COLA increases are based in part on current conditions but also on past conditions because of their cumulative nature. In addition, because they are contingent on only one dimension of current economic conditions — the change in the CPI — these provisions can make wages less responsive to general economic conditions rather than more, depending on the relationship between current economic conditions and changes in the CPI. (Wage indexation is discussed further below.) Only new settlements reached during the period are affected by changes in economic conditions (except possibly changes in the CPI).

This first factor suggests reasons for inertia in the economy-wide average wage but not necessarily in new settlements reached during the period. However, considerable persistence also exists in new settlements. That is, the time series of current settlements exhibits a high degree of autocorrelation. This is especially evident in the quarterly data in Table 2-1.

A second obvious way these institutional features may cause wage inertia results from the long-term nature of contracts. If wages were renegotiated each month, we would expect that economic conditions prevailing at the time of negotiation would have a greater influence than if wages were renegotiated each year. In the union sector, wage changes depend to some extent on current economic conditions because the relative bargaining power of each side is a function primarily of current conditions which affect the cost of a strike or lockout to the firm versus the cost to the workers. However, they also depend on the conditions expected to prevail during the term of the contract. Thus changes in current economic conditions, especially those which are regarded as being temporary rather than permanent, would be expected to exert less influence on long than on short contracts.[5]

The third reason these institutional features appear to be a major source of inertia is the most subtle, but possibly also the most important. This factor arises because of the interaction of the overlapping nature of contracts with the importance of relative wages to firms and workers. Relative wage considerations imply that in setting wages, firms and workers will take into account wages that will prevail or are expected to prevail in contracts that will overlap with the current contract. This implies looking backward at wages set previously but which will remain in effect through part or all of the present contract, and looking forward to wage negotiations that will arise during the present contract. This process produces considerable persistence in wage settlements and thus in employment and output. Starting in equilibrium, a shock to the economy produces deviations from equilibrium to both real and nominal variables (i.e., unemployment from the natural rate of unemployment and wage inflation from the underlying rate of wage inflation) that persist for several periods, even if those involved in wage and price setting have rational expectations. Indeed, in the context of a rational expectations model, Taylor (1980a) has shown that contracts as short as one year can account for the degree of persistence observed in postwar business cycles in the United States.

The intuition behind this point is straightforward. If recent wage settlements have been running at, say, 10 percent and an unanticipated decline in aggregate demand occurs, it will be difficult for firms to convince their workers and the union leaders that substantially lower settlements are in order. The depressed conditions will exert some downward pressure on wage settlements but not a large amount. As a result, much of the decline in aggregate demand will be met by reductions in output and employment.

A fourth source of inertia results from the fact that contracts extend for a predetermined length and involve non-contingent wage rates. However expectations are formed, they will almost always be incorrect to some degree. With contract length and the wage rate predetermined, any adjustment for unanticipated economic conditions must be postponed until the contract is renegotiated. As discussed in chapter 2, the empirical literature (see, e.g., Christofides et al., 1980b; Riddell and Smith, 1982) has found this "catch-up effect" to be an important factor in subsequent wage negotiations. This factor is not taken into account in simulations such as those by Taylor (1980a, 1983) and thus is an additional source of persistence.

This adjustment for unanticipated economic conditions can work both ways. In the late 1960s and early 1970s there were a large number of wage contracts signed that clearly failed to anticipate the large increase in inflation which subsequently occurred. Thus, real wages provided under outstanding contracts were lower than anticipated by employees, resulting in dissatisfaction with the lower than expected increase or actual reduction in purchasing power and in living standards. The opposite occurred in the early 1980s; contracts negotiated prior to the beginning of the recession were clearly based on both a higher level of expected inflation and stronger economic activity than in fact occurred. In this case, the profits of employers were squeezed as a result of paying higher real wages and facing weaker market conditions than they had expected.

These two examples point to one of the disadvantages of long-term, fixed-wage contracts. The terms agreed to at the time they are negotiated may turn out to be inappropriate to the economic conditions over the life of the contract. In these circumstances, some adjustments will be provided for in the negotiation of subsequent contracts. The process of adjustment to the original change in economic circumstances thus becomes spread out through time.

This discussion suggests that long-term overlapping nominal wage contracts are an important source of inertia in wage inflation and that they cause the short-term impact of changes in aggregate demand to be primarily on output and employment. The results obtained thus far from ongoing research provide empirical evidence to support this view. Industrial relations specialists have long emphasized the importance of relative wage considerations in wage negotiations. Terms such as "wage contours," "orbits of coercive comparisons," "spillovers," and "pattern bargaining" have been used to describe this phenomenon. In addition to a large amount of anecdotal evidence, there is also econometric evidence which supports the view that relative wage comparisons play an important role within the union sector (Flanagan, 1976; Christofides et al., 1980b).

Emphasizing these features of wage contracts invites intercountry comparisons, for the Canadian and U.S. economies are unique in the degree to which long-term overlapping contracts are common. Some countries (e.g., Italy) employ long-term contracts but these contracts do not overlap (e.g., a sequence of three-year "wage rounds" in 1969, 1972, 1975). Japan and several European countries (e.g., Sweden, Norway, Austria, Germany) have short contracts (typically one year) and synchronized bargaining, while the United Kingdom is characterized by short contracts without a predetermined expiry date and non-synchronized negotiations.[6] If long-term overlapping wage contracts are an important source of wage inertia, the response of nominal wages to aggregate demand should be more sluggish in North America than in Europe and Japan. Further, if sluggish nominal wage adjustment results in greater variation in output and employment, deviations of these real variables from their trend or natural levels should be larger in North America. Similarly, if synchronization is important there should be significant differences between Japan and the United Kingdom in the responsiveness of wages, prices, output and employment.

Several intercountry comparisons have recently been carried out (Sachs, 1979 and 1983; Branson and Rotemberg, 1980; Taylor, 1980b; Barber and McCallum, 1982; Gordon, 1982, 1983; Schultze, 1981, 1984; Wilcox, 1983; Kahn, 1984). Although there are many unsettled issues and some apparently conflicting results, there is a substantial amount of support for these predictions. Gordon (1982, 1983), for example, finds that nominal wages display substantially less variability in the United States than in either the United Kingdom or Japan, while output and employment display substantially more variability. In Riddell (1983) some evidence for Canada, together with that of Gordon for the United States, the United Kingdom and Japan, is presented. The degree of nominal wage inertia in Canada is less than that of the United States, but considerably greater than that of the United Kingdom or Japan. Similarly, the variability of output and employment is more like that of the United States than that of Japan or the United Kingdom. Japan, which is characterized by both short contracts and synchronized negotiations, displays the greatest variability in nominal wages relative to the variability in employment and hours worked.

The fact that these institutional features are a relatively recent phenomenon suggests intertemporal comparisons. Multiyear agreements were rare prior to World War II; indeed, prior to the Korean War. The pioneering settlement was the 1948 agreement between General Motors and the United Auto Workers. In Canada, one-year contracts were widely employed until the late 1950s; the move to two- and three-year agreements took place during 1956–59 in manufacturing, the sector in which multiyear agreements first became popular and in which they remain most popular. For the economy as a whole, the move toward multiyear contracts was not concentrated in the relatively brief period 1956–59, but continued throughout the early 1960s (Riddell, 1979; Christofides, n.d.).

Many observers have suggested that wages and prices have become less responsive to variations in aggregate demand during the post-World War II period. A number of U.S. empirical studies support this conclusion (Cagan, 1975; Sachs, 1980; Gordon, 1982, 1983; Mitchell, 1985a, b; Taylor, 1984b). For example, Gordon (1982, 1983) found that the degree of wage and employment variability in the United States prior to World War II was similar to that of Japan and the United Kingdom. Only in the postwar period did the United States display less variability in wages and greater variability in employment and hours.

There is thus a substantial amount of evidence indicating that U.S. wages and prices were more flexible prior to the 1940s. Modern macroeconomic theory would therefore predict greater cyclical fluctuations in the recent period, other factors being held constant. As is well known, the magnitude of cyclical fluctuations has been significantly smaller since the end of World War II. This remains true even if the Great Depression is excluded from the comparison. Thus the contribution of reduced wage and price flexibility to greater cyclical fluctuations, if any, must have been offset by other factors. Testing this issue is made difficult by the large number of other factors that have changed. One factor which is widely believed to have played an important role is the use, since World War II, of counter-cyclical stabilization policy and the growth of built-in stabilizers such as the progressive income tax, unemployment insurance, and other forms of social assistance. In addition, numerous other factors have contributed to macroeconomic stability. Agriculture, a highly unstable sector, has declined significantly in importance while public administration and related government services, a relatively stable sector, have grown in importance. The dramatic growth in private credit has allowed households more freedom to smooth out their consumption in spite of fluctuations in income. The development of deposit insurance has significantly reduced financial worries.

In a recent study using multivariate time-series analysis, Taylor (1984b) examines the behaviour of wages, prices and output during the periods 1891–1914 and 1952–83. In the later period, the magnitude of output fluctuations was smaller, and the duration of fluctuations in output and wage and price inflation was longer (i.e., output and inflation exhibited more persistence). Analysis of these data reveals that the disturbances to the economy were smaller in the later period, but these disturbances were translated into much larger and more prolonged fluctuations in output than would have occurred if the dynamics of the earlier period had applied. These findings can be interpreted as supporting the view expressed above — that increased wage and price persistence has resulted in greater cyclical fluctuations than would otherwise have occurred. Of course, as is true of any relatively unexplored hypothesis, further testing will be needed before a more definitive conclusion can be reached.[7]

While the empirical evidence does appear to support the view that long-term overlapping nominal wage contracts are an important source of inertia in wage and price inflation, there are other explanations of the intercountry and intertemporal findings. One competing explanation is that differences in the policy rules followed by the monetary and fiscal authorities can account for the observed differences in the slope of the short-run Phillips Curve, and thus in the variability of wages and prices versus employment and hours. Most of the intercountry studies (Taylor, 1980b, is an exception, but he does not allow for differences across countries in the length of wage contracts, degree of synchronization, etc.) have not allowed for the possibility that the willingness of the authorities to validate price and wage increases differs across countries and that those involved in wage and price setting infer the policy rule and take it into account when setting wages and prices.

Of course, these two factors — wage and price inertia and the policy stance of the central authorities — are unlikely to be independent. The widespread acceptance of Keynesian economics and the role of government in stabilization of the economy probably contributed to the adoption of long-term fixed wage contracts in the labour market (Baily, 1978). Perhaps more important for the empirical testing, central banks can credibly threaten not to accommodate shocks in economies with short contracts and synchronized negotiations. The role of this factor in Germany in the 1970s was pointed out clearly by Giersch (1979) and has been emphasized more recently by Tarantelli (1984).

Another competing explanation is that there are other cultural or institutional differences across countries which account for the observed differences in wage and employment variability. In chapter 4 we noted the more centralized bargaining structures in several European countries and their extensive reliance on incomes policies. Barber and McCallum (1982), for example, attribute the observed behaviour to differences in the degree of "social consensus." A potentially important factor accounting for the Japanese wage-employment variability is the substantial use of bonus payments. This point is elaborated below.

There is unlikely to be a single cause of the observed differences in wage and price inflation inertia across countries and time periods. The challenge for empirical research is that of assessing the contribution of each of these factors. On the basis of current knowledge it appears that long-term overlapping nominal wage contracts will continue to be recognized as a quantitatively major factor, but not the only factor.

This analysis suggests two alterations (shorter wage contracts and synchronized negotiations) to existing collective bargaining arrangements that would decrease the inertia in wage settlements and permit improved macroeconomic performance — in particular, greater stability in employment and output — in the future. Should these changes be made? Since this is a complex and difficult question, let us examine a number of the salient factors involved.

First, the arguments which link overlapping nominal wage contracts and wage inertia are symmetrical. Decreasing contract duration and synchronizing negotiations will make disinflation less painful, but will also make the economy more prone to rapid increases in wages and prices. This follows from the prediction that these changes will make the short-run Phillips Curve steeper. My view is that the symmetrical nature of the predictions is not a strong argument against these changes. Indeed, their adoption would make the consequences of inflationary policies apparent more quickly. An unfortunate consequence of the existing institutional arrangements is that the short-run costs of overly expansionary policies are deceptively low, a temptation the economy would be better off without. That is, wage and price inertia can lead to a situation in which a government could expand the economy during the period building up to an election, as most of the inflationary consequences will come later.

A second observation is that we need to know more than we now know about why overlapping nominal wage contracts are preferred by labour market participants before seriously considering altering these arrangements. Obviously these institutional arrangements are privately efficient; otherwise, they would have disappeared by now. Overlapping multiyear agreements seem to have become an enduring feature of North American labour markets. Even during the recent severe recession, when there have been numerous changes in collective bargaining, the tendency for firms and unions to negotiate long-term contracts has not changed in a noticeable fashion. Because they contribute to wage and price inertia, they may generate some social costs which are not taken into account by individual firms and unions in wage setting. However, to make a convincing case it needs to be shown that alternative institutional arrangements involve lower social costs and not substantially lower private benefits.

Why do long-term fixed wage contracts continue to be chosen by labour market participants? One obvious reason is to economize on negotiation and related costs. The major collective agreements data reveal that the average duration of negotiations in all industries varied from six to ten months over the period 1967–81. These durations would undoubtedly fall if sequences of shorter contracts were negotiated; nonetheless, they suggest that direct negotiation costs may be large and that contracts shorter than one year are not likely to be feasible.

Another explanation for long-term wage contracts is that they are the parties' preferred method of avoiding or reducing industrial disputes. In Canada, strikes and lockouts during the term of the agreement are prohibited in most jurisdictions. In the United States the parties typically include such a prohibition in the collective agreement. Since the expiry date of the contract is known, the firm can take action (inventory accumulation, for example) to minimize the potential costs of a strike. With shorter contracts, negotiations would occur more frequently and there would therefore be more opportunities for strikes or lockouts. It should be noted, however, that both theory and some recent evidence suggest that the probability of a strike occurring is an increasing function of the length of the previous agreement (Riddell, 1985b; Cousineau and Lacroix, 1983). Thus, shortening contracts would reduce the probability of a strike occurring in any given set of negotiations but would increase the number of negotiations.

Although it is by no means obvious that more frequent negotiations (imposed, say, by legislation banning long-term contracts) would result in an increase in strike activity[8] or a shift in bargaining power toward unions, a recent study indicates that most employers believe that this would be the outcome. Jacoby and Mitchell (1984) surveyed the attitudes of U.S. employers to long-term union contracts and found strong opposition to any attempt to force a shortening of contract duration. A substantial majority of employers apparently believe that union bargaining power would increase with more frequent negotiations, resulting in higher wage settlements, and that strike activity would increase. Part of the reason for this belief is a perceived non-linearity in strike costs to the employer; specifically, employers believe that a one-month strike every year would be more costly than a three-month strike every three years.

Employers also seem to prefer long-term wage contracts for long-range planning purposes and the marketing advantages of security of supply. This planning aspect was noted by Garbarino (1962) in his early analysis of long-term contracts. It also appeared to be an important reason for the employers' strong preference for long-term contracts in the Jacoby and Mitchell survey: "Management respondents to the survey are, if anything, oversold on the merits of long-term contracts from the employer viewpoint" (p. 226). Their results suggest that imposing shorter contracts would meet with strong opposition from employers.

While these private benefits of long-term contracts (reduced negotiations costs, possibly reduced work stoppages, long-term planning, security of supply) are not small or unimportant, they need to be compared to the costs associated with wage and price inertia. These costs are potentially very large. Moreover, because of their macroeconomic nature, they are to a considerable extent outside the control of any single firm or union. That is, the degree of wage and price inertia in the economy, and thus the extent of cyclical fluctuations in output and employment, will not be altered if one firm and union negotiate a shorter contract. However, if many were to do so, employers and employees generally could benefit. Thus the existing arrangements, although privately efficient, may not be socially efficient.

There is an intermediate possibility. A more flexible wage provision could be negotiated within the context of a long-term contract covering non-wage benefits, working conditions, and so on.

The discussion thus far has focussed primarily on contract length, and has said little about the overlapping feature of labour contracts. As mentioned earlier, the contribution of non-synchronization to inflation inertia depends on the strength of relative wage effects, the formation of expectations, and the importance of "catch-up" effects. While little is known about the marginal contribution of non-synchronization to inertia, it appears likely that it plays an important role. The effect of non-synchronization can be inferred from simulations such as those reported by Taylor (1980a, 1983), but these assume rational expectations and a particular structure for relative wage effects.

Even if synchronized negotiations could be shown to be in the national interest, the possibility of bringing it about in Canada is very remote indeed. The constitutional division of powers over labour relations, and the extremely decentralized structure of collective bargaining, factors which are by no means independent, would make synchronization difficult to achieve and enforce. Even in the limited number of cases in which centralized (and thus typically synchronized) bargaining has been attempted (usually on an industry-wide basis within a province), such arrangements have often broken down, especially recently under the pressures of the recession (see Davies, 1985, and Riddell, 1985c, for further discussion). Synchronized negotiations, although they would have some important benefits, thus appear to be a "non starter" from a public policy point of view. They would also have some important costs. Greater centralization would almost inevitably accompany synchronization, an outcome I would regard as a cost to society. Synchronization, especially if accompanied by centralization, might make the relative wage structure rigid. In addition, some worry that with Canada's record on labour-management disputes, synchronization would result in "shutting the country down every spring" (or whenever negotiations occur). This concern may well be exaggerated because it appears to ignore the fact that with synchronized negotiations, work stoppages become more costly to both sides. Thus, according to the information/joint-costs perspective, strikes and lockouts should become less frequent (Riddell, 1985c). Nonetheless, when they occurred they would involve a major disruption. Furthermore, the Quebec experience with centralized bargaining makes one wary of the practice (Hébert, 1984), although in this case there are other factors involved in addition to centralization.

Wage Indexation and Gain-Sharing Compensation Arrangements

Thus far the long-term and overlapping features have been discussed; I now wish to turn to the third feature mentioned above, the fact that nominal wage rates are predetermined in most collective agreements. An obvious way to reduce inertia would be to make wages contingent on realized economic conditions rather than being set in advance.

A distinction should be made between a contingent wage scheme and a gain-sharing or shared-compensation system. The former is a compensation system in which employees are paid an hourly wage, but this wage is contingent on realized economic conditions. The latter refers to a compensation system in which employees receive a share of the profits or revenue of the firm. As will become clear below, the latter is a more fundamental reform.

Contingent wage systems, or wage indexation, have been used in a variety of circumstances. The most common form is the COLA clause, which indexes the wage to changes in the cost of living. Much less common have been schemes that index wages to variables related to the employers' ability to pay, such as having the wages of gold miners related to the price of gold, or of steel workers to the price of steel.

Uncertainty about future economic conditions means that both employers and employees face risks. When the wage is set ex ante it will turn out to be too high for some states of the world and too low for others. If the state were observed by both parties, then both could gain from making the wage state contingent.[9] The logic behind this proposition is straightforward. The state contingent arrangement allows the wage rate to be tailored to the realized economic conditions. The options available with a non-state contingent wage are a subset of those available with a contingent wage; the two parties could decide to make the wage a constant function of the state. Thus, a state contingent arrangement dominates (in the Pareto sense) a non-state contingent arrangement.

Offsetting these gains are the additional costs of negotiating, writing up, and enforcing the contingent arrangement. While these may not be trivial, especially for the first such arrangement, they do not appear to be a serious obstacle to contingent arrangements. Rather, the most important difficulties appear to involve finding observable variables that are highly correlated with the more important dimensions of the state. There are two problems here: imperfect information and asymmetric information. The former refers to the fact that neither party will have complete information about the state of the world, while the latter refers to the situation in which the firm has better information about some aspects of the state and possibly the same is true for the workers.

The existence of imperfect information would imply that the wage cannot be made fully state contingent. The parties are restricted to a second best arrangement in which the wage is made contingent on variables that are correlated with the state. The appeal of a contingent wage scheme evidently depends on the magnitude of the correlation. A number of observed or observable variables have been suggested. On the demand side, firm or industry sales, profits, output, revenue, and output per hour or per worker have been suggested by Mitchell (1982) and value added per hour by Thurow (1983). On the supply side, the CPI is widely used as an indexation measure for the workers' cost of living. Measures of the opportunity cost of the workers' time would be another important supply side dimension; wages earned by comparable workers elsewhere and the value of workers' leisure time are the main aspects of opportunity cost.

Probably the most important consequence of imperfect information is that the firm will not be able to distinguish between changes in demand due to nominal shocks and those due to real shocks. The second difficulty with the demand side variables is that the firm often has much better information than the workers. The more widespread use of contingent payment schemes would require more sharing of information between employers and employees than currently exists. The alternative is to index the wage to some variable or variables which are observed by both parties and are correlated with the state. However, the demand side variables are typically collected and reported by the firm. In the absence of sufficient trust between the parties, the workers may anticipate manipulation of the variables by the firm. This (legitimate) fear implies the need for a potentially costly monitoring system. The same problem may exist on the supply side, although it is possible that the firm already monitors wage developments in related firms and industries.

The manipulation and associated monitoring cost problems will be most severe when firm specific disturbances are important. In industries with relatively homogeneous firms the wage could be indexed to demand side variables reported by Statistics Canada or other agencies. Even in this case, however, there is some scope for manipulation as the statistical agencies obtain the basic information from the firms.

Another important factor affecting the choice of compensation arrangements is risk. Workers dislike the risks associated with an uncertain income. However, whether contingent wage compensation schemes are more or less risky than fixed wage payments systems depends on how much the flexible wage system reduces the risk of layoff in response to fluctuations in demand.

Empirical evidence supports the view that more flexible wage payments systems imply a lower risk of layoffs, holding other factors constant. The evidence based on comparisons across a number of countries has already been cited. Additional evidence comes from comparing the behaviour of temporary layoffs and wages in the union and non-union sectors. Fixed wage contracts are common in unionized firms, while non-union firms can and typically do adjust wages upward and downward to reflect changes in economic conditions. Empirical studies confirm that unionized firms rely more on temporary layoffs to respond to fluctuations in demand than do non-union firms, holding other factors constant (Freeman and Medoff, 1984).

It is important to note that workers are not affected equally by the risk of layoff. In unionized firms, layoffs are typically in reverse order of seniority. Seniority is also used, though to a lesser extent, in the non-union sector. Thus, for the majority of workers, the risk of layoff is very low except in an unusually severe recession. The risk is high, even for moderate downturns in economic activity, for workers at the bottom of the seniority ladder. Changing from a fixed wage to a more flexible wage compensation system would result in somewhat increased risk of income fluctuations for the majority of workers, but would result in substantially reduced risk of income fluctuations for the minority of workers at the bottom of the seniority ladder.

The problem of optimal wage indexation has recently been studied by Karni (1983) in the context of a macroeconomic model used earlier by Gray (1976) to consider indexation of wages to the price level. This is a single output, single (labour) input economy subject to monetary and real shocks. Karni shows that wages can be indexed to the price level and the level of output such that all inertia or friction associated with predetermined nominal wages is removed. That is, the economy with an appropriately indexed wage attains the same output and employment levels as would be obtained if spot markets for labour and goods cleared after the state is realized (i.e., after the nominal and real disturbance has occurred). The proposition that all inertia can be removed through indexation results from the absence of imperfect information in this model; the structure of the economy is such that the exact magnitude of the otherwise unobservable stochastic disturbances can be inferred. However, Karni's result suggests that optimal wage indexation schemes will exist in more complex and realistic models. Of course, with imperfect information it will not be possible to remove all inertias through indexation. Nonetheless, even the second best may represent a substantial improvement over predetermined wages.

Given this potential gain from indexation, why is it not more common? One answer is that the transactions and monitoring costs which arise because of imperfect and asymmetric information are simply too large relative to the gains to make indexation of wages to variables other than the CPI worthwhile. This answer presumes that those involved in wage determination have assessed the costs and benefits of indexation and have decided that the expected costs exceed the expected benefits. A second answer is that those involved in wage determination have not been sufficiently imaginative or sophisticated to have considered or to appreciate the potential benefits of more elaborate indexation schemes. Although there is probably some truth in each of these answers, I suspect that the former carries the bulk of the explanation. Thus, I am skeptical about the potential for widespread adoption of indexation schemes. Several of the reasons for this skepticism were given above: the problems associated with imperfect and, especially, asymmetric information, and the absence of information-sharing and trust between employers and employees.

The theoretical literature on wage indexation, like most of the literature on labour market contracts, is set in a two period model: the present, which is known, and the future, which is unknown. However, the two parties do not need to choose between setting a wage or wage path for the entire future and a contingent wage schedule. Rather, they can and do choose a sequence of short (relative to the length of time the two parties expect the relationship to last) wage contracts so that the wage is revised as uncertainty is resolved. In this setting the distinction between contingent and non-contingent contracts is not clear cut. The sequence of shorter contracts could be argued to be an implicit contingent agreement covering the longer horizon, especially if on renegotiation there is a form of ex post "settling up" to adjust for unanticipated events during the previous contract. As mentioned earlier, there is considerable empirical evidence that such catch-up factors play an important role in wage determination.

Whether we consider the sequence of short contracts a contingent agreement or not, the point that the two parties have a variety of ways of dealing with uncertainty is beyond dispute. Each of these methods (explicit indexation, renegotiating more frequently, using wage reopener clauses) will also alter the degree of inertia in wage inflation. Thus, if we wish to know which of these means of reducing inertia has the greatest benefits relative to costs, at least as perceived by those involved in wage determination, we should look at the method chosen by the parties when making marginal adjustments to changes in uncertainty about the future. The evidence indicates that more frequent renegotiation and COLA clauses are chosen in these circumstances. This suggests that shortening contracts is preferred to wage indexation (other than to the cost of living) as a method of reducing inertia.

A related reason for being skeptical about the potential gains from more elaborate indexation comes from the view that, in spite of predetermined wage rates, existing contractual provisions may enable the parties to achieve a better approximation to a contingent wage scheme than is probably realized. The argument is laid out in detail in Hall and Lillien (1979), so I will simply summarize it briefly here. The point of departure is that with asymmetric information the wage must be indexed to a variable that is observed by both parties. Employment is a logical candidate. Hall and Lillien's argument is that contract provisions (overtime pay rates is the main one; provisions that require the promotion of existing workers and limit new hires to entry levels are others) imply that a "compensation rule" is imbedded in union contracts. The compensation rule relates hourly earnings (Hall and Lillien deal with total compensation but the argument can be formulated in terms of hourly compensation) to employment, even though wage rates are fixed. If there are only demand or supply fluctuations, a compensation rule exists such that if one party (the firm in the case of demand fluctuations; the union in the case of supply disturbances) unilaterally chooses employment subject to the rule, the efficient level of employment will be chosen for each realization of the demand or supply shock. However, if both demand and supply fluctuations occur, such a compensation rule does not exist. In this case a contingent agreement is needed to ensure efficient employment levels. However, the measurement, monitoring and enforcement costs make a contingent contract unattractive. Hall and Lillien's argument is that because demand fluctuations are relatively large and are often transitory while supply fluctuations occur gradually and are typically permanent, the parties choose an approximately efficient arrangement whereby the firm chooses employment subject to the compensation rule imbedded in the contract. This response does away with the need to index wages to demand disturbances. The arrangement is only approximately efficient because it does not incorporate supply fluctuations. To a considerable extent these fluctuations can be incorporated by allowing for expected inflation or explicitly indexing to the CPI. The wage is adjusted for the remaining supply fluctuations through periodic renegotiation of the contract.

Gain-Sharing

A share compensation system has considerably stronger tendencies to stabilize employment and output in response to various economic shocks than other forms of contingent wage systems. There are two general ways a gain-sharing compensation system could operate. One is to negotiate (or otherwise determine) in advance a sharing formula. The two most obvious candidates are revenue per employee or profits per employee. A share of, say, two-thirds would imply that the employee would receive two-thirds of the revenue per employee and the employer the remaining one-third. The second is to negotiate (or otherwise determine) the share at a subsequent date. This is the system used in Japan, where bonus payments are negotiated semi-annually for most regular industrial workers. The bonus is not related to profits or revenue by an explicit formula, but does vary somewhat with the company's market performance.

Either system is likely to have a fixed salary or wage component, with the share or bonus supplementing this base level of income. In Japan the bonus component is substantial. On average, bonuses exceed one-quarter of a worker's total earnings.

We will be concerned primarily with the implications of gain-sharing compensation arrangements for employment stability. However, it is worth noting that these types of payments systems have also been recommended as methods for improving employee morale and productivity. They are also viewed by some as an important part of a package leading to a more cooperative and consultative labour-relations environment. Discussion of these aspects occurs elsewhere (Riddell, 1985b).

The thesis that an economy in which a share-compensation system is widely used will exhibit a strong tendency to maintain full employment of labour is argued in detail in an important book by Martin Weitzman (1984). Without going into the details the reasoning can be sketched here.

There is a fundamental difference between an economy in which workers are paid a fixed hourly wage and one in which workers are paid a share of revenue or profit. In the wage economy, the labour market is in equilibrium when the demand for labour equals the supply of labour. In the share economy, however, in equilibrium there is unsatisfied demand or unfilled job vacancies at the prevailing negotiated shares. This excess demand for labour will act as a cushion, protecting the economy from significant deviations from full employment. Any reduction in labour demand will be offset by the existence of unfilled vacancies.

The reason for this important difference is that with the share compensation system the firm can always increase profits by expanding employment and output.[10] With the wage system the firm will expand employment only to the point at which the additional revenue generated by the extra employment equals the additional cost which is the hourly wage.

The main empirical evidence supporting the view that widespread use of a share-payments system will stabilize employment and output comes from postwar Japan. Japan weathered the contractions of 1954, 1957–58, 1962, 1965, 1971, 1974–75 and 1981–83 with relatively little change in registered unemployment. Of course, it would be a mistake to attribute this remarkable performance to the use of the bonus system alone. Japan also has annual synchronized bargaining which, as noted above, contributes to stability in employment and output. In addition, the Japanese labour force contains a secondary component that avoids unemployment as normally defined by moving out of the labour force in response to the downturns in economic activity.

Evidence from analysis of Japanese experience over time lends some further support to the positive role that can be played by the share payments system. The key wage-setting institutions (synchronized bargaining, annual contracts, substantial bonus payments) were adopted in the postwar era. Prior to World War II, the Japanese economy also suffered from substantial fluctuations in employment and output.

This suggests that there is a case for policy intervention to promote gain-sharing arrangements. The case is similar to that for shorter contracts and/or synchronized negotiations. It rests on the macroeconomic benefits to Canadian society as a whole of greater employment stability. Because of the cumulative or multiplier effects associated with business cycles, layoffs in one industry will reduce output demand and, thus, employment in other industries. These macroeconomic effects are not fully taken into account by individual firms and unions in making their choices. The situation is again that of a prisoner's dilemma where a coordinated change can benefit society as a whole.

The experience of the recent recession may well cause firms and unions to reconsider wage-setting arrangements. There is evidence to support the view that labour market participants are in the process of re-examining compensation schemes, although significant change has yet to occur in Canada. It seems likely that some form of government intervention would be required to achieve substantially more widespread use of gain-sharing arrangements if that were considered desirable.

Conclusions

This chapter has discussed three options for increasing stability in employment and output in Canada. All three would lead to increased flexibility and variability in wages and prices. They would not, however, necessarily cause real income to be any more variable because both wages and prices would become more flexible and because employment would fluctuate less.

Existing knowledge does not enable us to make precise predictions about the effects of these reforms. Among the three structural changes, gain-sharing compensation arrangements probably yield the best mix of benefits and costs. Further, and not entirely unrelated, this reform would probably be the easiest to bring about — although the obstacles to more widespread use of these arrangements should not be underestimated. Achieving synchronized wage negotiations or uniformly shorter contracts would require federal-provincial agreement on the wisdom of these structural reforms and would face other important barriers, as noted earlier.

Greater use of gain-sharing compensation arrangements could be brought about by offering employees more favourable tax treatment to earnings negotiated in the form of a share of profits or revenue.[11]

Research and debate as the consequences of this approach should receive high priority.

An important obstacle to the more widespread use of gain-sharing compensation arrangements, especially to firms that are privately owned, is the inadequate exchange of relevant information between employers and employees.

Chapter 7

Summary and Conclusions

Inflation and unemployment have dominated the policy agenda for the past two decades, and are likely to continue to receive high priority in the future. This study has examined the main policy options for dealing with inflation and unemployment in the Canadian setting. There are two related challenges: how to respond to various economic shocks without allowing a deeply imbedded inflationary spiral to develop, and how best to reduce an ongoing inflation should one develop. The key implications of this study for these two challenges are discussed in turn.

With respect to responding to economic disturbances in the future, the following conclusions appear warranted:

- Clearly it is important not to allow a recurrence of the experience of the 1960s and early 1970s when overly expansionary monetary and fiscal policies contributed to a sustained overheating of the economy and a buildup of inflationary pressures. The short-run benefits — output and employment temporarily above normal levels — of this approach are not worth the long-run consequences — a deeply embedded inflation which is difficult and extremely costly to reduce. This does not necessarily imply that macroeconomic policy should not attempt to reduce fluctuations around potential output — an issue not addressed here, but it does imply that attempting to maintain the economy above potential output on an extended basis is unwise.
- It is also important not to allow foreign inflationary developments to become translated into domestic inflation; that is, to use the exchange rate to insulate the economy from these disturbances to the extent possible.

- The experience of the past two decades has led some analysts to believe that Western economies have developed a bias toward operating the economy above potential output and thus toward increasing inflation. An alternative hypothesis is that these economies did have such a bias during the era of belief in a stable Phillips Curve, but that this tendency no longer exists. The experience since the mid-1970s does provide some support for this latter hypothesis.
- A policy of non-accommodation of inflation would have benefits in the form of increased price stability, but would also produce somewhat greater fluctuations in output and employment. In this context, institutional changes to wage-setting mechanisms are worthy of serious consideration as a means of achieving greater stability in output and employment.
- A permanent incomes policy in order to deal with inflationary pressures appears unnecessary and unwise.

On his 90th birthday, George Bernard Shaw was asked how he enjoyed old age. He replied: "It's not bad when you consider the alternative." The challenge of dealing with imbedded inflation has to be approached in a similar fashion. Perhaps the clearest implication of this study is that there is no costless way to reduce inflation. However, some alternatives do appear preferable to others:

- Demand restraint may become somewhat more effective in the future, given the recent experience of disinflation. However, this is by no means certain. Thus there is considerable risk that severe demand restraint will have substantial short-run and long-run costs, as was true in the recent disinflationary experience.
- Wage and price controls combined with appropriate monetary and fiscal restraint can bring about a reduction in inflation at less cost than reliance on demand restraint alone. Such programs should be clearly temporary, and should be used infrequently.
- Incentive-based incomes policies, such as those operating through the tax system, could also be used in combination with monetary and fiscal restraint to bring about a disinflation. While these have some advantages over direct controls, they are unlikely to involve significantly less administrative costs or to do substantially less damage to social goodwill. Nor is it clear that introducing a major complication to the tax system is wise. Thus direct controls probably represent a better choice than incentive based incomes policies as a means of bringing about a reduction in inflation.
- Demand restraint is a costly policy to pursue because of the momentum in the inflationary process. This momentum is in part associated with the institutional mechanisms for wage determination in Canada. Reforms to these institutional features — such as shorter contracts,

synchronized negotiations, and more flexible compensation arrangements — are worth considering both as means to facilitate disinflation in the future and to reduce fluctuations in output and employment in response to economic disturbances. Gain-sharing compensation arrangements appear particularly promising.

Notes

CHAPTER 1

1. The most recent period (1982–84) is dominated by the 1982–83 recession, and is thus not comparable (in the sense of being cyclically neutral) to the other postwar periods.
2. For details of these and related labour force developments see the papers in Riddell (1985a).
3. On postwar developments with respect to unionization and collective bargaining see Kumar (1985) and the overview paper in Riddell (1985b). The use of fixed wage contracts is discussed in chapter 6. Pensions, health care and unemployment insurance are covered in Vaillancourt (1985).
4. For alternative, and in most respects more detailed, reviews of the evolution of events and ideas see Gordon (1980), Feldstein (1982) and Grubel (1983).
5. Using the estimates of Bodkin et al. (1966) as an example, an unemployment rate of 3 percent implied wage inflation in excess of 5 percent. Unemployment of 5 percent was estimated to be needed to reduce wage inflation to 3 percent. Thus, if productivity growth was about 3 percent (a high rate of growth; see Table 1-1), an unemployment rate of 5 percent was estimated to be required for price stability.
6. For example, in its first annual review, the Economic Council of Canada (1964) stated that "In the light of careful studies, we have concluded that a 97 percent rate of employment, or a 3 percent rate of unemployment, of the labour force, would constitute a realistic objective to be aimed at over the balance of the 1960s, and that economic policies should be actively directed toward the achievement of this target" (pp. 37–39).

   The Royal Commission on Taxation (the Carter Commission) expressed the view that unemployment rates could usually be maintained below 4 percent without developing sustained inflationary pressures (Canada, Royal Commission on Taxation, 1964). The Commission recommended reducing unemployment to 3 to 3.5 percent and criticized the macroeconomic policy of the 1950s and early 1960s for over-concern with inflation. Similarly, in its recommendations the Task Force on Labour Relations stated that "On the basis of present knowledge we would be inclined to put relatively more emphasis on full employment than on price stability." (Canada, Task Force on Labour Relations, 1968, p. 188).
7. See, for example, Smith (1966), Economic Council of Canada (1966), and Canada, Task Force on Labour Relations (1968).
8. An advantage of a flexible exchange rate is that it enables Canada to insulate itself from foreign inflation, at least to some degree. In order to achieve a lower (higher) inflation rate than that of our major trading partners, our exchange rate must appreciate (depreciate) by the difference between the foreign and domestic inflation rates. Thus, allowing the Canadian dollar to appreciate in the late 1960s would have reduced the inflation imported from the United States. In the postwar period countries such as West Germany and Switzerland achieved considerable success in maintaining low domestic inflation by allowing their exchange rates to appreciate relative to those of their major trading partners.

9. For detailed discussions of strike activity in Canada see Lacroix (1985) and the overview paper in Riddell (1985c). There is some evidence that increases in worker militancy — usually measured by strike activity — result in higher wage settlements, though there is debate on the extent to which these increases are exogenous or determined by economic factors such as a decline in real wages due to unanticipated inflation.
10. For details on union growth in Canada with particular emphasis on the postwar period see Kumar (1985) and the overview paper in Riddell (1985c).
11. The union/non-union wage differential refers to the percentage difference in wages between unionized and comparable non-union workers. For the economy as a whole this differential is generally estimated to be 10 to 20 percent in Canada. For a summary of Canadian studies see the overview paper in Riddell (1985c).
12. As noted earlier, in the Keynesian dichotomy, any unemployment in excess of "full employment" was associated with deficient aggregate demand. Although the Phillips Curve tradeoff muddied the notion of full employment, the unemployment rate was used as the primary measure of the degree of excess demand or supply in the labour market. Lipsey's (1960) theoretical derivation of the Phillips Curve relationship made clear that the unemployment rate alone could be used providing there was a stable relationship between unemployment and job vacancies. Such provisos, however, can easily become forgotten. Furthermore, the job vacancy data available at the time were not as useful as subsequent data (see Figure 1-4 below) in identifying the change in the meaning of the aggregate unemployment rate.
13. Kaliski (1985) provides a detailed discussion of the reasons why these developments tended to raise the natural unemployment rate and a summary of the main empirical studies.
14. Figure 1-4 suggests a stable U-V relationship existed during the period 1955–71. Measured in terms of the unemployment rate, the U-V relationship shifted up by about 2 percent — compare 1975 to 1969 and 1972 to 1965/66. Reid and Meltz (1979) provide a statistical analysis of the behaviour of unemployment and job vacancies. They attribute most of the shift to the 1971/72 changes to the UI act.
15. Some of these studies are discussed in chapter 2 of this book. See also Kaliski (1985).
16. It is often stated that maintaining the economy below the natural rate will lead to accelerating inflation. The term NAIRU (non-accelerating inflation rate of unemployment) is an example. In fact, the natural rate hypothesis implies only that the inflation rate will increase (because actual inflation will exceed expected inflation, a situation which cannot be maintained indefinitely), not that it will increase at an increasing rate as would be required for the term "accelerate" to be appropriate.
17. In the U.S. context see Gordon (1975b), Phelps (1978b), Blinder (1979) and Solow (1980). In Canada see Helliwell (1984). Much of the research is comparative in nature; see in particular Bruno and Sachs (1984) and Helliwell (1985).
18. The rationale had been outlined several years earlier by the Prices and Incomes Commission, as noted above.
19. See the Annual Report of the Governor (Bank of Canada, 1975).
20. Lucas (1976) provides a detailed analysis of the point that econometric estimates are conditional on the policy regime in operation during the sample period used for estimation.
21. For the background to this policy change in the United Kingdom see Buiter and Miller (1981b, 1983); for the United States see Brimmer (1983).
22. For a more detailed discussion of these different schools of thought see O'Reilly (1985) and O'Reilly, White and Ford (1985).
23. A brief word on the definition of inflation is in order. It is important to distinguish between a once-and-for-all rise in the price level and a continuing rise in prices. Some economists use the term "inflation" to refer only to the latter. I will define inflation as a rise in prices, whether of a one-shot or continuing nature. The reasons for preferring this definition are spelled out well by Lipsey (1979). When it is important to do so, I will distinguish between a once-and-for-all and a continuing rise in prices by referring to the latter as an ongoing, continuing or sustained inflation.

CHAPTER 2

1. Under the assumptions of perfect competition and continuous market clearing, firms and workers are price and wage takers, respectively, and adjust output and employment in response to variations in perceived relative prices and wages. In these circumstances the causality would run from changes in aggregate demand or supply to changes in prices and wages (relative to expectations) to changes in output and employment. Thus, according to the modern classical approach, the dependent variable should be output, employment or unemployment and the explanatory variables should include the amount of unanticipated price or wage inflation; that is, the Phillips Curve is reversed (see Riddell (1980) and Wogin (1980) for examples of this approach in Canada). These modern classical models appear unable to account for the observed serial correlation in output and employment. Thus, this chapter focusses on the expectations-augmented Phillips Curve specification.
2. "Contract" is being used here in a generic sense to refer to either implicit or explicit agreements. Throughout this book terms such as "wage settlements" and "wage agreements" will be used in this generic sense.
3. The explanation of wage rigidity has attracted considerable attention, and continues to be a matter for debate and research. Okun (1981) and Gordon (1982) are useful references. Aspects of wage rigidity are also discussed further in chapter 6.
4. By joining the points in wage change-unemployment space from one year to the next, Phillips (1958) noted that there were systematic counter-clockwise loops around the curve.
5. See Christofides et al. (1980a) or Riddell (1979) for an elaboration of this point, which also holds in a firm-union setting.
6. O'Reilly (1983) provides a detailed discussion of alternative specifications of the price equation.
7. This aspect is described in more detail in chapter 6.
8. Two other groups of studies have been carried out. Most macroeconomic models have a wage-price sector similar to the equations being discussed here. See Helliwell (1983) for a survey. Also, there are several unpublished studies carried out by researchers at the Bank of Canada. Neither of these groups of studies obtains results which are contradictory to those discussed here.

CHAPTER 3

1. For a description of the U.S. policy change and some of its effects see Brimmer (1983). See Buiter and Miller (1981b, 1983) for details of the approach of the Thatcher regime and for an assessment of its impact.
2. Of course, the oil price decline is not entirely exogenous. However, if Canada alone were to undertake a disinflationary policy, favourable reductions in world prices could not be anticipated.
3. Cooper (1982) provides a useful summary and assessment of the various gold standard proposals that have been made. Hall (1981) describes a commodity standard that would better stabilize the value of the dollar than would the gold standard. However, like most economists, Hall emphasizes that there are problems in managing a commodity standard. While a properly managed commodity standard can ensure reasonable price stability, so can a properly managed fiat money system. "Simply switching from our existing badly managed fiat money to a badly managed commodity standard might well be a step backward" (p. 1).

CHAPTER 4

1. As opposed to policies which attempt to control or prevent price increases in particular sectors; for example, rent controls.
2. Note that, in principle at least, this policy does not require deviating from potential output. This point is elaborated below.
3. If the controls are to be flexible in order to allow relative wages and prices to change this may require a norm of less than y percent.

4. For statements of this view see Carr (1982) or Mayer (1984).
5. For statements of this view see Gordon (1973) or Blinder and Newton (1981).
6. Of course there are sources of non-synchronization in price setting also, but the wage case appears quantitatively more significant.
7. This section was written jointly with Keith Banting of the University of British Columbia and draws on Banting (1985) and Riddell (1985b).
8. A recent survey of labour and business leaders by Maital and Meltz (1984) shows more support for a social contract to restrain wage and prices increases in Canada than in the United States. However, even in Canada a majority of both labour and business leaders were opposed.
9. Both systems provide for a union to be recognized as the exclusive bargaining representative of a group of employees if a majority of employees favour this outcome. For a further discussion of the similarities and differences see the overview paper in Riddell (1985c) and the references cited therein.
10. For reviews of the American experience with incomes policies see Pencavel (1981) and Russell (1983).
11. The Korean War program had many of the features of wartime attempts to control wage and price inflation during a period of general excess demand.
12. The program contained a government contract compliance provision, but this threat became less credible as time passed.
13. See, for example, Perry (1970, 1980), Blinder and Newton (1981), Reid (1981), Gordon (1975a), Frye and Gordon (1981), Pencavel (1981), and Hagens and Russell (1985).
14. See the government's white paper *Attack on Inflation: A Program of National Action* (Ottawa: Department of Finance, 1975).
15. Bank of Canada, *Annual Report of the Governor* (Ottawa: Bank of Canada), p. 11. See also Canada, Department of Finance, *Canada's Recent Inflation Experience* (Ottawa: The Department, 1978) for a clear statement of the rationale for the AIP.
16. This calculation does not allow for any feedback or lagged effects. A recession of this magnitude would clearly affect more than wages and these additional effects (price changes, expectations) would reduce wage changes.
17. Letourneau (1979) and Fortin and Newton (1982) have sample periods ending in 1978, and thus are not able to allow for this possibility.
18. Average rollbacks were 2.5, 2.0, 1.1 and 0.6 percent in the years 1975–78, respectively (Christofides and Wilton, 1985).
19. Wilson and Jump (1979) also examined the impact of the AIP on wages and prices. However, because their sample ends in the middle of the AIB's term, the estimated impact on prices is small. Given their sample period, their results are comparable to Letourneau's.
20. Largely on the basis of the disappointing performance of previous incomes policies in other countries, many Canadian economists were skeptical about the controls component of the AIP. The accumulation of empirical evidence, as summarized in Table 4-1, has caused several to alter their views on the wisdom of such policies. Compare, for example, Lipsey (1977) and Lipsey (1981). A survey of 40 economists who had opposed the creation of the AIB provides examples of several other "converts" (Weldon, 1983).
21. Indeed, McCallum (1985b) has recently argued that the estimated effects of the AIP may be substantially understated. Briefly, his argument is that in the absence of the AIB, the fiscal and monetary restraint employed to reduce inflation would not only have caused a severe recession but would have led to an appreciation of the exchange rate (via high interest rates). This implies a decline in international competitiveness which is not taken into account by existing studies of the AIP. To restore balance of payments equilibrium would require either more inflation or additional unemployment. For a formal analysis which supports this view see Buiter and Miller (1981a).
22. Christofides and Wilton (1985) find that AIB *rollbacks* did tend to be reversed in the first wage agreement following the controls program. They found, however, that the "counterfactual effect" of the program, which accounts for the bulk of the policy's estimated impact, showed no tendency to be reversed.

23. The observation that a substantial component of the price effects of the AIB occurred after the expiry of the program makes the counterfactual assessment even more difficult.

24. Empirical evidence on the magnitude of this variation is presented in the next chapter (Table 5-3), where this point is discussed in more detail.

CHAPTER 5

1. Below I argue that (2) and (3) really amount to the same thing. They are listed as separate rationales here because they appear to be viewed as such by their proponents.

2. Maital and Benjamini (1980) interpret earlier writings of Keynes and Baumol as implying that inflation externalities exist.

3. By "rationale for intervention" I mean that there is a logical argument which indicates that intervention could yield a socially preferable outcome. Whether the intervention is worth the costs is an additional question that must be addressed before a policy decision is made.

4. Throughout this discussion the term "inefficient" is used in the Pareto sense; that is, an outcome is Pareto inefficient if one or more individuals can be made better off without making anyone worse off. The (non-cooperative) Nash equilibrium refers to a situation in which each player in the game chooses his best move, given the choices made by the other players.

5. The following situation yields the utility payoffs shown in Figure 5-1. Two criminals are arrested, charged with murder, and put in separate cells. The police have enough evidence to convict both of a lesser crime (breaking and entering) for which each would receive a five-year sentence. Without a confession, the police will be unable to obtain a conviction on the murder charge. The officer tells each prisoner that if he alone confesses, and testifies against the other, he will receive a light sentence (two years) while his accomplice will receive the maximum sentence (30 years). If both confess the crown attorney will recommend less than the maximum sentence (20 years).

6. This conclusion needs to be qualified if the game is repeated. Experiments indicate that players frequently choose the optimal outcome in repeated prisoner's dilemma situations — a form of tacit collusion. On the last play, however, the inefficient outcome obtains.

7. By "underlying" inflation rate I mean the inflation rate that will tend to persist if the economy is maintained at the natural unemployment rate.

8. See Maital (1984) for macro model simulations of U.S. wage and price behaviour which produce outcomes such as those in Figure 5-2. Maital also discusses other game situations which can arise.

9. See Phelps (1979) for a further discussion.

10. Jackman and Layard (1982b, p. 47) state this quite explicitly: "It is essential to have an incomes policy that *can* be permanent. For the inflation problem is certainly not a temporary one. We would of course like to reduce the inflation rate. But when we do, we shall not have solved the problem. We shall still have to hold inflation steady year after year. If we have got unemployment to an acceptable level and then relax our incomes policy, inflation will inevitably increase."

11. The firm's concession function shows the highest wage the firm would be willing to pay to avoid a strike of a given length. The union's concession function shows the lowest wage the union would be willing to receive to avoid a strike of a given length. In this model, strikes need never occur, but the anticipation of a strike causes convergence to a negotiated settlement.

12. These authors actually analyze the effects of a tax on the wage rate rather than on the wage increase. This point is elaborated below.

13. By assuming the union's utility is a function of the rate of growth of wages and of employment, Kotowitz and Portes (1974) do incorporate the dynamic nature of the optimization problem. However, one might well question whether this is the appropriate way to go about it.

14. See Ashenfelter and Layard (1983) for details of the intended and realized effects of the United Kingdom incomes policies adopted in the 1970s. The Canadian AIP also attempted to narrow differentials through a maximum $2,400 increase provision. It appears that this intent was realized (Frank, 1979).

Chapter 6

1. For a detailed assessment of the Canadian experience with stabilization policy see the studies in Sargent (1985).
2. Price determination matters too, of course. Issues relating to the macroeconomic consequences of price behaviour are examined in O'Reilly et al. (1985).
3. Another exception is the reopener provision. While many contracts contain reopener provisions, most provide for predetermined nominal wage rates with the reopener being available only in emergencies. Contracts which do not specify the nominal wage to be paid during the second and third years of the contract, leaving this to be determined at a later date, are rare.
4. Further details of these institutional features for Canada are provided in Christofides (n.d.) and Riddell (1983). Taylor (1983) provides similar information for the United States. At present, there does not appear to be any tendency for these features to change.
5. This point has a simple but potentially important implication: the effect of demand restraint on wage settlements will depend not only on the current economic conditions produced not only by restraint (measured, for example, by the deviation of the actual unemployment rate from the natural rate) but also by the expected duration of those conditions.

   It is possible to interpret the recent behaviour of wage settlements in Canada as confirming this tendency. The current recession began in 1981Q3 but it was not until 1982Q2 that forecasts of recovery being "just around the corner" stopped being made, and a general view of a lengthy recession became common. Lipsey (1983) argues that the private sector did not seem to appreciate (until after the June 1982 budget) that the recession was policy-induced and that it was unlikely to be short-lived. As is evident from Table 2–1, the steep decline in wage settlements did not begin until 1982Q2.
6. For more details on wage-setting institutions in selected industrial countries see Sachs (1979), Barber and McCallum (1982), or Flanagan, Soskice and Ulman (1983).
7. There are both theoretical and empirical issues: A theoretical issue is what structural interpretation to give to these empirical findings. Delong and Summers (1984) question Taylor's interpretation, and in fact argue that price inflexibility could even contribute to output stability in some cases. Specifically, they are concerned with the possibility that more flexible prices could result in greater fluctuations in real interest rates. The poor quality of prewar data creates problems for empirical research. Indeed, Romer (1984) suggests that the prewar volatility may be an artifact of old data construction procedures.
8. In fact, the two countries with long-term overlapping contracts, Canada and the United States, have the longest average strike duration among industrial countries and are among the most dispute prone, as measured by time lost due to labour disputes per union member. Italy, which has ranked with Canada as the most dispute prone in recent periods, also employs long-term contracts. Of course, there are other important factors which affect differences in strike and lockout activity across countries. For further discussion see Lacroix (1985) and Riddell (1985a).
9. Here I am using the terms "state of the world," "state of nature," or simply "state" in the language of decision theory. Arrow (1971) defines a state as a "description of the world so complete that, if known, the consequences of every action would be known." Thus, all uncertainty is incorporated in the notion of a state.
10. In a share system the marginal cost of labour is declining so that increasing employment reduces the average cost of labour.
11. The February 1984 Federal budget proposed a measure along these lines, but it no longer appears to be under active consideration.

Bibliography

Adams, R.J. 1985. "Industrial Relations and the Economic Crisis: Canada Moves Toward Europe." In *Industrial Relations in a Decade of Economic Change*, edited by H.A. Jarvis, M. Thompson and W. Daniels. Madison, Wisc.: Industrial Relations Research Association.

Arrow, K.J. 1971. *Essays in The Theory of Risk Bearing*. Chicago: Markham.

Ashenfelter, O. 1983. "The Withering Away of a Full Employment Goal." *Canadian Public Policy* 9 (March): 114–25.

Ashenfelter, O., and G.E. Johnson. 1969. "Bargaining Theory, Trade Unions and Industrial Strike Activity." *American Economic Review* 79: 35–43.

Ashenfelter, O., and R. Layard. 1983. "Incomes Policies and Wage Differentials." *Economica* 50 (May): 127–44.

Ashley, R. 1979. "Anti-Inflation Taxation Policy: An Alternative to Wage and Price Controls." *Journal of Macroeconomics* 1 (Fall): 417 – 21.

Baily, M.N. 1976. "Contract Theory and the Moderation of Inflation by Recession and by Controls." *Brookings Papers on Economic Activity*: 585–633.

———. 1978. "Stabilization Policy and Private Economic Behavior." *Brookings Papers on Economic Activity* 1: 11–50.

Bank of Canada. *Annual Report of the Governor*, various years. Ottawa: Bank of Canada.

Banting, K.G. 1985. *The State and Economic Interests*, volume 32 of the research studies prepared for the Royal Commission on the Economic Union and Development Prospects for Canada. Toronto: University of Toronto Press.

Barber, C.L., and J.C.P. McCallum. 1982. *Controlling Inflation: Learning from Experience in Canada, Europe and Japan*. Toronto: James Lorimer.

Bellan, R. 1983. "Stable Prices with Employment." *Policy Options* (July/August): 42–44.

Blackaby, F., ed. 1980. *The Future of Pay Bargaining*. London: Heinemann.

Blanchard, Olivier J. 1984. "The Lucas Critique and the Volcker Deflation." *American Economic Review* 74 (May): 211–15.

Blinder, A.S. 1979. *Economic Policy and the Great Stagflation*. New York: Academic Press.

Blinder, A.S., and W.J. Newton. 1981. "The 1971–1974 Controls Program and the Price Level: An Econometric Post-Mortem." *Journal of Monetary Economics* 8: 1–23.

Bodkin, R.G. 1981. "The Challenge of Inflation and Unemployment in Canada during the 1980s: Would a Tax-Based Incomes Policy Help?" *Canadian Public Policy* 7 (April) (supplement): 202–14.

———. 1982. "Is Tax-Based Incomes Policy an Answer?: A Rejoiner." *Canadian Public Policy* 8 (Winter): 102–105.

Bodkin, R.G., E.P. Bond, G.L. Reuber and T.R. Robinson. 1966. *Price Stability and High Employment: The Options for Canadian Economic Policy*. Study prepared for the Economic Council of Canada. Ottawa: Queen's Printer.

Boyer, A. 1975. "La serisette : un impôt français au coeur de la formation des prix." *Public Finance* 30 (3): 452–59.

Branson, W.H., and J. Rotemberg. 1980. "International Adjustment with Wage Rigidities." *European Economic Review* 13 (3): 309–32.

Brimmer, A.F. 1983. "Monetary Policy and Economic Activity: Benefits and Costs of Monetarism." *American Economic Review* 73 (May): 1–12.

Bruno, M., and J. Sachs. 1984. *The Economics of Worldwide Stagflation*. Cambridge, Mass.: Harvard University Press.

Buiter, W.H., and M. Miller. 1981a. "Real Exchange Rate Overshooting and the Output Cost of Bringing Down Inflation." Warwick Economic Research Papers No. 204. Warwick: University of Warwick. Department of Economics.

———. 1981b. "The Thatcher Experiment: The First Two Years." *Brookings Paper on Economic Activity* 2: 315–67.

______. 1983. "Changing the Rules: Economic Consequences of the Thatcher Regime." *Brookings Paper on Economic Activity* 2: 305–65.

Burns, A. 1951. "Introduction." In *What Happens During Business Cycles*, edited by W.C. Mitchell. Cambridge, Mass.: National Bureau of Economic Research.

Cagan, P. 1979. "Changes in the Cyclical Behavior of Prices." In P. Cagan, *Persistent Inflation: Historical and Policy Essays*. New York: Columbia University Press.

Cagan, P., and W. Fellner. 1983. "Tentative Lessons from the Recent Disinflationary Effort." *Brookings Papers on Economic Activity* 2: 603–608.

Calmfors, L. 1985. "Trade Unions, Wage Formation and Macroeconomic Stability: An Introduction." *Scandinavian Journal of Economics* 87 (2).

Canada. Department of Consumer and Corporate Affairs. 1968. *Policies For Price Stability*. Ottawa: Queen's Printer.

______. Department of Finance. 1974. *Budget Speech*. Ottawa: The Department.

______. Department of Finance. 1975. *Attack on Inflation: A Program of National Action*. Ottawa: The Department.

______. Department of Finance. 1978. *Canada's Recent Inflationary Experience*. Ottawa: The Department.

______. Department of Finance. 1983. *The Economic Outlook for Canada*. Ottawa: Minister of Supply and Services Canada.

______. Department of Reconstruction and Supply. 1945. *Employment and Income*. Ottawa: King's Printer.

______. Prices and Incomes Commission. 1972. *Inflation, Unemployment and Incomes Policy*. Final report. Ottawa: Information Canada.

______. Royal Commission on Taxation. 1964. *Report*, vol. 2, *The Use of the Tax System to Achieve Economic and Social Objectives*. Ottawa: Queen's Printer.

______. Task Force on Labour Relations. 1968. *Canadian Industrial Relations: The Report of the Task Force on Labour Relations*. Ottawa: Queen's Printer.

Carr, J. 1982. "Tax-Based Incomes Policy: A New Way of Packaging an Old Solution to an Old Problem." In *Tax-Based Incomes Policies: A Cure for Inflation*, edited by M. Walker. Vancouver: Fraser Institute.

Chatterji, M. 1984. "Unions, Employment and the Inflation Tax." Discussion Paper no. 238. Essex: University of Essex.

Christofides, L.N., and D.A. Wilton. 1979. *Wage Controls in Canada (1975–1978): A Study of Their Impact on Negotiated Base Wage Rates*. Ottawa: Minister of Supply and Services Canada.

______. 1985. "Wage Determination in the Aftermath of Controls." *Economica* 52 (February): 51–64.

Christofides, L.N., R. Swidinsky, and D.A. Wilton. 1980a. "A Microeconometric Analysis of the Canadian Wage Determination Process." *Economica* 47 (May): 165–78.

______. 1980b. "A Microeconometric Analysis of Spillovers Within the Canadian Wage Determination Process." *Review of Economics and Statistics* 62 (May): 213–21.

Claudon, M.P., and R.H. Cornwall, eds. 1981. *An Incomes Policy for the United States: New Approaches*. Boston: Martinus Nijhoff.

Coe, D.T., and F. Gaglierdi. 1985. "Nominal Wage Determination in Ten OECD Countries." OECD Working Paper No. 19, March. Paris: OECD.

Coe, D.T., and G. Holtham. 1983. "Output Responsiveness and Inflation: An Aggregate Study." *OECD Economic Studies* 1 (Autumn): 93–145.

Colander, D.C. 1979. *Solutions to Inflation: A Reader*. New York: Harcourt Brace Jovanovich.

Coleman, W.D. 1985. "Canadian Business and the State." In *The State and Economic Interests*, volume 32 of the research studies prepared for the Royal Commission on the Economic Union and Development Prospects for Canada. Toronto: University of Toronto Press.

Cooper, R.N. 1982. "The Gold Standard: Historical Facts and Future Prospects." *Brookings Papers on Economic Activity* 1: 1–56.

Cornwall, J., and W. Maclean. 1984. *Economic Recovery for Canada*. Ottawa: Canadian Institute for Economic Policy.

Courchene, T.J. 1983. "Monetarism: The Canadian Experiences." Paper presented at the 1983 Regional Meeting of the Mount Pelerin Society, Vancouver, B.C.

Cousineau, J.M., and R. Lacroix. 1977. *Wage Determination in Major Collective Agreements in the Private and Public Sectors*. Ottawa: Economic Council of Canada.

______. 1978. "L'impact de la politique canadienne de contrôle des prix et des revenus sur les ententes salariales." *Canadian Public Policy*.

______. 1983. "Why Does Strike Activity Vary over Time and between Industries?" Montreal: Université de Montréal.

Crispo, J. 1984. *National Consultation: Problems and Prospects*. Montreal: C.D. Howe Institute.

Davies, R.J. 1985. "The Structure of Collective Bargaining in Canada." In *Canadian Labour Relations*, volume 16 of the research studies prepared for the Royal Commission on the Economic Union and Development Prospects for Canada. Toronto: University of Toronto Press.

Delong, J.B., and L.H. Summers. 1984. "The Changing Cyclical Variability of Economic Activity in the United States." NBER Working Paper No. 1450. Cambridge, Mass.: National Bureau for Economic Research.

Denny, M.G.S. 1985. "The Prospects for Productivity." In *Economic Growth: Prospects and Determinants*, volume 22 of the research studies prepared for the Royal Commission on the Economic Union and Development Prospects for Canada. Toronto: University of Toronto Press.

Denton, F., et al. 1975. "Patterns of Unemployment Behaviour in Canada." Discussion Paper No. 36. Ottawa: Economic Council of Canada.

Dildine, L.L., and E.M. Sunley. 1978. "Administrative Problems of Tax-Based Incomes Policies." *Brookings Papers on Economic Activity* 2: 363–89.

Donner, A.W., and D.D. Peters. 1979. *The Monetarist Counter-Revolution: A Critique of Canadian Monetary Policy 1975–1979*. Toronto: James Lorimer.

Eckstein, Otto. 1984. "Foundations of Aggregate Supply Price." *American Economic Review* 74 (May): 216–20.

Economic Council of Canada. 1964. *Economic Goals for Canada to 1970*. First Annual Review. Ottawa: Queen's Printer.

______. 1966. *Prices, Productivity and Employment*. Third Annual Review. Ottawa: Queen's Printer.

______. 1976. *People and Jobs: A Study of the Canadian Labour Market*. Ottawa: Economic Council of Canada.

Fallick, J.L., and R.F. Elliott, eds. 1981. *Incomes Policy, Inflation and Relative Pay*. London: George Allen and Unwin.

Feldstein, M. 1982. "Inflation and the American Economy." *The Public Interest* 67 (Spring): 63–76.

Fellner, W. 1980. "The Valid Core of Rationality Hypotheses in the Theory of Expectations." *Journal of Money, Credit and Banking* 12 (November): 763–87.

Fischer, S. 1977. "Long Term Contracts, Rational Expectations, and the Optimal Money Supply Rule." *Journal of Political Economy* 85 (April): 191–206.

______. 1984. "Contracts, Credibility, and Disinflation." Working Paper No. 1339. Cambridge, Mass.: National Bureau of Economic Research.

Flanagan, R.J. 1976. "Wage Interdependence in Unionized Labor Markets." *Brookings Papers on Economic Activity* 3: 635–73.

Flanagan, R.J., D.W. Soskice, and L. Ulman. 1983. *Unionism, Economic Stabilization and Incomes Policies: The European Experience*. Washington, D.C.: Brookings Institution.

Fogarty, M. 1973, "Fiscal Measures and Wage Settlements." *British Journal of Industrial Relations* 2: 29–65.

Ford, R.P. 1985. "Overlapping Contracts and Spillover Effects." Research Department, Bank of Canada. Mimeo.

Fortin, P. 1983. "Why Has Inflation Been So High and Persistent in Canada?" *Cahier 8303*. Quebec City: Université Laval, Département d'économique.

______. 1985. "Unemployment in Canada: A Macroeconomic Disease in Need of a Macroeconomic Cure." In *Unemployment: Can It Be Reduced? An International Perspective*, edited by M. Gunderson, N. Meltz and S. Ostry. Toronto: University of Toronto Press, forthcoming.

Fortin, P., and K. Newton. 1982. "Labour Market Tightness and Wage Inflation in Canada." In *Workers, Jobs and Inflation*, edited by N.M. Baily. Washington, D.C.: Brookings Institution.

Fortin, P., and L. Phaneuf. 1979. "Why Is the Unemployment Rate so High in Canada?" Paper presented at the Canadian Economics Association, Saskatoon.

Fortin, P., and D. Prud'homme. 1984. "La courbe de Phillips canadienne contre rents et marées." Université Laval, Groupe de Recherche en Politique economique, Cahier No. 8410.

Fournier, P. 1985. "Consultation in Canada: Case Studies and Perspectives." In *The State and Economic Interests*, volume 32 of the research studies prepared for the Royal Commission on the Economic Union and Development Prospects for Canada. Toronto: University of Toronto Press.

Frank, J.G. 1979. *Compensation and Industrial Relations — Into the 1980s*. Ottawa: The Conference Board of Canada.

Freeman, R.B., and J.L. Medoff. 1984. *What Do Unions Do*? New York: Basic Books.

Friedman, B.M. 1984. "Lessons from the 1979–82 Monetary Policy Experiment." *American Economic Review* 74 (May): 382–87.

Friedman, M. 1968. "The Role of Monetary Policy." *American Economic Review* 58: 1–17.

Frye, J.F., and R.J. Gordon. 1981. "Government Intervention in the Inflation Process: The Econometrics of 'Self-Inflicted Wounds.'" *American Economic Review* 71 (May): 288–94.

Garbarino, J. 1962. *Wage Policy and Long-Term Contracts*. Washington, D.C.: Brookings Institution.

Giersch, H. 1979. "Aspects of Growth, Structural Change, and Employment — A Schumpeterian Perspective." *Weltwirtschaftliches Archiv* 115 (4): 629–52.

Gordon, R.J. 1973. "The Response of Wages and Prices to the First Two Years of Controls." *Brookings Papers on Economic Activity* 3: 765–78.

______. 1975a. "The Impact of Aggregate Demand on Prices." *Brookings Papers on Economic Activity* 3: 765–78.

______. 1975b. "Alternative Responses of Policy to External Supply Shocks." *Brookings Papers on Economic Activity* 6: 183–206.

______. 1980. "Postwar Macroeconomics: The Evolution of Events and Ideas." In *The American Economy in Transition*, edited by M. Feldstein. Chicago: University of Chicago Press.

______. 1982. "Why U.S. Wage and Employment Behaviour Differs from that in Britain and Japan." *Economic Journal* 92 (March): 13–44.

______. 1983. "A Century of Evidence on Wage and Price Stickiness in the United States, the United Kingdom, and Japan." In *Macroeconomics, Prices and Quantities*, edited by J. Tobin. Washington, D.C.: Brookings Institution.

______. 1985. "Understanding Inflation in the 1980s." *Brookings Papers on Economic Activity* 1: 263–99.

Gray, J.A. 1976. "Wage Indexation: A Macroeconomic Approach." *Journal of Monetary Economics* 2 (April): 221–35.

Grubb, D., R.A. Jackman, and P.R.G. Layard. 1982. "Causes of the Current Stagflation." *Review of Economics Studies* 49 (Special Issue): 707–30.

______. 1983. "Wage Rigidity and Unemployment in OECD Countries. *European Economic Review* (March/April): 11–39.

Grubel, H.G. 1983. "Canadian Monetary Policy as a Reflection of Major Trends in Economic Theory: 1951–1981." *Western Economic Review* 2 (April): 1–27.

Hagens, J.B., and R.R. Russell. 1985. "Testing for the Effectiveness of Wage-Price Controls: An Application to the Carter Program." *American Economic Review* 75 (March): 191–207.

Hall, R.E. 1981. "Explorations in the Gold Standard and Related Policies for Stabilizing the Dollar." Paper presented at NBER Conference on Inflation, Washington, D.C., February 1981.

Hall, R.E., and D. Lillien. 1979. "Efficient Wage Bargains Under Uncertain Supply and Demand." *American Economic Review* 69 (December): 868–79.

Hébert, A. 1984. "Public Sector Bargaining in Quebec: A Case of Hyper-centralization." In *Conflict or Compromise: The Future of Public Sector Labour Relations*, edited by G. Swimmer and M. Thompson. Montreal: Institute for Research on Public Policy.

Helliwell, J.F. 1983. "Recent Evidence from Macroeconomic Models of the Canadian Economy." In *Macroeconomics: Theory, Policy and Evidence*, edited by G. Mason. Winnipeg: Institute for Social and Economic Research.

______. 1984. "Stagflation and Productivity Decline in Canada, 1974–82." *Canadian Journal of Economics* 17 (May): 191–216.

______. 1985. "Comparative Macroeconomics of Stagflation." Vancouver: University of British Columbia. Mimeographed.

Helliwell, J., M.E. MacGregor, and T. Padmore. 1985. "Economic Growth and Productivity in Canada: 1955–90." In *Economic Growth: Prospects and Determinants*, volume 22 of the research studies prepared for the Royal Commission on the Economic Union and Development Prospects for Canada. Toronto: University of Toronto Press.

Henry, S.G.B. 1981. "Incomes Policy and Aggregate Pay." In *Incomes Policy, Inflation and Aggregate Pay*, edited by J.L. Fallick. London: George Allen and Unwin.

Henry, S.G.B., and P.A. Ormerod. 1978. "Incomes Policy and Wage Inflation: Empirical Evidence for the U.K. 1961–1971." *National Institute Economic Review* 85: 31–39.

Holt, C.C., C.D. MacRae, S.O. Schweitzer, and R.E. Smith. 1971. *The Unemployment Inflation Dilemma: A Manpower Solution*. Washington, D.C.: The Urban Institute.

Howard, J.V. 1976. "A Method of Controlling Inflation." *Economic Journal* 86 (December): 832–44.

Howitt, P. 1985. "Indexation and the Adjustment to Inflation in Canada." In *Post-War Macroeconomic Developments*, volume 20 of the research studies prepared for the Royal Commission on the Economic Union and Development Prospects for Canada. Toronto: University of Toronto Press.

Isard, P. 1978. "The Effectiveness of Using the Tax System to Curb Inflationary Collective Bargains: An Analysis of the Wallish-Weintraub Plan." *Journal of Political Economy* 81: 729–40.

Jackman, R.A. 1984. "Counter-Inflationary Policy in a Unionised Economy with Non-Synchronized Wage Setting." Seminar Paper No. 302. Stockholm: University of Stockholm, Institute for International Economic Studies.

Jackman, R.A., and P.R.G. Layard. 1982a. "Trade Unions, the NAIRU, and a Wage-Inflation Tax." *Economica* 49 (August): 232–39.

______. 1982b. "An Inflation Tax." *Fiscal Studies* 3: 47–59.

Jacoby, S.M., and D.J.B. Mitchell. 1984. "Employer Preferences for Long-Term Union Contracts." *Journal of Labour Research* 5 (Summer): 215–28.

Johnston, J. 1980. "The Elusive Phillips Curve." *Journal of Macroeconomics* 2: 265–86.

______. 1985. *Public Opinion and Public Policy in Canada*. Volume 35 of the research studies prepared for the Royal Commission on the Economic Union and Development Prospects for Canada. Toronto: University of Toronto Press.

Kahn, G.A. 1984. "International Differences in Wage Behavior: Real, Nominal, or Exaggerated?" *American Economic Review* 74 (May): 155–59.

Kaliski, S.F. 1984, "Why Must Unemployment Remain So High?" *Canadian Public Policy* 10 (June): 127–41.

______. 1985. "Trends, Changes and Imbalances: A Survey of the Canadian Labour Market." In *Work and Pay: The Canadian Labour Market*, volume 17 of the research studies prepared for the Royal Commission on the Economic Union and Development Prospects for Canada. Toronto: University of Toronto Press.

Karni, E. 1983. "On Optimal Wage Indexation." *Journal of Political Economy* 91 (April): 282–92.

Keynes, J.M. 1936. *The General Theory of Employment Interest and Money*. London: Macmillan, Papermac Edition 1964.

Kotowitz, Y., and R. Portes. 1974. "The Tax on Wage Increases: A Theoretical Analysis." *Journal of Public Economics* 3 (May): 113–32.

Kumar, P. 1985. "Union Growth in Canada: Retrospect and Prospect." In *Canadian Labour Relations*, volume 16 of the research studies prepared for the Royal Commission on the Economic Union and Development Prospects for Canada. Toronto: University of Toronto Press.

Lacroix, R. 1985. "Strike Activity in Canada." In *Canadian Labour Relations*, volume 16 of the research studies prepared for the Royal Commission on the Economic Union and Development Prospects for Canada. Toronto: University of Toronto Press.

Lacroix, R, and F. Dussault. 1984. "The Spillover Effect of Public Sector Wage Contracts in Canada". *Review of Economics and Statistics* 66 (August).

Latham, R.W., and D.A. Peel. 1979. "The 'Tax on Wage Increases' When the Firm is a Monopsonist." *Journal of Public Economics* 8 (October): 274–83.

Layard, R.A. 1982a. "Is Incomes Policy the Answer to Unemployment?" *Economica* 49 (August): 219–39.

______. 1982b. *More Jobs, Less Inflation: The Case for a Counter-Inflation Tax*. London: Grant McIntyre.

Lerner, A.P. 1977a. "Stagflation: Its Cause and Cure." *Challenge* (September/October).

______. 1977b. "From Pre-Keynes to Post-Keynes." *Social Research* 44 (Autumn): 387–415.

______. 1978. "A Wage Increase Permit Plan to Stop Inflation." *Brookings Papers on Economic Activity* 2: 491–505.

Lerner, A.P., and D. Colander. 1980. *MAP: A Market Anti-Inflation Plan*. New York: Harcourt Brace Jovanovich.

Letourneau, R.S. 1979. *The Impact of the Anti-Inflation Program: A Framework for Analysis*. Ottawa: The Conference Board of Canada.

Lipsey, R.G. 1960. "The Relation between Unemployment and the Rate of Change of Money Wage Rates in the United Kingdom, 1862–1957: A Further Analysis." *Economica* 27: 1–31.

______. 1977. "Wage-Price Controls: How to Do a Lot of Harm by Trying to Do a Little Good." *Canadian Public Policy* 3 (Winter): 1–13.

______. 1979. "World Inflation." *Economic Record* 55 (December): 283–96.

______. 1981. "The Understanding and Control of Inflation: Is There a Crisis in Macroeconomics?" *Canadian Journal of Economics* 14 (November): 545–76.

______. 1983. "The Great Anti-Inflation War 1975–?" Woodward Lectures, University of British Columbia, March 1983.

______. 1984. "After Monetarism." In *After Stagflation*, edited by J. Cornwall. New York: M.E. Sharpe.

Lipsey, R.G., and M. Parkin. 1970. "Incomes Policy: A Reappraisal." *Economica* 37 (May): 1–31.

Lipsey, R.G., and D.D. Purvis. 1982. "If Controls Must Come, TIP Would Be Wrong Choice." *Financial Post*, May 15.

Lucas, R.E. 1976. "Econometric Policy Evaluation: A Critique." In *The Phillips Curve and Labor Markets*, edited by K. Brunner and A.H. Meltzer. Amsterdam: North-Holland.

McCallum, J. 1983a. "Inflation and Social Consensus in the Seventies." *Economic Journal* 93 (December): 784–805.

______. 1983b. "A Generalized Credibility Hypothesis: Theory and Evidence." Université du Québec à Montréal, Département de Science économique cahier no. 8309.

———. 1984. "Some International Evidence on the Lucas Critique." *American Economic Review*, forthcoming.

———. 1985a. "Wage Gaps, Factor Shares, and Real Wages." *Scandinavian Journal of Economics* 87 (2).

———. 1985b. "Two Cheers for the Anti-Inflation Board." *Canadian Public Policy*, forthcoming.

McMenamin, J.S., and R.R. Russell. 1983. "Measuring Labor Compensation in Controls Programs." In *The Measurement of Labor Cost*, edited by J.E. Triplett. Chicago: University of Chicago Press.

Macurdy, T., and J. Pencavel. 1983. "Testing between Competing Models of Wage and Employment Determination in Unionized Markets." Stanford University. Mimeo.

Maital, S. 1984. "Reducing Unemployment in the NonZero-Sum Society." Paper presented at the conference "Unemployment: Can It Be Reduced?" Centre for Industrial Relations, University of Toronto.

Maital, S., and Y. Benjamini. 1980. "Inflation as Prisoner's Dilemma." *Journal of Post-Keynesian Economics* 2 (Summer): 459–81.

Maital, S. and N.M. Meltz. 1984. "Labour and Business Attitudes Towards a New Social Context." Paper presented at Canadian Industrial Relations Association Annual Meeting, Guelph, Ontario.

Malinvaud, E. 1978. "Some Problems of Prices and Incomes Policy in France." In *Econometric Contributions to Public Policy*, edited by R. Stone and W. Peterson. London: Macmillan.

———. 1982. "Wages and Unemployment." *Economic Journal* 92: 1–12.

Martin, A. 1985. "The Politics of Employment and Welfare: National Policies and International Interdependence." In *The State and Economic Interests*, volume 32 of the research studies prepared for the Royal Commission on the Economic Union and Development Prospects for Canada. Toronto: University of Toronto Press.

Martinello, F. 1984. "Wage and Employment Determination in a Unionized Industry: The IWA and the B.C. Wood Products Industry." Ph.D. thesis, University of British Columbia.

Maslove, A.M. 1982. "The Political Economy of a Canadian Incomes Control Policy: A Microeconomic Perspective." *Western Economic Review* 1 (December): 46–66.

Maslove, A.M., and G. Swimmer. 1980. *Wage Controls in Canada 1975–78*. Montreal: Institute for Research on Public Policy.

Mayer, T. 1984. "Fervent Hopes vs. Dismal Reality." *Challenge* (March/April): 49–52.

Meade, J.E. 1984. *Wage Fixing*. London: George Allen and Unwin.

Mitchell, D.J.B. 1980. "The Rise and Fall of Real Wage Insurance." *Industrial Relations* 19 (Winter): 64–73.

———. 1982. "Gain-Sharing: An Anti-Inflation Reform." *Challenge* (July/August): 18–25.

———. 1985a. "Wage Flexibility in the United States: Lessons from the Past." *American Economic Review* 75 (May): 36–40.

———. 1985b. "Wage Flexibility: Then and Now." *Industrial Relations*, forthcoming.

Mortensen, D.T. 1970. "A Theory of Wage and Employment Dynamics." In *Microeconomic Foundations of Employment and Inflation Theory*, edited by E.S. Phelps et al. New York: Norton.

———. 1984. "Job Search and Labor Market Analysis." Discussion Paper 594. Evanston, Ill.: Northwestern University.

Muth, J.F. 1961. "Rational Expectations and the Theory of Price Movements." *Econometrica* 29: 315–35.

Nichols, D.A. 1979. "Comparing TIP to Wage Subsidies." *American Economic Review* 69 (May): 207–11.

———. 1983. "Wage Measurement Questions Raised by an Incomes Policy." In *The Measurement of Labor Cost*, edited by J.E. Triplett. Chicago: University of Chicago Press.

Noll, R.G. 1981. "The Feasibility of Marketable Emissions Permits in the United States." Social Science Working Paper, No. 397. Los Angeles: California Institute of Technology.

Nordhaus, W.D. 1983. "Macroconfusion: The Dilemmas of Economic Policy." In *Macroeconomics, Prices, and Quantities*, edited by J. Tobin. Washington, D.C.: Brookings Institution.

Okun, A. 1977. "The Great Stagflation Swamp." *Challenge* 20 (November/December): 6–13.

______. 1978. "Efficient Disinflationary Policies." *American Economic Review* 68 (May): 348–52.

______. 1981. *Prices and Quantities: A Macroeconomic Analysis*. Washington, D.C.: Brookings Institution.

O'Reilly, B. 1985. "Prices in the Post-War Period." In *Post-War Macroeconomic Development*, volume 20 of the research studies prepared for the Royal Commission on the Economic Union and Development Prospects for Canada. Toronto: University of Toronto Press.

O'Reilly, B., W.R. White, and R. Ford. 1985. "Price Flexibility and Business Cycle Fluctuations in Canada: A Survey." In *Post-War Macroeconomic Developments*, volume 20 of the research studies prepared for the Royal Commission on the Economic Union and Development Prospects for Canada. Toronto: University of Toronto Press.

Oswald, A.J. 1984a. "Three Theorems on Inflation, Taxes and Marginal Employment Subsidies." *Economic Journal*, forthcoming.

______. 1984b. "Trade Unions and the Welfare Economics of Wages and Incomes Policy." Working Paper 177. Princeton, N.J.: Princeton University, Industrial Relations Section.

Panitch, L. 1985. "The Tripartite Experience." In *The State and Economic Interests*, volume 32 of the research studies prepared for the Royal Commission on the Economic Union and Development Prospects for Canada. Toronto: University of Toronto Press.

Parkin, M., M.T. Sumner, and R.A. Jones. 1972. "A Survey of the Econometric Evidence of the Effects of Incomes Policy on the Rate of Inflation." In *Incomes Policy and Inflation*, edited by M. Parkin and M.T. Sumner, pp. 1–29. Manchester: Manchester University Press.

Pencavel, J.H. 1981. "The American Experience with Incomes Policies." In *Incomes Policies, Inflation and Relative Pay*, edited by J.L. Fallick and R.F. Elliott. London: George Allen and Unwin.

______. 1982. "The Effects of Incomes Policies on the Frequency and Size of Wage Changes." *Economica* 49: 147–59.

Perry, G.L. 1970. "Changing Labor Markets and Inflation." *Brookings Papers on Economic Activity* 3: 411–48.

______. 1980. "Inflation in Theory and Practice." *Brookings Papers on Economic Activity* 1: 207–41.

______. 1983. "What Have We Learned About Disinflation?" *Brookings Papers on Economic Activity* 2: 587–602.

Phelps, E.S. 1968. "Money Wage Dynamics and Labor Market Equilibrium." *Journal of Political Economy* 76: 678–711.

______. 1978a. "Disinflation Without Recession: Adaptive Guideposts and Monetary Policy." *Weltwirtschaftliches Archiv* 114 (4): 783–809.

______. 1978b. "Commodity-Supply Shock and Full-Employment Monetary Policy." *Journal of Money Credit and Banking* 10: 206–21.

______. 1979. "Obstacles to Curtailing Inflation." In *Essays in Post-Keynesian Inflation*, edited by J.H. Gapinski and C.E. Rockwood. Cambridge, Mass.: Ballinger.

Phillips, A.W. 1958. "The Relation between Unemployment and the Rate of Change of Money Wage Rates in the United Kingdom, 1861–1957." *Economica* 25: 283–99.

Pissarides, C.A. 1985. "Taxes, Subsidies and Equilibrium Unemployment." *Review of Economic Studies* 52 (January): 121–33.

Portes, R. 1977. "The Control of Inflation: Lessons from East European Experience." *Economica* 44 (May): 109–30.

Possen, U.M. 1978. "Wage and Price Controls in a Dynamic Macro Model." *Econometrica* 46 (January): 105–26.

Purvis, D.D., and C. Smith. 1985. "Fiscal Policy in Canada: 1963–84." In *Fiscal and Monetary Policy*, volume 21 of the research studies prepared for the Economic Union and Development Prospects for Canada. Toronto: University of Toronto Press.

Reid, F. 1976. "Canadian Wage and Price Controls." *Canadian Public Policy* 2: 103–33.

______. 1979. "The Effect of Controls on the Rate of Wage Change in Canada." *Canadian Journal of Economics* 12 (2): 214–27.

______. 1981. "Control and Decontrol of Wages in the United States: An Empirical Analysis." *American Economic Review* 71 (March): 108–120.

______. 1982. "Price and Wage Controls in Canada." In *Union-Management Relations in Canada*, edited by John C. Anderson and M. Gunderson. Don Mills: Addison-Wesley.

Reid, R., and N.M. Meltz. 1979. "Causes of Shifts in the Unemployment-Vacancy Relationship: An Empirical Analysis for Canada." *Review of Economics Statistics* 61 (August): 470–75.

Riddell, W.C. 1979. "The Empirical Foundations of the Phillips Curve: Evidence from Canadian Wage Contract Data." *Econometrica* 47: 1–24.

______. 1980. "Unanticipated Inflation and Unemployment in Canada, Ontario and Newfoundland." Economic Council of Canada, Discussion Paper No. 182.

______. 1983. "The Responsiveness of Wage Settlements in Canada and Economic Policy." *Canadian Public Policy* 9 (March): 9–23.

Riddell, W.C., research coordinator. 1985a. *Work and Pay: The Canadian Labour Market*. Volume 17 of the research studies prepared for the Royal Commission on the Economic Union and Development Prospects for Canada. Toronto: University of Toronto Press.

______. 1985b. *Labour-Management Cooperation in Canada*. Volume 15 of the research studies prepared for the Royal Commission on the Economic Union and Development Prospects for Canada. Toronto: University of Toronto Press.

______. 1985c. *Canadian Labour Relations*. Volume 16 of the research studies prepared for the Royal Commission on the Economic Union and Development Prospects for Canada. Toronto: University of Toronto Press.

______. 1985d. *Adapting to Change: Labour Market Adjustment in Canada*. Volume 18 of the research studies prepared for the Royal Commission on the Economic Union and Development Prospects for Canada. Toronto: University of Toronto Press.

Riddell, W.C., and P.M. Smith. 1982. "Expected Inflation and Wage Changes in Canada, 1967–81." *Canadian Journal of Economics* 15 (August): 377–94.

Romer, C. 1984. "Spurious Volatility and Historical Unemployment Data." MIT, Department of Economics, mimeo.

Russell, R.R. 1983. "Can Incomes Policies Work?" In *The Political Process and Economic Change*, edited by K.R. Munroe. New York: Agathon Press.

Sachs, J.D. 1979. "Wages, Profits, and Macroeconomic Adjustment: A Comparative Study." *Brookings Papers on Economic Activity* 2: 269–319.

______. 1980. "The Changing Cyclical Behavior of Wages and Prices." *American Economic Review* 70 (March): 78–90.

______. 1983. "Real Wages and Unemployment in OECD Countries." *Brookings Papers on Economic Activity* 1: 255–89.

Samuelson, P.A. 1974. "Worldwide Stagflation." In *The Collected Scientific Papers of Paul A. Samuelson*, Volume 4. Cambridge, Mass.: MIT Press.

Sargent, J., research coordinator. 1985. *Fiscal and Monetary Policy*. Volume 21 of the research studies prepared for the Royal Commission on the Economic Union and Development Prospects for Canada. Toronto: University of Toronto Press.

Sargent, T.J. 1981. "The Ends of Four Big Inflations." NBER Conference Paper No. 90, January 1981, presented at the NBER Conference on Inflation, Washington, D.C., October 1980.

Scarth, W.M. 1982. "An Evaluation of Tax-Based Incomes Policies." In *Tax-Based Incomes Policies: A Cure for Inflation*? edited by M. Walker. Vancouver: Fraser Institute.

Schelling, T.C. 1982. "Establishing Credibility: Strategic Considerations." *American Economic Review* 72 (May): 77–80.

Schultze, C.L. 1981. "Some Macro Foundations for Micro Theory." *Brookings Papers on Economic Activity* 2: 521–76.

______. 1984. "Cross-Country and Cross-Temporal Differences in Inflation Responsiveness." *American Economic Review* 74 (May): 160–65.

Scott, H.F. 1961. "A Tax on Price Increases?" *Economic Journal* 71 (June): 350–66.

Seidman, L.S. 1976a. "A New Approach to the Control of Inflation." *Challenge* 19 (July/August): 39–43.

______. 1976b. "A Payroll Tax-Credit to Restrain Inflation." *National Tax Journal* 29 (December): 398–412.

______. 1978a. "Tax-Based Incomes Policies." *Brookings Papers on Economic Activity* 2: 301–348.

______. 1978b. "Would Tax Shifting Undermine the Tax-Based Incomes Policy?" *Journal of Economic Issues* 12 (September): 647–76.

______. 1979a. "The Role of a Tax-Based Incomes Policy." *American Economic Review* 69 (May): 202–206.

______. 1979b. "TIP: Feasibility and Equity." *Journal of Post Keynesian Economics* 1 (Summer): 24–37.

______. 1981. "Equity and Tradeoffs in a Tax-Based Incomes Policy." *American Economic Review* 71 (May): 295–300.

Sheahan, J. 1967. *The Wage-Price Guideposts*. Washington, D.C.: Brookings Institution.

Shupp, F.R. 1976. "Optimal Policy Rules for a Temporary Incomes Policy." *Review of Economic Studies* 43 (June): 249–60.

Smith, D.C. 1966. *Incomes Policies: Some Foreign Experiences and Their Relevance for Canada*. Special study No. 4, Economic Council of Canada. Ottawa: Queen's Printer.

Solow, R.M. 1978. "Summary and Evaluation" in *After the Phillips Curve*, Federal Reserve Bank of Boston, Boston, Mass., 203-09.

______. 1980. "What to Do (Macroeconomically) When OPEC Comes." In *Rational Expectations and Economic Policy*, edited by S. Fischer, pp. 249–67. Chicago: University of Chicago Press.

Sparks, G.R. 1985. "The Theory and Practice of Monetary Policy in Canada, 1945 to 1983." In *Fiscal and Monetary Policy*, volume 21 of the research studies prepared for the Royal Commission on the Economic Union and Development Prospects for Canada. Toronto: University of Toronto Press.

Steuer, M.D. 1962. "Economic Policy and Union Activity." In *Industrial Relations — Contemporary Problems and Perspectives*, edited by B.C. Roberts. London: Methuen.

Sumner, M.T. 1975. "Le Prélèvement Conjoncturel." *Public Finance* 30 (3): 461–65.

Sumner, M.T., and R. Ward. 1983. "The Reappearing Phillips Curve." *Oxford Economic Papers* 35: 306–320.

Tarantelli, E. 1984. "The Credibility of Monetary Policy and the Regulation of Inflation and Unemployment in Western Countries." In *Unemployment: Can It Be Reduced? An International Perspective*, edited by M. Gunderson, N. Meltz and S. Ostry. Toronto: University of Toronto Press forthcoming.

Taylor, J.B. 1979. "Staggered Wage Setting in a Macro Model." *American Economic Review* 69 (May): 108–113.

______. 1980a. "Aggregate Dynamics and Staggered Contracts." *Journal of Political Economy* 88 (February): 1–23.

______. 1980b. "Output and Price Stability: An International Comparison." *Journal of Economic Dynamics and Control* 2: 109–132.

______. 1982. "Establishing Credibility: A Rational Expectations Viewpoint." *American Economic Review* 72 (May): 81–85.

______. 1983. "Union Wage Settlements During a Disinflation." Princeton University. *American Economic Review* 73 (December): 981–93.

———. 1984a. "Recent Changes in Macro Policy and its Effects: Some Time Series Analysis." *American Economic Review* 74 (May): 206–210.

———. 1984b. "Improvements in Macroeconomic Stability: The Role of Wages and Prices." National Bureau of Economic Research, Working Paper No. 1491. Cambridge, Mass.

Thurow, C.C. 1983. "An International Keynesian Yank." *Challenge* (March/April): 36–39.

Tobin, J. 1972. "Inflation and Unemployment." *American Economic Review* 62 (March).

———. 1977. "How Dead Is Keynes?" *Economic Inquiry* 15 (October): 459–68.

———. 1980a. "Stabilization Policy Ten Years After." *Brookings Papers on Economic Activity* 1: 19–71.

———. 1980b. *Asset Accumulation and Economic Activity*. Chicago: University of Chicago Press.

———. 1982. "After Disinflation, Then What?" Killam Lecture, Dalhousie University, October.

———. 1984. "A Social Compact for Restraint." *Challenge* (March/April): 52–54.

Vaillancourt, F., research coordinator. 1985. *Income Distribution and Economic Security in Canada*, volume 1 of the research studies prepared for the Royal Commission on the Economic Union and Development Prospects for Canada. Toronto: University of Toronto Press.

Vanderkamp, J. 1982. "Wage and Price Controls: Some Basic Macro Issues." Paper presented at the conference "Economic Policies for Canada in the 1980s." Winnipeg, Manitoba.

von Weizsäcker, C.C. 1975. "Grenzen der traditionellen Globalsteuerung." *Jahrbuch für Nationalökonomie und Statistik* 189: 1–41.

Vroman, W. 1983. *Wage Inflation: Prospects for Deceleration*. Washington, D.C.: The Urban Institute Press.

Waldie, K.G. 1985. "The Evolution of Labour-Government Consultation on Economic Policy." In *Labour-Management Cooperation in Canada*, volume 15 of the research studies prepared for the Royal Commission on the Economic Union and Development Prospects for Canada. Toronto: University of Toronto Press.

Wallich, H.C. 1966, 1970. Articles in *Newsweek*, September 5, 1966, and December 14, 1970. Article in *New York Times*, December 16, 1970.

———. 1972. "Alternative Strategies for Price and Wage Controls." *Journal of Economic Issues* (December): 89–104.

Wallich, H.C., and S. Weintraub. 1971. "A Tax-Based Incomes Policy." *Journal of Economic Issues* 5 (June): 1–19.

Weintraub, S. 1970. "An Incomes Policy to Stop Inflation." *Lloyds Bank Review* (January): 1–12.

———. 1972. "Incomes Policy: Completing the Stabilization Triangle." *Journal of Economic Issues* (December): 105–22.

———. 1978. *Capitalism's Inflation and Unemployment Crisis*. Reading, Mass.: Addison-Wesley.

———. 1982. *Our Stagflation Malaise*. Westport, Conn.: Quorum Books.

Weitzman, M.L. 1984. *The Share Economy*. Cambridge, Mass.: Harvard University Press.

Weldon, J.C. 1983. "Wage Controls and the Canadian Labour Movement." Publication No. 10. Ottawa: Canadian Centre for Policy Alternatives.

Wilcox, J.A. 1983. "Demand Shocks, Supply Shocks, and Wage-Setting Institutions: An International Comparison." Berkeley: University of California. Mimeo.

Wilson, T.A., and G.V. Jump. 1979. *The Influence of the Anti-Inflation Program on Aggregate Wages and Prices*. Ottawa: Anti-Inflation Board.

Wilton, D.A. 1980. *Wage Inflation in Canada, 1955–75*. Study prepared for the Economic Council of Canada. Ottawa: Minister of Supply and Services Canada.

______. 1982. *An Assessment of Canada's Experience with Wage and Price Controls in 1975–78*. Study prepared for the Department of Finance. Ottawa: Minister of Supply and Services Canada.

______. 1984. "An Evaluation of Wage and Price Controls in Canada." *Canadian Public Policy* 10 (June): 167–76.

______. 1985. "Public Sector Wage Compensation." In *Canadian Labour Relations*, volume 16 of the research studies prepared for the Royal Commission on the Economic Union and Development Prospects for Canada. Toronto: University of Toronto Press.

Wogin, G. 1980. "Unemployment and Monetary Policy under Rational Expectations. *Journal of Monetary Economics* 6: 59–68.

Wood, A. 1978. *A Theory of Pay*. Cambridge: Cambridge University Press.

You, J.S. 1982. "Is Tax-Based Incomes Policy an Answer?" *Canadian Public Policy* 8 (Winter): 95–102.

The Collected Research Studies

Royal Commission on the Economic Union and Development Prospects for Canada

Economics

Income Distribution and Economic Security in Canada (Vol. 1), *François Vaillancourt, Research Coordinator*

Vol. 1 Income Distribution and Economic Security in Canada, *F. Vaillancourt* (C)*

Industrial Structure (Vols. 2-8), *Donald G. McFetridge, Research Coordinator*

Vol. 2 Canadian Industry in Transition, *D.G. McFetridge* (C)
Vol. 3 Technological Change in Canadian Industry, *D.G. McFetridge* (C)
Vol. 4 Canadian Industrial Policy in Action, *D.G. McFetridge* (C)
Vol. 5 Economics of Industrial Policy and Strategy, *D.G. McFetridge* (C)
Vol. 6 The Role of Scale in Canada–US Productivity Differences, *J.R. Baldwin and P.K. Gorecki* (M)
Vol. 7 Competition Policy and Vertical Exchange, *F. Mathewson and R. Winter* (M)
Vol. 8 The Political Economy of Economic Adjustment, *M. Trebilcock* (M)

International Trade (Vols. 9-14), *John Whalley, Research Coordinator*

Vol. 9 Canadian Trade Policies and the World Economy, *J. Whalley with C. Hamilton and R. Hill* (M)
Vol. 10 Canada and the Multilateral Trading System, *J. Whalley* (M)
Vol. 11 Canada–United States Free Trade, *J. Whalley* (C)
Vol. 12 Domestic Policies and the International Economic Environment, *J. Whalley* (C)
Vol. 13 Trade, Industrial Policy and International Competition, *R. Harris* (M)
Vol. 14 Canada's Resource Industries and Water Export Policy, *J. Whalley* (C)

Labour Markets and Labour Relations (Vols. 15-18), *Craig Riddell, Research Coordinator*

Vol. 15 Labour-Management Cooperation in Canada, *C. Riddell* (C)
Vol. 16 Canadian Labour Relations, *C. Riddell* (C)
Vol. 17 Work and Pay: The Canadian Labour Market, *C. Riddell* (C)
Vol. 18 Adapting to Change: Labour Market Adjustment in Canada, *C. Riddell* (C)

Macroeconomics (Vols. 19-25), *John Sargent, Research Coordinator*

Vol. 19 Macroeconomic Performance and Policy Issues: Overviews, *J. Sargent* (M)
Vol. 20 Post-War Macroeconomic Developments, *J. Sargent* (C)
Vol. 21 Fiscal and Monetary Policy, *J. Sargent* (C)
Vol. 22 Economic Growth: Prospects and Determinants, *J. Sargent* (C)
Vol. 23 Long-Term Economic Prospects for Canada: A Symposium, *J. Sargent* (C)
Vol. 24 Foreign Macroeconomic Experience: A Symposium, *J. Sargent* (C)
Vol. 25 Dealing with Inflation and Unemployment in Canada, *C. Riddell* (M)

Economic Ideas and Social Issues (Vols. 26 and 27), *David Laidler, Research Coordinator*

Vol. 26 Approaches to Economic Well-Being, *D. Laidler* (C)
Vol. 27 Responses to Economic Change, *D. Laidler* (C)

* (C) denotes a Collection of studies by various authors coordinated by the person named.
(M) denotes a Monograph.

Politics and Institutions of Government

Canada and the International Political Economy (Vols. 28-30), *Denis Stairs and Gilbert R. Winham, Research Coordinators*

Vol. 28 Canada and the International Political/Economic Environment, *D. Stairs and G.R. Winham* (C)
Vol. 29 The Politics of Canada's Economic Relationship with the United States, *D. Stairs and G.R. Winham* (C)
Vol. 30 Selected Problems in Formulating Foreign Economic Policy, *D. Stairs and G.R. Winham* (C)

State and Society in the Modern Era (Vols. 31 and 32), *Keith Banting, Research Coordinator*

Vol. 31 State and Society: Canada in Comparative Perspective, *K. Banting* (C)
Vol. 32 The State and Economic Interests, *K. Banting* (C)

Constitutionalism, Citizenship and Society (Vols. 33-35), *Alan Cairns and Cynthia Williams, Research Coordinators*

Vol. 33 Constitutionalism, Citizenship and Society in Canada, *A. Cairns and C. Williams* (C)
Vol. 34 The Politics of Gender, Ethnicity and Language in Canada, *A. Cairns and C. Williams* (C)
Vol. 35 Public Opinion and Public Policy in Canada, *R. Johnston* (M)

Representative Institutions (Vols. 36-39), *Peter Aucoin, Research Coordinator*

Vol. 36 Party Government and Regional Representation in Canada, *P. Aucoin* (C)
Vol. 37 Regional Responsiveness and the National Administrative State, *P. Aucoin* (C)
Vol. 38 Institutional Reforms for Representative Government, *P. Aucoin* (C)
Vol. 39 Intrastate Federalism in Canada, *D.V. Smiley and R.L. Watts* (M)

The Politics of Economic Policy (Vols. 40-43), *G. Bruce Doern, Research Coordinator*

Vol. 40 The Politics of Economic Policy, *G.B. Doern* (C)
Vol. 41 Federal and Provincial Budgeting, *A.M. Maslove, M.J. Prince and G.B. Doern* (M)
Vol. 42 Economic Regulation and the Federal System, *R. Schultz and A. Alexandroff* (M)
Vol. 43 Bureaucracy in Canada: Control and Reform, *S.L. Sutherland and G.B. Doern* (M)

Industrial Policy (Vols. 44 and 45), *André Blais, Research Coordinator*

Vol. 44 Industrial Policy, *A. Blais* (C)
Vol. 45 The Political Sociology of Industrial Policy, *A. Blais* (M)

Law and Constitutional Issues

Law, Society and the Economy (Vols. 46-51), *Ivan Bernier and Andrée Lajoie, Research Coordinators*

Vol. 46 Law, Society and the Economy, *I. Bernier and A. Lajoie* (C)
Vol. 47 The Supreme Court of Canada as an Instrument of Political Change, *I. Bernier and A. Lajoie* (C)
Vol. 48 Regulations, Crown Corporations and Administrative Tribunals, *I. Bernier and A. Lajoie* (C)
Vol. 49 Family Law and Social Welfare Legislation in Canada, *I. Bernier and A. Lajoie* (C)
Vol. 50 Consumer Protection, Environmental Law and Corporate Power, *I. Bernier and A. Lajoie* (C)
Vol. 51 Labour Law and Urban Law in Canada, *I. Bernier and A. Lajoie* (C)

The International Legal Environment (Vols. 52-54), *John Quinn, Research Coordinator*

Vol. 52 The International Legal Environment, *J. Quinn* (C)
Vol. 53 Canadian Economic Development and the International Trading System, *M.M. Hart* (M)
Vol. 54 Canada and the New International Law of the Sea, *D.M. Johnston* (M)

Harmonization of Laws in Canada (Vols. 55 and 56), *Ronald C.C. Cuming, Research Coordinator*

Vol. 55 Perspectives on the Harmonization of Law in Canada, *R. Cuming* (C)
Vol. 56 Harmonization of Business Law in Canada, *R. Cuming* (C)

Institutional and Constitutional Arrangements (Vols. 57 and 58), *Clare F. Beckton and A. Wayne MacKay, Research Coordinators*

Vol. 57 Recurring Issues in Canadian Federalism, *C.F. Beckton and A.W. MacKay* (C)
Vol. 58 The Courts and The Charter, *C.F. Beckton and A.W. MacKay* (C)

FEDERALISM AND THE ECONOMIC UNION

Federalism and The Economic Union (Vols. 58-72), *Mark Krasnick, Kenneth Norrie and Richard Simeon, Research Coordinators*

Vol. 59 Federalism and Economic Union in Canada, *K. Norrie, R. Simeon and M. Krasnick* (M)
Vol. 60 Perspectives on the Canadian Economic Union, *M. Krasnick* (C)
Vol. 61 Division of Powers and Public Policy, *R. Simeon* (C)
Vol. 62 Case Studies in the Division of Powers, *M. Krasnick* (C)
Vol. 63 Intergovernmental Relations, *R. Simeon* (C)
Vol. 64 Disparities and Interregional Adjustment, *K. Norrie* (C)
Vol. 65 Fiscal Federalism, *M. Krasnick* (C)
Vol. 66 Mobility of Capital in the Canadian Economic Union, *N. Roy* (M)
Vol. 67 Economic Management and the Division of Powers, *T.J. Courchene* (M)
Vol. 68 Regional Aspects of Confederation, *J. Whalley* (M)
Vol. 69 Interest Groups in the Canadian Federal System, *H.G. Thorburn* (M)
Vol. 70 Canada and Quebec, Past and Future: An Essay, *D. Latouche* (M)
Vol. 71 The Political Economy of Canadian Federalism: 1940–1984, *R. Simeon and I. Robinson* (M)

THE NORTH

Vol. 72 The North, *Michael S. Whittington, Coordinator* (C)

Commission Organization

Chairman

Donald S. Macdonald

Commissioners

Clarence L. Barber
Albert Breton
M. Angela Cantwell Peters
E. Gérard Docquier
William M. Hamilton
John R. Messer
Laurent Picard
Michel Robert
Daryl K. Seaman
Thomas K. Shoyama
Jean Casselman-Wadds
Catherine T. Wallace

Senior Officers

Executive Director
J. Gerald Godsoe

Director of Policy
Alan Nymark

Secretary
Michel Rochon

Director of Administration
Sheila-Marie Cook

Senior Advisors
David Ablett
Victor Clarke
Carl Goldenberg
Harry Stewart

Director of Publishing
Ed Matheson

Directors of Research
Ivan Bernier
Alan Cairns
David C. Smith

Co-Directors of Research
Kenneth Norrie
John Sargent

Research Program Organization

Economics

Research Director
David C. Smith

Executive Assistant & Assistant Director (Research Services)
I. Lilla Connidis

Coordinators
David Laidler
Donald G. McFetridge
Kenneth Norrie*
Craig Riddell
John Sargent*
François Vaillancourt
John Whalley

Research Analysts
Caroline Digby
Mireille Ethier
Judith Gold
Douglas S. Green
Colleen Hamilton
Roderick Hill
Joyce Martin

Politics and the Institutions of Government

Research Director
Alan Cairns

Executive Assistant
Karen Jackson

Coordinators
Peter Aucoin
Keith Banting
André Blais
Bruce Doern
Richard Simeon
Denis Stairs
Cynthia Williams
Gilbert R. Winham

Research Analysts
Claude Desranleau
Ian Robinson

Office Administration
Donna Stebbing

Law and Constitutional Issues

Research Director
Ivan Bernier

Executive Assistant & Research Program Administrator
Jacques J.M. Shore

Coordinators
Clare F. Beckton
Ronald C.C. Cuming
Mark Krasnick
Andrée Lajoie
A. Wayne MacKay
John J. Quinn

Administrative and Research Assistant
Nicolas Roy

Research Analyst
Nola Silzer

*Kenneth Norrie and John Sargent co-directed the final phase of Economics Research with David Smith